THE FORTUNE HUNTER

THE FORTUNE HUNTER

A German Prince in Regency England

PETER JAMES BOWMAN

Signal Books
Oxford

First published in 2010

This paperback edition first published in 2014 by
Signal Books Limited
36 Minster Road
Oxford
OX4 1LY
www.signalbooks.co.uk

A catalogue record for this book is available from the British Library

ISBN 978-1-909930-03-2 Paper

Design & Production: Devdan Sen
Cover Design: Devdan Sen
Cover Image: 'An Election Ball'. Caricature by William Heath, 1827 or
1828; in the author's possession.
Printed in India

'In the past of one's country one is a foreigner, and it is naturally with other foreigners that one identifies.'
J. W. Burrow, *The Times*, 20 June 1970

FOR MY PARENTS

Contents

LIST OF ILLUSTRATIONS

ACKNOWLEDGEMENTS

In telling the previously untold story of Prince Pückler's matrimonial tour of England, I have adhered to the documentary evidence and avoided imaginative reconstruction. This policy was made easier by the richness of the sources in the Archive of the Pückler Foundation in Branitz. In using these sources I was assisted by the Archive's staff, initially Volkmar Herold and subsequently Christian Friedrich and Anne Schäfer, for whose hospitality, patience and manifold generosity it is a pleasure to express my gratitude here. The Archive is housed in the pretty neo-Gothic former estate forge, and my workroom there, with its view of the park and the mansion house where Pückler spent his last twenty-six years, will always be a happy memory. I also benefited from *Englandsouvenirs*, the companion volume to an exhibition on Pückler's stay in England held at Muskau and Branitz in 2005, particularly from the essays therein by Nicole and Michael Brey.

To Dr Nikolaus Gatter, director of the Varnhagen Society in Cologne, I am deeply obliged for photocopies of Pückler-related newspaper and periodical articles in the Society's collection and for many other acts of kindness. Also in Germany, Ulf Jacob provided information and references and brought my research to the attention of his fellow Pückler scholars.

The bulk of my work with British newspapers, journals and books was done at the Cambridge University Library, facilitated by the unfailing efficiency of its staff. Were it not for the magnanimous policy of allowing graduates of the University lifelong membership of the Library, this book would have taken far longer to write.

I have also been helped by the staffs of the British Library, the British Library Newspapers (Colindale), the Guildhall Library, the Family Records Centre, the National Archives (Kew), the London Metropolitan Archives, and several Public Record Offices and other institutions in the UK as well as the Jagiellonian Library in Cracow, Poland.

For welcoming me into their homes and giving me access to family papers I extend my warmest thanks to Sir John and Lady Hervey-Bathurst, Somborne Park; Captain and Mrs Bell, Llangedwyn

Hall; and Mr and Mrs Somerset, Castle Goring.

Those who provided information in response to written en-
quiries are too numerous to list, but I must at least mention Robin
Elliott, Berkshire Record Office; Nigel Everett, Hafod Press; Kate
Fielden, Bowood Estate Office; Sheena Jones, Windsor Reference
Library; Sheila Markham, The Travellers Club; Malcolm Underwood,
St John's College, Cambridge; John Wardroper, Shelfmark Books; and
Emma Whinton, National Monuments Record. Bia von Doetinchem
answered my questions about Wilhelm von Biel and sent me a copy
of her privately printed book about his family.

I am very grateful to those who read some or all of the manuscript at various stages for their comments: Richard Aronowitz, Lizzie
Collingham, Carmel Curtis, Marion Piening, Reehana Raza, Thomas
Seidel, Deb Truscott and my parents John and Silvia Bowman. My
greatest debt in this regard is to Richard T. Kelly, whose eight pages
of remarks on an early draft prompted me to rewrite several chapters.
I further profited from the editorial input of James Ferguson of Signal
Books, who did everything possible to make the journey into print
speedy and smooth. As well as being the first to read the full manuscript, Claude Piening gave me invaluable help and encouragement
from the inception of this project. John Cornwell placed his long experience as a writer at my disposal in various ways.

About a third of the illustrations are taken from Pückler's travel
albums, and their reproduction here is by gracious permission of the
Pückler Foundation in Branitz (vol. I) and Count Hermann von
Pückler (vols II & III). Erika Ingham of the Archive and Library of the
National Portrait Gallery tracked down several portraits for me,
Sotheby's and Christie's sent on blind letters to current owners, and
private individuals and curators of collections kindly furnished me
with images of items in their possession or care. Further acknowl-
edgements are made in the list of illustrations.

Note: Following common practice, I use the term 'Regency' to describe the
first three decades of the nineteenth century, not just the years from 1811 to
1820 when the Prince of Wales acted as Regent for his father George III.

PROLOGUE

L ate in the evening of 28 September 1826 the steam packet from
Rotterdam finally dropped anchor near London Bridge. Rather
than the usual twenty hours the crossing had taken forty, six of
them spent beached on a sandbank in the Thames Estuary. The conditions were so stormy, the motion of the boat so unsettling and the
stench from the engines so foul that all the passengers were violently
ill. On arrival they were told they must not remove their luggage until
the Custom House in Lower Thames Street opened at ten o'clock the
next day. Some slept alongside their possessions, but Prince Hermann
von Pückler-Muskau passed the night in a sailors' tavern next to the
moored boat. As he lay in his dingy room, unchanged and unwashed,
he must have wondered why he could not be at home, enjoying the
comforts of a well-run chateau with his beloved Lucie. But England
was his only hope; if he could not repair his fortunes here he faced
bankruptcy and the loss of his life's work. In the morning he went
back on board for the inspection of his effects and succeeded in
bribing the customs men to ignore the pairs of French gloves he had
packed as gifts for ladies. Then he drove to the Clarendon Hotel in
Bond Street. He could not afford to stay there for long, but it would
be a good base from which to begin his campaign.

A decade earlier he had married Lucie von Pappenheim, a moderately wealthy divorcee. Both were passionately attached to Muskau,
his large estate in the eastern German region of Lusatia, which, with
her help, he would turn into a magnificent park. But before the work
was complete they had poured all their money into the soil and were
deep in debt. To avoid the dire necessity of selling the estate the couple
devised a bizarre, but to their minds perfectly sensible, scheme: they
would divorce so that Pückler could marry an heiress who would
finance his continued landscaping and, after a decent interval, be per-

suaded to let Lucie carry on living at Muskau with them.

The likeliest place to find a suitably dowered bride was England, Europe's richest country, and as soon as the divorce came through he sailed for London. In his favour he had a grand title, a handsome appearance and a charming personality; against him was the fact that England was already full of titled, handsome and charming Continental noblemen with exactly the same intentions.

Moreover, their presence was causing considerable alarm. A letter printed in the *Morning Post* just three weeks after Pückler's arrival makes this clear: 'As the commencement of the fashionable season now approaches, and families are returning fast to town, may it not be proper to warn the British Fair as to the place being now, as is really the case, swarming with aliens of the description of mere fortune hunters, who have come over for the sole purpose of inveigling women of property.' A few months earlier the diarist Clarissa Trant, on hearing that her cousin had bestowed her hand and £20,000 on a Count Orsini of Turin, voiced the widespread view that 'Italian Counts and German Barons are a suspicious, or at best a suspected race.' As were Frenchmen, and the *Court Journal* of 1829 went as far as to claim that while many London heiresses had been taken as wives by Parisians, no portionless Englishwoman had ever had a suitor from the rival metropolis. Not all aspirants were even real aristocrats, chimed in *Fraser's Magazine* in 1832, but fraudsters who boasted of their pedigrees, feudal castles and rent-rolls so as to 'kidnap some artless girl's affections'.[1]

The problem was not new. As early as 1740 a published sermon cautioned young English ladies against Irish adventurers, who were coming over in large numbers 'to make a Property of you, to enrich themselves, though thereby they undo you.' A second threat was posed by the émigrés arriving from France after 1792, described by one commentator as using their innate duplicity to seduce unwary females and filch their fortunes. But it was in the two decades after the defeat of Napoleon that concern became acute. The renewed accessibility of the island nation from the Continent of Europe prompted a large influx of visitors, mostly titled and almost all men. According to the *Quarterly Review* in 1831, the 'cold nights of November do not more surely portend to the anxious sportsman in the country the approach of woodcocks, than do the balmy zephyrs of May foretell the arrival of illustrious foreigners in London.' The swallow season blows in countless visitors, agreed *Fraser's Magazine* the following year: 'Scarcely does a steam-boat cross the channel, or stage-coach wend its weary way from Dover to town, without bringing its due complement of whiskered aliens.'[2]

Of course not all these men had the same motive. Some came to see the sights, others to hunt or shoot, a few to study Britain's politics and economy, rather more to taste the pleasures of London society. But many, very many, were drawn by the fabled wealth of Albion's daughters. For at least a century travellers had been struck by the country's prosperity, and now, despite the cost of the twenty-two year struggle against Napoleonic France, in which Britain had often funded its allies' military efforts, it was wealthier than any of its neighbours by far. While other nations had suffered the depredations of a war fought on their own soil, Britain had experienced a golden age of innovation: farming yields had improved rapidly; the power of steam was harnessed for the mining of coal, copper and iron ore; and improvements to the road network wrought by Telford and McAdam doubled the speeds at which coaches could travel. Most importantly, manufacturing output was growing apace, with little competition from the still pre-industrial Continent and a superb merchant fleet, backed by the unrivalled power of the navy, to bring in raw materials from Britain's colonies and export finished goods all over the world.

In exchange for a share of these riches, wooers from abroad offered to turn a marriageable woman into a baroness, a countess or even a princess. And it was not just their titles that were seductive. To many potential brides they had the fascination of the unfamiliar and, as most spoke more French than English, the glamour that had long attached itself to French culture. The author of a contemporary survey of London life censures the higher classes for getting their cooks and governesses, and even their theatrical tastes, from abroad, while 'to be escorted to any place of public amusement by a foreign Count, is still one of the most desirable objects in the estimation of our aristocratic dames.' The visitors were also associated with a highly fashionable import—the waltz. Already somewhat known during the war years, the new dance now became a craze, and one observer recalls that 'the handsome Germans and accomplished Frenchmen who had the *entrée* to good society in England were constantly seen whirling with the prettiest women of rank.'[3] Native waltzers attended daily practice sessions at Devonshire House, but could never match the deft footwork of men who for years had been gyrating round the assembly rooms of Europe.

The appeal of Continental suitors was further enhanced by an attentiveness and suavity of manner to which Englishwomen were not accustomed. The memoirist Captain Gronow recalls that in the years after Waterloo 'female society amongst the upper classes was most notoriously neglected; except, perhaps, by romantic foreigners.' Among overseas observers, Talleyrand's niece the Duchess of Dino and the travel writer Astolphe de Custine praise the reserve of the English male, finding in it more true chivalry than in the fiery glances and purling flatteries of Frenchmen; but many more agree with the translator Madame d'Avot, who complains that men in London lack the '*nuances de délicatesse*' that make the charm of their Parisian counterparts.[4] The general impression was that well-born Englishmen simply did not enjoy spending time with women, or at least women of their own class. Even when the two sexes dined together they divided after the dessert, the ladies retiring to another room for coffee while the gentlemen continued drinking and gave a freer turn to their conversation. By midnight even those still capable of finding their beds unassisted were in no state to present themselves anew to the ladies.

The visiting American journalist Nathaniel Parker Willis was so shocked at the want of attention paid to women of rank that he actually asked one of them about it: 'I detest England for that very reason,' she told him. 'It is the fashion in London for young men to prefer every thing to the society of women. They have their clubs, their horses, their rowing matches, their hunting and betting, and every thing else is a *bore*!' The suggestion here that such conduct was dictated by convention as much as inclination is certainly valid for the dandies, whose show of self-sufficiency was part of a group identity. Often they would loll on sofas and exchange saucy quips while ignoring a nearby party of ladies, and the Frenchman Joseph Pichot notes that 'instead of coming forward as protectors of the fair sex, some of them affect to treat the ladies with contempt, and they may occasionally be seen, linked arm in arm, and rudely driving a timid female from the footpath into the horse-road.' Not all men were dandies, of course, but the problem was considered general enough to merit discussion in an essay entitled 'Courtship and Marriage' in the *London Magazine* of 1826.[5]

In these circumstances, foreigners had plentiful opportunities to sigh at the feet of their chosen belle. But they needed to do more. As eloping with a girl carried the risk that she would be disinherited, and wealthy widows who could marry as they pleased were in short supply, lucrative English alliances could usually be formed only if the bride's parents were won over. The early nineteenth century was, as we know from Jane Austen, the age of the marrying mother, and this energetic personage tended to prefer native sons-in-law. Not always, though. The Countess of Shrewsbury, for example, was so enamoured of foreign titles that she united both of her daughters with Italian princes and acquired a reputation as an Anglo-European matchmaker. There was also the rather different case of Lady Strachan, an adventuress who hoped that well-born husbands would confer respectability on her three illegitimate girls. Her protector the Marquess of Hertford obligingly settled large sums on them and thereby tempted a trio of necessitous noblemen: Count Zichy-Ferraris, a Hungarian, married Charlotte and got £86,000; Count Berchtold, another Hungarian, married Matilda and got £80,000; and Prince Ruffo, an Italian, married Louisa and got £40,000.[6]

Nonetheless the general attitude towards connubially inclined foreigners, even those with imposing names, was one of distrust. Whereas in Britain only one man, his wife and his widowed mother bore a particular title, the children of a European nobleman tended all to be of the same rank as he, giving the impression that the Continent was awash with aristocrats. Hence the sentiment expressed in *Fraser's Magazine* in 1832 that blue-blooded foreigners were 'as cheaply estimated, as a plentiful crop of mushrooms after a shower of rain'. It was also undeniable that these men had less money than home-grown sprigs of nobility. The *Quarterly Review* of 1837 questions the real worth of French and Italian titles, while setting even these above the nomenclature of Poland and Russia, 'where, by an imperial ukase, no semi-barbarian may write himself prince, unless qualified by the possession of lands, estates, domains, territories, lordships, palatinates, and principalities to the clear value of forty pounds sterling per annum.'[7]

It was suspicions like these that dogged the young Frenchman Charles-Henri de Mornay, who spent much of 1829 and 1830 in England. Calling himself a count fifteen years before he was one, he became a common sight riding along the Marine Parade in Brighton and swirling around the ballrooms of London, and appears from contemporary accounts to have been handsome, clever and good-natured. During his stay he made a number of matrimonial essays, one of them, according to the *Court Journal*, with 'the daughter of an opulent blacking-maker, commonly known as the Emperor of Japan. A marriage of this description will form a new process of whitewashing for the broken-down dandies of Paris.' He also paid his addresses to Louisa Smythe, a niece of George IV's secret wife Maria Fitzherbert. She liked him, but her mother found him unsuitable and chased him away, leaving Miss Smythe to fume in her diary that her mother's 'whole absurd conduct to & about Mr. de Mornay made me so indignant that I could not help shewing how *very* much I was annoyed by it.' Mornay returned home wifeless and took up a diplomatic career, later becoming ambassador to Sweden.[8]

Matrimonial tourists had, then, much in their favour but much to contend with. It is difficult even to guess what proportion carried off a prize.[9] Given the sheer numbers plying the fashionable locales of London, it is likely that most of them drew a blank. Not all gained access to good society, and some were reduced to advertise, like the 'Foreign Gentleman of respectability, mature age, and well disposed' looking for an equally respectable lady who 'must have some property'; one doubts that such offers tempted many brides to the altar. All the same, the soldiers, diplomats and dandies willing to take time and trouble often secured their object. Men of letters did well too: the eminent French poets Alphonse de Lamartine and Alfred de Vigny married, respectively, Miss Marianne Birch and Miss Lydia Bunbury;

Count Carlo Pepoli, a versifier of ancient Bolognese family, married Miss Elizabeth Fergus; and Count Giuseppe Pecchio, an exiled patriotic writer reduced to giving Italian lessons, married Miss Philippa Brooksbank.[10]

In terms of nationality, there is no doubt that Frenchmen came off best. Their champion was Auguste Charles Joseph, Count Flahaut, a Napoleonic hero and natural son of Talleyrand who wed the enormously wealthy Margaret Mercer Elphinstone in 1817. Intelligent, lively and attractive, and the heiress to a peerage in her own right, Miss Mercer had already rejected many prominent suitors, including the Duke of Clarence, before accepting the dashing ex-soldier. Next came the Italians, led off by Francesco di Platamone, Count San Antonio, ambassador of the Two Sicilies in London during the Napoleonic Wars and thus able to seek a wife before the peacetime influx of fortune hunters. With his good looks and distinguished air he was well equipped for the task, and Sophia Johnstone, the rather plain daughter of a former Governor of Pensacola who inherited a fortune from her brother, did not resist his blandishments for long, becoming his countess in 1811.[11]

Germans made relatively fewer bridal tours of England, though old Field Marshal Blücher must have returned home from the victory celebrations of 1814 full of tales of London's riches, for both his grandson and his grand nephew took British spouses.[12] There was no reason why enterprising sons of the still fragmented Germany could not do as well as their French and Italian counterparts. Indeed, the decision of Prince Pückler-Muskau to try his luck in England had been prompted by the recent triumphs there of two friends, one from Bavaria and the other from Mecklenburg. Neither would ever have to worry about money again, and nor, if he could match their achievements, would he.

1

SUNDAY'S CHILD

*'The way my father went to absolutely every length to ruin
the fortune and position of his family is truly pitiful!'*

When Hermann Ludwig Heinrich von Pückler-Muskau
was born on Sunday 30 October 1785 at Muskau in
Upper Lusatia, then part of Saxony, his mother, Countess
Clementine, was just fifteen years old. She was the only child of the
last Callenberg of Muskau, and had been given away the previous year
to the thirty-year-old Count Ludwig Erdmann von Pückler, who by
the terms of the marriage changed his name to Pückler-Muskau and
moved to his bride's property. The Callenbergs were an old Lusatian
family known for their urbane cosmopolitanism and generous patronage of the arts, and Clementine's French mother, a Countess de
la Tour du Pin, was of similarly distinguished stock. The Pücklers
equalled the Callenbergs in lineage, with a family tree dating back to
the fourteenth century, but not in wealth or social standing. They were
a family of exclusively local, mainly agricultural interests, with a reputation for avarice, pushiness and boorish manners.

The marriage was a disaster. At first glance Count Ludwig
Erdmann might appear to have done well for himself. The Muskau
estate was many times bigger than the Pücklers' nearby property of
Branitz, and its owners had almost sovereign power in the small town
and forty-five villages and hamlets that fell within it, making church
appointments, administering justice through tribunals and keeping
order with liveried gendarmes. However, according to the marriage
contract it was not Count Ludwig Erdmann but his wife who exercised these powers. His only function, it seemed, was to sire children.
This humiliating status as subordinate consort, which his father had

carelessly negotiated on his behalf more or less without consulting him, exacerbated his naturally suspicious, resentful nature, as did his sense, shared by everyone else, that he was a poor match for his lively, beautiful child-wife. She bore him a second son, who died in infancy, and three daughters, Clementine, Bianca and Agnes, but always made it clear that she detested her awkward, earthbound husband, who from long bachelor habit was more at ease with servant girls than women of his own rank. Her own temperament was less angelic than her appearance, for she was spoilt, silly, pert and frivolous.

At the time such ill-assorted marriages were common among the German nobility, which allied itself for dynastic reasons with scant regard for personal compatibility. As their domestic life descended into acrimony, neither parent took much interest in the young hero of our story. His father had other preoccupations, and his mother, whose responsibility his upbringing was, had barely left the nursery herself. Now she played with him, now she struck him, without herself quite knowing why. Most of the time he was, as he later recalled, 'in the hands of rough, often stupid servants, who did with me pretty well as they pleased.'[1] In time the spirited child rebelled against this regime. One day he was locked in a room in one of the chateau's turrets despite his threats to fling himself into the moat. Finding some loose straw to hand, he removed his outer clothes and stuffed them to make a doll. Soon afterwards a splash was heard and everyone rushed outside and saw what looked like his drowned body floating on the surface.

At the age of seven he was sent away to a school run by the pietistic Moravian Brothers in Uhyst. His lifelong contempt for the parade of religious feeling may be dated from his experiences at this school, which he later called an 'institute for hypocrisy'.[2] Hating the place, its ethos and his teachers, young Hermann nonetheless had one thing to be grateful for: like every other boy he was allotted a small part of the school garden to tend as he wished. Soon he was completely absorbed in the task, pacing round his little plot until a planting scheme suggested itself to his mind, and then seizing his tools and working furiously until he had created the combination of shapes and colours he desired. Before long he would tire of what he had

not least as it threatened the prospects of his daughters, who had grown up under his roof and were much closer to his heart, and so he determined to leave the property in the control of trustees or transfer the succession to his eldest daughter Clementine. He secured Countess Seydewitz's approval for this scheme, probably by presenting their son's debts as a threat to the continuation of her income, and then set legal wheels in motion. In a letter of 1804 to a court official he called Pückler a wastrel who would gladly decimate Muskau's forests, run down its manufactories and sell off its assets to raise cash— a strange way to describe a man who would turn his patrimony into an internationally renowned landscape park, though not an entirely unreasonable prediction based on his conduct up to that point.[5] This threat of disinheritance was narrowly averted when its intended victim attained his majority.

Finding little taste for garrison life and manacled by debts, Pückler resigned his commission in the autumn of 1804 with the rank of cavalry captain. His relations with his father made Muskau an unwelcoming abode, and he spent the next few years in Prague, Vienna, Augsburg and Munich, often in very straitened circumstances. The lowest point in his fortunes saw him renting a seedy garret from a maker of playing cards in Ulm, washing his own clothes and calling himself Secretary Hermann so as not to disgrace his rank. His movements during this period can be traced in the letters he wrote to his father's secretary Ludewig Wolff, who had a soft spot for the young wanderer. It was thanks to Wolff that his father committed himself to a regular if meagre quarterly allowance of 300 thalers in 1808. Count Ludwig Erdmann had a ready excuse for his parsimony in the Napoleonic Wars, and although he exaggerated their effects times were hard for Saxon landowners. Wolff told Pückler the estate was so encumbered that if he wished to avoid selling it after his father's death he should find a rich bride. In his reply Pückler laughed at this suggestion and asked how he could possibly go courting in his indigent state. All the same, he was intrigued and reverted to the idea several times in the following months, calling to mind all the wealthy families he knew with daughters to wed.[6]

During these years he developed a lifelong love of travel, with its constant novelty and eternal promise of good fortune at the next stopping-place. In the spring of 1808, with his allowance settled, he purchased a pair of stout boots and a portmanteau and set off on a walking tour of Switzerland. He enjoyed the physical exercise, the mountain air and, despite its discomforts, the freedom of life on the road. His most intense joy came from the beauty of the natural world, a joy commingled with religious awe—for in contemplating nature he became aware of the presence of God. Throughout his life people mistakenly assumed Pückler to be uninterested in religion or even an atheist, and certainly he enjoyed laughing at ostentatious piety and the woodenness of the Lutheran tradition into which he was born. The truth was that, like many intelligent men and women of his time, he had a pantheistic faith, that is to say a belief that God is coextensive with nature (or the universe) rather than outside it.

In Lucerne Pückler made the acquaintance of a young medical student from Bremen named Müller, and for a while they journeyed together, riding up and down the Alpine landscape while laughing at the comical donkeys they had hired for the purpose. With class distinctions in Germany more rigid than in Britain, the two men were unusual companions, but the count was little given to class snobbery, and, as he showed many times in his life, had the talent of attuning himself to whoever he was with while staying true to his own nature. In Geneva he met Alexander von Wulffen, another Saxon nobleman reduced to touring on foot, and together they trudged to Marseille in twenty-six days. From Nice they took a boat to Genoa, followed by another long walk via Florence to Rome, where Pückler was unable to resist joining in the pleasures of society.

Then they continued to Naples, where Pückler witnessed an eruption of Vesuvius and had an affair of the heart: 'Countess G— is a true angel,' he wrote in his travel journal, 'and I fear that this living beauty will make me neglect all the beauties of nature and antiquity.' This is the only one of his youthful amours who can be identified: she was Beethoven's former muse Julie von Gallenberg, who lived in Naples with her husband and children. Pückler's personal papers from this period also include outpourings to an Adele, a Jeanette, a Lisette and a Diana, bundled together as 'Drafts of old love letters to be re-used as appropriate'; full of eternal devotion, hot tears, sleep-less nights, daggers to the heart and black despair, some no doubt had the desired effect, but the full names of the recipients will never be known.[7] Later he acquired a reputation as a heartless philanderer, but this is not quite fair; although a sensualist and no respecter of mar-riage, he neither tricked nor bullied his way into anyone's bed and was always honourable in his treatment of present and former loves.

To fund his social life in Rome and Naples Pückler had resorted to borrowing again, and the need to retrench, as well as the news that his father was ill, made him decide to return to Muskau after an absence of many years. Still, he did not relish the prospect, and dawdled for a few months in Strasburg and Paris before Wolff's ever graver reports of his father's health finally brought him home. Plagued by a gallstone and miserable in his isolation, Count Ludwig Erdmann had softened in his feelings towards his son, though their estrange-ment was too complete for a true reconciliation to take place.

Pückler found life under the paternal roof as depressing as he had expected, and before long he was off again, this time to the Prussian capital Berlin. He was drawn there for political reasons: Prussia had fought and lost against France, but was sullen in defeat and would soon revolt, whereas his own state of Saxony was allied with Napoleon, who had turned it from an electoral duchy into a kingdom as a reward. Like many others in disunited Germany, Pückler felt the humiliation of this foreign domination and was eager to join any force that opposed it.

It was in Berlin in January 1811 that he learned of his father's death at the age of fifty-six. Just over a week later he arrived in Muskau as its new master. After his formal investiture he addressed the municipal and estate officials in his service, promising firm but humane treatment for all. It was only now, in going through the ac-counts, that he realised his father's mismanagement was worse than he had feared, swelling considerably the 300,000 thalers that the estate had owed at the time of his birth. Count Ludwig Erdmann had sys-tematically leached money from the inheritance he was supposed to pass on intact, as documents Pückler saw later made even clearer: 'The way my father went to absolutely every length to ruin the fortune and position of his family is truly pitiful!' He also found 'incontro-vertible proofs' that his sisters Clementine and Agnes, but not Bianca, had tried to despoil him, presumably by egging their father on to dis-inherit him.[8] The resulting sibling quarrel was resolved, and though they met infrequently he remained in correspondence with all of his sisters. Each of them made an appropriate aristocratic marriage but only Agnes bore a child, a son who died as a young man.

The two or three years after his succession were frustrating ones for Pückler. His best moments were in Berlin, where he enjoyed a romance with the wife of a Russian diplomat, but for most of the time he was at home trying to bring order to his estate, an effort ham-pered by the ongoing hostilities. The Saxon economy was on its knees, and in 1812 French troops were billeted in Muskau, the men in the town and the officers in the chateau. He longed to play his part in throwing off the emperor's yoke, but before he could do so he was seized as a Prussian sympathiser and sentenced to house arrest. It was only after French defeat at the Battle of Leipzig in 1813 that he was finally free to take up arms. He was gazetted a major in the Russian army's third German corps under Grand Duke Charles Augustus of Weimar and took part in the battle for Antwerp and the storming of Merksem, as well as leading a detachment that raided Cassel and seized six enemy cannon. For these services he was made a Prussian lieu-tenant-colonel and awarded the Order of Vladimir by Tsar Alexander. After the ceasefire at the end of March 1814 he acted as a military governor in Bruges and then spent six weeks in Paris as a liaison officer between the tsar and the grand duke.

By now he was nearing the end of his third decade. In appearance he was decidedly handsome, far taller than average, with a muscular but slender physique, finely chiselled features and large, expressive blue eyes. He was highly strung and prone to minor ailments, but his con-stitution was basically sound. His manners were pleasing, with a mind both agile and incisive, though neither profound nor original. Despite his distant relations with his mother he owed more to the Callenbergs—especially their breadth of culture and love of travel and the arts—than to the narrow, philistine Pücklers. He had also inher-ited the Callenberg inconsistency of mood. He was quick to take fire, but his enthusiasms and pleasures were short-lived, often followed by depression, and even when fortune smiled on him he sometimes gave way to motiveless brooding.

In his relations with others he was probably right to call himself good-natured rather than good. He had a defensive, almost hygienic attitude to the stirrings of the heart—a legacy of his loveless child-hood—and never truly lost himself in feelings for another person. Instinctively selfish, he could also be cynical. On the other hand he was capable of warm friendship, for his timidity evaporated when he met with real affection. His best qualities were a basic honesty that made him recoil from humbug; a benign curiosity about his fellow human beings; a strong, often mischievous sense of humour; a will-ingness to turn the needle of his irony against himself; and, in com-munication with those he trusted, a deep modesty about his abilities and achievements.

By the beginning of June 1814 his work in Paris was over, and he joined the suite of victorious sovereigns bound for England. According to Karl von Nostiz, who had known him at school in Halle, he had been fascinated by the country even then.[9] Now he would see it for himself.

2

To England: The Jolly Marchioness

'A Vulgar Irish woman near fifty and larger than Mrs Fitzherbert'

On a June evening in 1814 Alexander I and Frederick William III, Russian tsar and Prussian king, crossed the Channel from Boulogne to Dover, where three regiments of the British Army and a large crowd stood ready to welcome them. 'God be praised!' exclaimed the tsar on disembarking, 'I have set foot upon the land that has saved us all.' Next morning they drove to London, where Frederick William moved into Clarence House and Alexander, preferring his own quarters, put up at the Pulteney Hotel in Piccadilly. Soon they were joined by the Austrian chancellor Prince Metternich, Prussia's Field Marshal Blücher, Hetman Platov of the Don Cossacks and a number of lesser crowned heads, including Count Pückler-Muskau's commander the Grand Duke of Weimar. All were received with euphoria. Every day the tsar appeared at his hotel balcony to receive the crowd's acclamations, and when Blücher drove out men unharnessed the horses from his carriage and bore it along themselves. As the diarist Mary Frampton remembers, 'The madness to see persons who had become so famous was carried to an extravagant height: people from the most distant parts of England flocking to London to get a peep from a garret window or even an area grating at a hero or a Prince as they passed.'[1]

After drinking in this adulation for a few weeks most of the dignitaries left, soon to foregather again in Vienna for the great Congress. But some of the soldiers, diplomats and hangers-on who had come with them lingered for months, enjoying the pleasures of the capital and their own popularity. The victory celebrations continued all summer. There was a masked ball at Watier's Club, of which George Bryan 'Beau' Brummell was president, and for the general public fireworks and illuminations without end in Hyde Park, Green Park and St James's Park; marquees and pagodas were erected, and there was a mock naval battle fought by miniature frigates on the Serpentine. The high point was a fête given by the Regent for 2,500 guests at Carlton House in the Duke of Wellington's honour. A hall designed by John Nash was draped in muslin for the occasion, at its centre a temple girt with artificial flowers housing two military bands, while in the gardens covered walks led to supper tents decorated with allegorical tributes to the allies' feats of arms.

Pückler must have been present at many of the festivities, but this summer is one of the most poorly documented periods of his adult life and his movements are hard to trace. He certainly attended the victory parade in Hyde Park on 12 June, and it was at about this time that he took off his uniform and returned to civilian life. He renewed an old friendship with Prince Wilhelm Malte zu Putbus, an adjutant of the Swedish crown prince, and they both stayed at the Clarendon Hotel in Bond Street, described by Captain Gronow as the only hotel in London 'where you could get a genuine French dinner, and for which you seldom paid less than three or four pounds.'[2] From this base they made trips to the races, joined the *beau monde* for its afternoon rides in Hyde Park, attended gala dinners, and went to one of the Duke of Devonshire's famous garden parties at Chiswick. Like other visitors they probably looked around the Tower of London and Westminster Abbey, and admired the Parthenon Marbles lately brought over from Athens by Lord Elgin and displayed in the British Museum. In the Royal Exchange and the Bank of England they could see the symbols of the nation's wealth, and in Whitbread's giant brewery and the new East and West India Docks the edifices of its industrial and commercial achievement.

It would be interesting to know whether Pückler met Beau Brummell. Certainly he later showed a great familiarity with the emblematic dandy's life and the many witticisms attributed to him. A younger son of the private secretary to Prime Minister Lord North and the grandson of a shopkeeper, Brummell had only a small fortune and no pedigree, but raised himself up to be the undisputed arbiter of fashion entirely by dint of his skill in self-promotion. His sartorial code—starched cravats, country-washed linen, simple but perfectly cut coats, Hessian boots and tight pantaloons—was a well-timed reaction against the extravagance of the previous generation in favour of a practical, essentially manly style; but he would not have succeeded in imposing it if he had not exploited the insecurity of rich young men by projecting a self-possessed air and putting into circulation a series of anecdotes testifying to an imperious, rather snobbish wit. By this time Brummell had already fallen out with the Regent, probably because of his sympathy for his neglected wife Princess Caroline, but his star in elegant society was shining as brightly as ever. Its sudden and final eclipse lay less than two years in the future.

Some of his evenings Pückler passed in the theatre. At Covent Garden he saw the tragic actress Eliza O'Neill in her spectacularly successful first London season, and was enraptured by her performances in *Romeo and Juliet* and Thomas Otway's *Venice Preserved*. He was also presented to the Regent, and like many others was struck by his easy, graceful charm. One evening he went to a men's dinner given by the Regent's hearty brother the Duke of York. Also present were the duke's aide-de-camp Colonel 'Kangaroo' Cooke, who had reputedly got his nickname by letting loose a cagefull of marsupials from Peacock's menagerie, and the diplomats Count Merveldt of Austria and Count Beroldingen of Württemberg. At midnight the duke, who had downed six bottles of claret, decided to show his guests his collection of exotic weapons. By this time no one had a steady hand, and both he and Merveldt cut their fingers on an Indian sword. Then Merveldt tried to slice a lighted candle down to its socket with one blow of a Turkish sabre, but instead knocked over and extinguished all the candles on the table. As the men stumbled around in the dark, Cooke suddenly called out, 'By God. I remember the sword is poisoned!' An uncomfortable few moments passed before the colonel admitted that the wine had prompted his words.[3]

No doubt our hero witnessed a number of authentic Regency scenes like this, but he was not one to spend all his time in such revelry. A more serious activity was visiting England's great parks, for the boy who enjoyed tending a corner of the school garden had grown into a keen horticulturalist. In Germany the fashion for formal or 'architectonic' gardens, associated above all with Louis XIV's France, had waned in favour of the landscaped style of Lancelot 'Capability' Brown and Humphry Repton, in which loose clusters of trees, expanses of greensward and carefully designed waterways suggested nature transfigured by art. During his youthful peregrinations in Central Europe and Italy Pückler had made a point of seeing important parks and gardens that lay on his route. In line with the times he came to prefer the English style, and it dawned on him that Muskau, most of which was made over to forestry, offered a canvas for landscaping on a grand scale. This idea was already well formed by 1810 when he went to Weimar to pay homage to Goethe. The great man listened with interest to the young count's schemes and then produced one of those Delphic utterances that he liked to bestow on his visitors: 'Follow this path. You seem to have a talent for it. Of all objects of study Nature is the most unfathomable, but also the most grateful, for she gives happiness to him who seeks it.'[4]

The following year Pückler became master of Muskau and appointed his childhood friend the poet Leopold Schefer as its superintendent. The ravages of war kept his landscaping ambitions in check during the next three years, but in England he was determined to gain as much technical knowledge as possible. In September 1814 he called Schefer to his side and they saw no fewer than thirty-six properties in six weeks, including Stourhead, Longleat, Wilton and Blenheim.[5] His own total was even higher, for he started before Schefer arrived and continued after he left. At Holland House the porter told him the gardens were never open to visitors, but he gave the man a five-shilling bribe and saw as much as he could before being spotted from the house by Lord Holland and ordered off the premises. Everywhere he went he made sketches and took measurements; he observed the difficult operation of transplanting mature trees; and at Stourhead he had several talks with the distinguished topographer Sir Richard Colt Hoare about the use of wooded areas, water and open spaces.

If he was ever to apply the information he hereby acquired he would need far more money than he currently possessed. In the spring of 1814, while still in Bruges and Paris, he had received letters from Schefer bewailing the pitiful condition of the Muskau estate, which had long quartered French troops and lately been requisitioned by the Russians. But a solution appeared to be at hand. Now aged twenty-eight, Pückler recalled the advice his father's secretary Ludewig Wolff had given him years earlier: to salvage his fortunes with an heiress. England was the place to find one, and before long he could claim to have done so: 'Marriage negotiations with Lady Lansdowne,' wrote Wolff, who was still following the count's progress, in his diary for September. Three months later the affair seemed settled, and Pückler wrote to Schefer, now back in Muskau, describing his fiancée as 'an excellent woman, forty-four years old, still reasonably good-looking and very agreeable in her conversation'.[6]

Lady Lansdowne was born Maria Arabella Maddock, the daughter of a Welsh clergyman who moved to Ireland. Her first husband was 'Sir' Duke Gifford, a County Meath squireen calling himself a baronet, whom she bore five daughters. After his death she became the mistress of Lord Wycombe, the eldest son of the first Marquess of Lansdowne. Wycombe's main aim in life appears to have been to gain a reputation for eccentricity, which he achieved with political opinions so radical that for a time he was followed by government spies, and with libertine pursuits that were extreme even for that unbuttoned age. He liked to use gross language when speaking of women, and in letters to friends he referred to Lady Gifford as 'the old sow' and described her physical attractions in comical terms. She may not have been aware of this crudity, or, if she was, chose not to take umbrage at it; either way she held his affections and when he succeeded to the marquisate in 1805 he married her. The society gossip Lady Bessborough reported that among marriages 'the only extraordinary one is the present Ld. Lansdowne and Ly. Gifford—a Vulgar Irish woman near fifty and larger than Mrs Fitzherbert [...]. I suppose it is point d'honneur, for she has liv'd with him publickly as his Mistress for some years past.'[7]

It probably did not occur to the new marchioness to consider her age and size as detracting from her fascinations, for this was the era of matronly beauty. The Regent's well-known taste was for 'fair, fat and forty', and two of his favourites, Lady Hertford and Lady Conyngham, were in their fifties at the height of their power over him. Boisterous and roguish, Lady Lansdowne was much admired. Soon she was on the market again, for after a childless four-year marriage the marquess died of dropsy. His will broke with convention in that everything not positively entailed was left to his wife and the grown daughters from her first marriage rather than to his own family, infuriating the half-brother who succeeded him in the title. In the following years Lady Lansdowne lived principally in the bizarre mock-Gothic tower house her husband had built in Southampton using stones from the existing Norman castle. In 1813 Lord Glenbervie saw her there:

> I have just called on the Dowager Marchioness of Lansdowne in her castle which seems to overlook the world. It is a fine day, and the view was magnificent, both by land and water. She had not break-fasted, and had on a night-cap which I thought very knowing, but which every one of the four daughters, coming into the breakfast room one after the other, exclaimed on as frightful, which her Ladyship humbly acknowledged, adding that she scarcely ever wore anything over her hair. She certainly looked very fresh and hand-some in spite, or with the aid of her night-cap, and being towards twenty years younger than Lady Hertford, and nearly of her size, I cannot help thinking that notwithstanding her vulgarity and Irish brogue, she may prove a dangerous rival to that superb and puissant princess. That she is so already was the chronicle last winter, and the report continues to gain ground.

And Lady Bessborough, visiting the town, was surprised at the sight of the coquettish marchioness, 'who, with her three daughters following her, wrapt in thin lace Veils, blue silk shoes, and bare headed, not only brav'd the wind and the rain, but the sharp stones and muddy streets of Southampton, and the astonish'd gaze of the passengers.'[8]

Pückler must have met Lady Lansdowne within weeks of his arrival in England. Compensating for his cheese-paring youth, he was already spending far too much. His suite at the Clarendon and day-to-day living in the world's most expensive city were more than he could afford, and he was unable to resist buying various luxuries for Muskau. This would not have mattered if he could win Lady Lansdowne's hand, and by Christmas it looked as though he had. He told Schefer that they had signed a marriage contract with terms highly favourable to himself: first, he assumed control of her annual income of £5,000 on the understanding that he give her £1,000 in pin money; second, her furniture and artworks, valued at over £12,000, were to be auctioned and the proceeds paid to him; third, if she died first her claims on property in Yorkshire, her diamonds worth £40,000, and her silver service worth £6,000 were made over to him; and fourth, in the case of a divorce all assets and income reverted to her if he was at fault, but if she was the guilty party she would pay him a large sum in penalty.

> As you can see, my dear friend, I have not done badly for myself, and have made as much use as I could of an old woman's love, but I honestly confess that I dread this marriage despite all the wealth it will bring me. If the constraint I have already had to impose on all my actions is anything to go by, I fear that I am preparing a splendid misery for myself. Furthermore the marchioness's whole family is furious at her folly, as they call it, and she, assailed from all sides by people criticising me, is in the greatest anxiety and uncertainty. They are doing all they can to prevent the marriage, and although I am certain of the marchioness's attachment I know not whether I shall prevail against her family.

He was right to identify Lady Lansdowne's family, that is to say her daughters Ann, Harriet, Eliza, Louisa and Maria, as the force that stood between him and his goal. Ann and Harriet were already married, and the former had personal experience of a foreign wooer, having fended off Count Holmar, a Dane, during three months in 1808.[9] Lady Lansdowne was a fond mother, and the ferocity of her daughters' opposition to her plans, which would of course harm them financially, put her in a sad quandary. Soon they were able to plant doubts in her mind about her suitor's motives and spoil the delight she had taken in her new romance. The vivacious widow's spirits were crushed, but rather than betray her suspicions to Pückler she explained away her misgivings by saying she had grown used to independence and was having second thoughts about living abroad. He sought to allay her fears and strengthen her resolve, knowing how fond of him she was. Harassed on all sides, she begged her friend Lord Lauderdale for help.

James Maitland, eighth Earl of Lauderdale, was a successful politician and economic theorist of West Lothian origins and radical tendencies. Known for his shrewdness, keen temper and abilities as a talker, he also had a mania for getting involved in other people's affairs. An acquaintance recalled that 'if a family *imbroglio* occurred, whatever its nature, in the large circle in which Lord Lauderdale lived, he was sure to be found in the midst of it, as adviser, mediator, or controller. I never knew him more alert and happy than when he had a matter of this kind in hand.' Soon he had the measure of his friend's predicament and undertook to manage everything on her behalf. He and Pückler began to correspond, the Scotsman in English and the German in French, and it is from this exchange, as well as a long letter from Pückler to Lady Lansdowne and a short one from her to him, that the latter stages of their odd courtship can be pieced together.[10]

Straight away Pückler set out his financial position for Lauderdale, explaining that he owned considerable assets even though his income was modest by English standards. He rather implausibly denied wanting to marry the marchioness for her money, but quite reasonably pointed out that her implacable daughters already enjoyed independent incomes. As for Lady Lansdowne's fear that he might divorce her after a few years, he protested that he could scarcely do more to allay it than agree, as he had, to renounce all right to her fortune in that eventuality. His best argument, given the age gap between the parties, was that the contract's terms were needed to protect him in the case of her predeceasing him. Lauderdale wrote his replies with the wails of his friend's married and unmarried children in his ears. What horrified them most was the clause stipulating the transfer of their mother's income, and it was here that he opened his attack. In this he was backed up by Lady Lansdowne herself, who told Pückler she had been wrong to commit herself to such complete dependency. After a while he ceded the point, but to his surprise she was not satisfied. In fact she had more or less lost her head. Within a few months she pledged to marry him and then changed her mind no fewer than four times.

This was a tense period for Pückler. When he signed the marriage contract he had debts with a tailor, a glazier, a coach-maker, a gold-smith and others amounting to £871. He continually pressed Schefer for money, 'for it would create a bad impression if, having passed myself off as a German Croesus, about to marry into a family where no one asks what a thing costs, only if it pleases, I had to go to court for a debt of a hundred or a few hundred pounds and then borrow the sum from the marchioness to avoid a spell in King's Bench Prison.' Schefer eked out what he could from Muskau's still anaemic revenues, but was only able to send small amounts, leading his master to cry out that this 'arrival of money drop by drop is driving me to despair, as it evaporates before it can gain any consistency.' By February 1815 his debts stood at £1,057 and he had to ask his fiancée for a short-term loan. Soon afterwards he was in the awkward position of having to defer repayment, claiming that an extraordinary post-war levy had swallowed up £1,200 he had expected to receive from home.

When it became clear that Lady Lansdowne would yield to her family's opposition to their marriage, Pückler had to consider his options. Having deposited a signed copy of the contract with his lawyer, he was in a position to sue for breach of promise, a serious offence at that time, and secure a large sum in compensation. His lawyer thought he should do just that, as he told her afterwards, but he rejected the idea; meanwhile she, unaware of this decision, got hold of the document by devious means and refused to give it back. A more ruthless man would not have surrendered his trump card, but Pückler's feelings revolted at the thought of playing it. All the same it made him furious, as he told Lauderdale, to think of 'the time I have so fruitlessly spent in England being tormented in vain and being more ill used than ever a man was at the hands of a woman.' Lady Lansdowne now asked for the return of the £2,100 she had advanced to him to set up their household, but he countered that the cost of his stay in England, greatly extended for her sake, and of the injury his absence had done to the management of his estate, amounted to nearly twice as much. Certainly he could have got far more in an action for breach of promise.

Pückler sent his last letter to Lady Lansdowne soon after his return home in April 1815. He had not got over his vexation, and said there were things he would write if his respect for the female sex did not restrain his pen. Still, he did not wish their relations to end thus, and washed away the acrimony with soft soap: 'I had a sincere attachment for you and my conscience tells me to this day that I should have made you happy. [. . .] Maybe you are wrong to congratulate yourself on having escaped in time from the danger of marrying me.' He even told her he would restore the sum he had kept 'so as not to have even a shadow of wrong on my side', though he warned that it would take him two years to raise it. The matter was concluded, and Lord Lauderdale could preen himself on his negotiating skills. He magnanimously assured the count that he would 'ever mention his conduct in the recent unfortunate transactions concerning his marriage with the utmost respect.' Lady Lansdowne too was relieved, but also sad, as she told Pückler shortly before his departure:

I have sacrificed myself, to what I am told I ought—to my *family*, and *friends*. What becomes of me *now* can be of little consequence to any body, but I will never deny my attachment to you, and that I had looked to being United to you, and to having found that happiness which I have long been a stranger to. All this can be of no consequence to you, except a sort of satisfaction it gives me, of letting you know, that whatever you may think to the contrary I am wretched.

Ever Ever yours,
M. A. L.

3

MARRIAGE AND DIVORCE

'Whoever you love comes to belong to you and cannot get by without you'

D espite the tribulations of his failed courtship Pückler returned from his nine-month stay in England full of admiration, especially for the art of living and the customs of elegant society he found there. He became a confirmed dandy, and engaged a London agent named John Blum to send over the accoutrements he needed to play the part, including a blue coat, a cashmere waistcoat, white summer pantaloons, black silk pantaloons for evening wear, white silk stockings and washable leather gloves. Blum was succeeded at some point by W. M. Hunt, the valet of the Duke of York's adjutant 'Kangaroo' Cooke. Hunt's service with such a prominent Regency buck qualified him to give sartorial tips to his German client—on the cut of trousers, the colour of handkerchief to sport during the day and with evening dress, the folding collars of waistcoats and even what sort of watch chain to use and how it should hang.[1]

All this finery served him well at a party given by Lady Castlereagh, the British foreign secretary's wife, at the Congress of Aachen in 1818, for in elegance of dress he eclipsed all the other guests, at least in his own estimation. And it was not just his clothes that were English. In London he had rediscovered his boyhood love of English horses and purchased several at Tattersall's auctions by Hyde Park Corner. He also brought home a curricle—a fast, open, two-wheeled vehicle—and a larger carriage with his coat of arms painted on the panels, 'for this can only be so finely done in England'. To look after these treasures he acquired a groom by the name of Child, of whom he said that 'no one else knows how to drive in such a fashionable way or sit on a box seat with such *grandezza*.'[2] It is hardly surprising that Pückler was sometimes taken for an Englishman. A patriotic French landlady refused to let him over her threshold on that assumption, and in Göttingen a young English student approached him and asked if he had the pleasure of speaking to a compatriot.

If in appearance he was English, in fact he was now Prussian. In punishment for Saxony's French alliance over half of its territory was confiscated by the victorious powers. Upper Lusatia, and with it Muskau, fell to Prussia, and Pückler's new capital was Berlin, eighty-five miles to the north-west of his seat. Because of agrarian reforms recently introduced in Prussia, Pückler now lost some of his old semi-feudal rights, as well as revenue-raising powers and tax privileges, reducing his net income by about two-fifths. But neither this blow nor the heavy mortgages he inherited could deflect him from his determination to transform Muskau into a great park, and on 1 May 1815 he issued a proclamation to the burghers of the town:

> As I have now decided to make Muskau my fixed residence for the rest of my life, to attend to the welfare of my good burghers and subjects with paternal care, and to use my income to benefit them rather than strangers, so I doubt not that the inhabitants of this town will afford me the satisfaction of working strenuously towards my most cherished goal, the accomplishment of which will give them pleasure and true utility both now and, even more, in the future. I mean the laying out of a park.[3]

His 'subjects' did not disappoint him. They sold him parcels of land in their ownership that he needed for his project at prices fixed by arbitration, and over the succeeding decades they watched in amazement as their little town became the centre of a majestic new landscape.

Though not an area of great natural beauty, Muskau had the advantages of undulating terrain and a river, the Neisse, running through it. In transforming it he drew plans and then directed their realisation, spending whole days riding from one site to another and going into every detail of the work in progress. Labour was cheap, and he employed a workforce of over a hundred to drain marshes and fertilise the sandy soil; excavate land to create hills; clear expanses of closely-packed, lanky pines to make way for elms, maples and oaks; and channel water into small lakes, a stream flowing through a meadow near the chateau, and an expanded moat. Everything was organised around a small number of carefully placed paths, which meandered in an unforced way across the landscape and, like silent guides, revealed new perspectives at every turn. In tribute to the country that had inspired him, Pückler built a thatched 'English' cottage with its own flower garden and pretty views of the Neisse valley.

As with most beginners there were lapses of taste—like putting up a hermitage and engaging as its inhabitant a bearded old guards-man with an enormous nose who had to wear a monkish habit and was only allowed out on Mondays. All the same when John Adey Repton, the son of Humphry Repton and himself a noted architect and landscaper, was invited to Muskau in 1822, he was impressed with what he found. Repton removed coach houses, stables and a tree-lined avenue from the vicinity of the chateau and erected a fence between the pleasure ground and the park, but said there was little else for him to contribute to a creation that seemed to be evolving in an unforced way from local conditions.[4] Pückler's use of these was his signal achievement, according to the prolific park-designer Eduard Petzold:

> The entire secret of his style lies in the study of nature, and his deep understanding of it. He studied the peculiarities of every terrain and brought its finest qualities to the fore, never yielding to the temptation to try and create nature anew. In this way his park, for all its simplicity, bore the stamp of naturalness and grandeur—a unified whole that the observer could immediately see was the product of a single mind.[5]

Not quite a single mind, for early on in his labours Pückler found a long-term partner. She was Lucie Countess Pappenheim, and he met her in April 1816 in Berlin, where, having separated from her husband, she lived with her daughter Adelheid and ward Helmina. In her youth she had been a comely blonde, but at forty her looks were faded and she had grown rather stout, so Berlin society was surprised to learn that she and Pückler, nine years her junior and one of the kingdom's most eligible bachelors, were to marry. Some said it was her money he coveted, others the patronage of the Prussian State Chancellor Prince Hardenberg, whose only daughter she was. The cynics were right on both counts, but what none foresaw was the enduring strength of the couple's bond. The sexual element was either non-existent or short-lived, for Pückler's decided preference was for slender women in their first youth. Nor did he profess a passion he did not feel, telling her at the outset that he would not be faithful. Nevertheless his regard for her was real and profound. Lucie was a clever, cultivated woman of refined tastes, immediate and strong feelings, generosity of spirit and a talent for friendship. Prone to anxiety, she had the strength to overcome it when the situation demanded. She was, everyone agreed, a great lady to her fingertips.

Moreover she loved him deeply. She had not been a blameless wife to Count Pappenheim, and offered to tolerate her second husband's infidelities as long as he did not conceal them. Soon he was in the habit of telling her his every thought, and when they were apart he wrote her daily letters that were artless and expansive, for such was his nature when he met with affection. He did not lie when he told her he loved her no less when pursuing another, and demonstrated his feeling with a constant stream of inventive gifts. Soon their pet names were in place: she was 'Schnucke' (lambkin), and he was 'Lou', possibly from 'loup' (wolf) or short for 'filou' (rascal). Lucie took up the role of comforter to her volatile husband, who between bouts of energy and ebullience was given to depression, but sometimes she needed to be soothed herself, for she had a tendency to misinterpret what he said, take needless offence, and in general overshoot the mark emotionally. The key to their lifelong attachment was that he was like a son to her, while she was the mother he had never had, 'the mother of your choosing', as she put it.[6] Sadly we only have direct testimony for one half of this unusual partnership until 1833, as Lucie's letters before that date are lost and only come into view as reflected in his.

They could not marry until she was divorced, and while she stayed in Berlin to expedite the legal process he worked feverishly to get Muskau ready for her arrival. His engagement letters breathe not a word of love, concentrating instead on grass seed, pineapple cultivation, parrots and monkeys for a menagerie, servants' liveries, crystal glasses, china services and wallpaper. In England there were separate summer and winter carpets, he told her, and they must have them too. He sent her on errands to buy various luxuries and jokingly called her his commissioner, though it was her money that was being spent, by him in Muskau and her in Berlin. She did not stint in her efforts or the sums she provided, so fascinated was she by his descriptions of her future home. Finally she obtained her divorce and they were married in October 1817. He feared that Muskau might not live up to her expectations, but need not have worried—her love for it was immediate and enduring.

After a life at the centre of society Lucie found the park a blissful idyll. She stood at her husband's side as he made landscaping plans and issued instructions, helped to manage the many projects in hand at any one time, and took sole charge when he was away. With a keen eye for beauty, she was soon able to suggest improvements of her own. Pückler encouraged her interest and talent without jealousy, and gave her a free rein when she told him she wanted to take advantage of the estate's iron-rich springs to create a spa. A large bathing house, chalets, a restaurant and assembly rooms were built under her supervision. The new facilities, intended to attract the wealthy classes and provide a new source of income, were opened in June 1823.

Despite her pleasure in the park Lucie was not bedded on roses. If she had hoped her husband would let a decent period elapse before enjoying the freedoms he had insisted on she was soon disabused. Even during their engagement he showed her a *billet doux* from a married woman who was chasing him and asked her to order a dress for a local girl, 'a real goddess of health' with 'iron thighs', after taking her measurements himself. Lucie's acquiescence was not cheaply bought, since she had been attractive to men and found it hard to make do with the friendship-love he offered. Her hardest trial came shortly after they married when he grew besotted with Helmina, the girl she had adopted as a sister for her daughter Adelheid. Lucie tried valiantly to keep the elfin seventeen-year-old out of his reach, but at last he succeeded in making her his mistress. The main consequence of Lucie's almost superhuman forbearance during this episode, and his subsequent repentance, was to strengthen his attachment to her and give her the moral leverage of the selfless over the selfish: 'Every day,' he told her, 'I sense all too deeply how truthfully you spoke when you said that whoever you love comes to belong to you and cannot get by without you.' He resolved never to hurt her so much again.[7]

As the years passed his emotional reliance on her increased, and her loving support became the mainspring of his ambition. He did not mind if she urged him to reform, though sometimes he reacted light-heartedly: 'I could not help laughing at your asking me to try to be sensible for just one year; you must think this would require a most arduous effort on my part. Unfortunately you are quite right!'[8] In the early years of their marriage he responded just as breezily to her concern about their spending on the park, but the persistence of her fretting began to irk him as he saw its cause but did not want to face up to it. He said she was too ready to lose her head over a trifle, and because she had a unique power to elate but also to paralyse his spirits she must never reproach him or give way to lamentations. She often ignored this demand, as the number of times he reiterated it shows. Her will was too firm for subservience, and she had a ready temper, for which he jokingly called her a powder-keg. On the other hand, if she followed up criticism with tenderness he was delighted and told her she had swept all his sadness away.

They had not been married long when Pückler began trying to persuade Lucie's father Prince Hardenberg to launch him into a lucrative career in the state service. After some prevarication the wily old politician did what he could, but failed to get the idea past his colleagues, who no doubt perceived that the young man's mercurial nature and dislike of constraint made him unfit for public life. Furthermore, although Frederick William III quite liked him, the powerful crown prince, the great hope of the clerical reaction and the future Frederick William IV, hated him for his independent views and

raffish lifestyle. Once it was clear that he would not enjoy the emol-
uments of office, Pückler pinned his hopes on a commission set up to
determine the indemnity payable to Prussia's formerly Saxon
landowners for their loss of privileges. However, progress was very
slow and after years of wrangling only about a fifth of his claim was
met. In compensation, and much at Hardenberg's insistence, he was
raised from a count to a prince, the highest rank of the nobility and
sometimes, though not in his case, a royal title.

There were other business matters that took him to Berlin during
these years, such as discussions with his banker about mortgages and
securities and with treasury officials about taxes. While he was there
he saw friends, pursued amatory diversions, and performed various
stunts: he won a wager by riding his English horse Sprightly from the
village of Zehlendorf to the city gates in under thirty minutes; he harnessed a foursome of stags to his carriage and drove to a central street,
where he sat reading a book as if oblivious to the staring onlookers;
and on a cloudless autumn day he and the aeronautical pioneer
Reichard went up in a balloon with a crowd of thousands watching
from the streets and squares (a few hours later they landed in a spruce
tree near Potsdam, where they were spotted by a soldier on a country
road and helped down with ladders). These and other escapades won
him renown, but his very desire to garner such attention also made
him vulnerable, based as it was on an insecurity, a vanity without self-
confidence, that was the legacy of parental neglect. Even in more
mature years he often tried to seem more brilliant and fascinating than
he really was, and when he failed, or was faced with the superior
claims to admiration of another, he would freeze in company and
suffer in private.

Pückler was at his happiest, and most relaxed, among Berlin's cultural circles, especially at the parties of the banker's wife Madame Beer
and the smaller gatherings of the city's foremost literary hostess Rahel
Varnhagen von Ense. The latter in particular thought him an excellent
acquisition, declaring him to be 'clever, elegant and handsome',[9] and
he also made a good impression on her husband Karl August, an influential writer and literary mentor whose biographical essays, diaries
and letters provide the best picture of Berlin's political and cultural life

at that time. A kindly man behind a mask of sober reserve, he was charmed by his guest's refinement and obvious pleasure in stimulating company. They did not at this time move beyond the mutual regard of congenial acquaintances, but a few years later they began a warm, unbroken friendship that would make a deep impact on Pückler's life.

Much less enjoyable was the courtly and aristocratic milieu to which our hero properly belonged. Narrowly focused on ritual and precedence, it had neither the nuances of fashion nor the cultural brilliance without which social elites lack glamour. The entertainments of his own class were, he felt, 'a ghastly, unforgivably empty exercise in killing time', and his view was so widely shared that the Berlin court had a Europe-wide reputation for dullness. To quote from Varnhagen's diary: 'People complain of the bitterest boredom; court ladies and adjutants are in despair.' And again: 'Everyone complains of the vacuity and tedium of court days, of the so-called festivities of the carnival holidays, and of high society as a whole.' When the Earl of Clanwilliam arrived as British ambassador in 1823 he could scarcely believe the desert he had entered. In his own recollection he was the first diplomat who even invited women to embassy dinners, and Varnhagen records that he gravely offended the strict notions of hierarchy by inviting Madame Beer and the opera singers Henriette Sontag and Angelica Catalani to a reception at his residence.[10]

All this was a world away from Regency London, where a shopkeeper's grandson like Beau Brummell could be a leader of fashion and a poet like Thomas Moore might dine with dukes and think the favour was on his side. The former's case was especially striking, as Pückler later reflected: 'The influence that Br[ummell], without birth or fortune, without a handsome figure or an outstanding mind, was able to exert for many years in London simply by genteel impertinence, droll originality, love of sociability and skill in dress, even now gives an excellent measure of the nature of that society.'[11] And if such brittle achievements also spoke to a superficiality and moral decadence, and though Pückler would eventually grow disenchanted with the dandy ideal, he continued to see in Brummell the embodiment of English high society's capacity to renew itself by embracing fresh

talent, a capacity that made it very different from its Prussian counterpart.

While Berlin society was crimped and dreary, so were the politics of the Berlin government, which after the Restoration of
1814–1815 ruled on the principle of absolute monarchy, almost as if
the French Revolution and the ideas it bore forth had never existed.
Especially after the Carlsbad Decrees of 1819, which put an end to
hopes that Frederick William III might promulgate a constitution, the
state became ever more authoritarian, with bureaucrats, censors and
police spies setting the tone. Ranged against this reactionary system in
Prussia as elsewhere in the German lands were the liberals, who believed in democratic participation and national self-determination.
The two forces would clash in the Europe-wide revolutions of 1848.

Accustomed to the jittery anti-democratic impulses of their own
government, Prussians visiting Britain in the 1820s found it a haven
of freedom and progress: Lieutenant von Willisen of the General Staff
returned from a stay of 1826 full of praise for the sanctity of individual rights he found there; and Prussia's ambassador Baron Maltzahn
joked that he hardly knew what to put in his dispatches, as anything
he heard through private channels was sure to have been in the *Courier*
two days before. Of a piece with this, or so it appeared, were the deeds
of the foreign secretary George Canning, who recognised the independence of the South American states, supported liberals against absolutism in Portugal and sheltered newly emancipated Greece from
Turkish aggression. Varnhagen recorded that his friends felt 'sympathy,
almost enthusiasm, for England's powerful, honourable, and freethinking role'; and the poet Heinrich Heine wrote that 'when the ra-
diance of Canning's words penetrated all the way to us, the few hearts
in which hope still dwelt jumped for joy.'[12]

Pückler supported the reformists' aspirations, but in a fairly detached way, giving little sign of the interest in politics he later developed. It was landscaping that consumed his energies at this time. The
results were spectacular, and Muskau's fame spread far and wide; but
as the park blossomed, so did his debts. Lucie's fortune had been spent,
and wages, which poor harvests in 1816 and 1817 had kept low, gradually rose; meanwhile the price of alum mined on the estate fell and

some tenants became insolvent. He could not sell Branitz, his smaller seat, because an entail restricted its possession to members of his own family, and Lucie's hopes of a sizeable bequest from her father were dashed when he died leaving everything to his young mistress, a baker's daughter of ruthless methods. Pückler signed a contract with a timber merchant and only realised subsequently how unfavourable it was; unable to meet his obligations, he had to pay a stiff penalty to escape from them. Lucie's spa was more successful, but the revenue it generated was too small to justify the outlay, partly because potential visitors were put off by the atrocious roads in the area.

Pückler should have been a very rich man, for Muskau's annual revenue in the 1820s exceeded 100,000 thalers, or £15,000. To give an idea of what this means, Mr Darcy in Jane Austen's *Pride and Prejudice* (1813) has an income of £10,000 and is considered extremely wealthy despite the far higher cost of living in England. Indeed, even £1,000 a year sufficed for a genteel existence if carefully managed, providing for a carriage and four or five servants. The problem was that by 1823 the estate carried debts of about 500,000 thalers, or over £75,000. Once Pückler had paid the interest on this sum, numerous salaries and pensions and his land tax bill he was left with only 12,000 thalers, less than £2,000, for his own expenditure, nothing like enough to live according to his rank and create a park.[13] With creditors swirling ever closer, it seemed that the only way to fend off bankruptcy without selling up was to wind down their household and live modestly in a small town somewhere, returning periodically to carry on such landscaping as the availability of ready money allowed. It never quite came to this, but they greatly reduced their spending and parted with many of their servants; the prince also sold his prized tilbury, curricle and English horses, and the princess her jewellery and plate. With characteristic fervour she even planned drastic cuts in their heating and lighting expenses, but he told her not to get carried away.

Then she had another idea. On 31 October 1823, a day after his birthday, she handed him a letter she had written in her room, the only one of hers that survives from this period. It was nothing less than an offer of divorce so that he could remarry:

I believe that your sentiments are such that no outward events or circumstances can alter or dissolve them, and it is only in this firm conviction that I draw the strength to make you a sacrifice that is difficult beyond words, but without which *I can find no relief.* May God give His blessing to this—and let it yield for you the purest, most undisturbed happiness, and for your maternal friend the consciousness of her faithful devotion and submission unto death to the most *precious* and *beloved* being she ever possessed in this world.[14]

Finding a wealthy bride, she reasoned, was the only way he could avoid having to give up his half-completed park. As she later wrote in her diary, 'I, in my love for the prince, made him the terrible sacrifice of a divorce so as to give him happier prospects in the dire straits in which he found himself.' He was deeply moved. The feeling her words gave him was sublime and indescribable, he told her, but separation was too hard a fate and he was unwilling to accept her offer. Instead he gave it a new twist: he would divorce her, but only pro forma, and then marry a naïve, pliable heiress who would in due course be cajoled into accepting her continued presence at Muskau. In this way Lucie could carry on helping him with the park, and, far from driving a wedge between them, their divorce would bind them faster than ever: 'For as long as we live, whatever the circumstances, our two souls in love and understanding will form a single, undivided whole.' And again: 'O Schnucke, now that it is decided I am to lose you, even if only in name, I have fallen completely in love with you.'[15]

Dissolving their marriage could take months, even years, and he decided to use that time to look for suitable parties. He made a few tentative efforts in Berlin, but soon his thoughts turned to England, where two friends of his had recently had rich pickings. Baron Heinrich von Maltzan from Munich (not the ambassador Maltzahn) had married a merchant's daughter, Julia Poulett Thomson, and now led a life of tasteful leisure in Dresden. Pückler visited them there and found the baroness an excellent woman who had furnished her house in a fine English style. Then Baron Wilhelm von Biel of Mecklenburg secured her sister Sophia, with a dowry of at least £30,000 and more in prospect. On being admitted to the secret of Pückler's plans, Biel told him that if he wished to see heiresses growing on trees he should hurry to England. The Thomsons, he said, were related by marriage to the financier Alexander Baring, who had three unwed daughters worth a minimum of £80,000 each.[16]

Of course to succeed in England he must be properly divorced. Achieving this became more urgent in January 1826 when the bankruptcy of a Berlin banking house further weakened his finances, while from London his agent W. M. Hunt wrote that 'all your Trades people weres me to death for thear money'.[17] In February Lucie made a direct appeal to the king, who hastened things along and signed the decree absolute. In March Pückler summoned his estate officials to inform them that his ex-wife remained their mistress and should be treated with the same deference as before. In Berlin his divorce and travel plans were now well known, and to evade wagging tongues he retreated to Muskau, where he spent a dispiriting few months turning some of his remaining effects into money to pay for his journey.

There cannot be many couples who are closer when they divorce than when they wed, or who enter into a marriage of convenience only to undergo a divorce of convenience nine years later. However, they knew their mind, and there seemed every reason to hope that Pückler would win his venture. At forty he was a shade mature for a fortune hunter, but with his tall, supple physique and handsome, lively features he looked much younger, some said ten years younger. Only his greying hair would have given him away, and two years before he had taken to dyeing it black. And while he did not relish the prospect of courting women he felt nothing for, he knew he would have Lucie's constant encouragement. He was, he said, like a leaky vessel that might founder before reaching port, 'but my Schnucke's love will swell the sails, and despite sandbanks and rocky coasts the little ship will fly along. And then, good Schnucke, we will have a long, comfortable rest, for it has truly been an arduous voyage!'[18]

He and Lucie made the most of each other's company before what they knew would be a long separation, and then he got into his travelling carriage and set off. She accompanied him as far as Bautzen some twenty-five miles from Muskau. On 7 September 1826 they parted, and she headed back home.

4

To England Again

*'This is what comes of hospitality that springs from
ostentation'*

On Friday 29 September 1826 the *Morning Chronicle* reported
that Lord Amherst, governor-general of India, had publicly
thanked Major-General Sir Archibald Campbell and the
British Army, 'by whose gallant and persevering exertions the recent
contest with the Burmese Empire' had been won. As well as securing
territorial gains and the renunciation of Burmese claims on Assam,
Campbell's victory on difficult terrain over a numerically superior
enemy had, said Lord Amherst, 'nobly sustained our military reputation'. Meanwhile in London the home secretary Robert Peel informed the House of Commons that although the incidence of petty
offences like pilfering and pocket-picking was increasing, violent
crime had recently declined. The latter trend was, however, not evident
the previous day at the Middlesex Sessions, where the case of a
'Daring Outrage on a Female' excited 'a very powerful interest'
among the county magistrates. They heard Charlotte Gunnell, 'about
20 years old, of good figure and prepossessing appearance', testify that
John Taft, an ostler at the King's Arms at Uxbridge, had sought to take
'improper liberties with her person', and when she resisted had hurled
her from a bridge into the Frays River, from which she was rescued
by two passers-by. After hearing various witnesses the jury needed
only fifteen minutes to return a guilty verdict.

Among the great men of the realm, the Duke of York had just
averted the humiliation of foreclosure on the London mansion he was
building (now Lancaster House) when the government agreed to
defray all further expenses connected with the work and refund him

the sums he had already spent. The Duke of Devonshire, on the other hand, had just relinquished his plan of erecting houses on his Chiswick estate, yielding to the advice that 'to increase the population in that neighbourhood might inconvenience the visitors to the Palladian Villas, on the occasion of great *fêtes*.' The news from the money markets was that Mexican bonds had risen during the last half-monthly account by a staggering fourteen per cent, with several of the South American securities doing nearly as well. On the other hand Prussian stock had offered few bargains of late, and variation on do-mestic funds was negligible. Finally, for theatregoers the main novelty was the revival of Sheridan's *The Rivals* at Drury Lane to showcase the talents of the newcomer Mr Burke as Sir Lucius O'Trigger. The paper's reviewer was unimpressed by his performance, finding that he had 'not a very good person, nor an easy deportment, and his voice certainly wants power.'

On the day readers of the *Morning Chronicle* were digesting all this, Pückler wrote his first letter to Lucie from England. Accompanied by his manservant Berndt he had travelled through Germany and the Netherlands, and on arriving in Rotterdam sent her a lithograph of the steamboat that would take him across the Channel: 'A † marks [. . .] the spot where I shall stand, and if you use your imagination you can see me waving my handkerchief to bid you goodbye, shouting back a thousand loving, heartfelt greetings from afar.'[1] After a stormy, forty-hour journey he arrived near London Bridge late on 28 September. The following morning, after giving the customs officers a guinea to hurry along their inspection of his luggage, he drove to the West End and the Clarendon Hotel, where he had stayed in 1814, and whose French-Swiss owner Monsieur Jacquier had been succeeded by his son. His first call, later the same day, was to the offices of Nathan Mayer Rothschild, from whom he drew £150 on the letter of credit he had brought with him.

His arrival went largely unnoticed, though the *New Times* re-ported on 5 October that 'Prince Buckler from Berlin' was residing at the Clarendon. As London was empty of fashionable society he decided to go on a round of sightseeing. New since his earlier visit were Waterloo Bridge, with its nine imposing granite arches, and Sir

Richard Westmacott's nude bronze of Achilles, erected in homage to the Duke of Wellington by a committee representing the women of England and made ridiculous by the fig leaf appended after much deliberation by said committee. The dominant force behind recent changes in London's appearance was John Nash. Pückler found his new Regent Street and Portland Place a little gimcrack in detail but superbly grand in composition, and much admired Regent's Park, especially the incorporation of houses in its layout, which prefigured his own pioneering ideas on the integration of parkland with living and working space. He also praised the lake:

> Here Art has fully overcome the difficult problem of concealing her operations in a seemingly free Nature. One fancies a broad river banked with dense bushes flowing into the distance and dividing into several streams, while in fact it is merely a standing, though clear, body of water contained in a laboriously excavated basin. This delightful landscape, with hills rising up in the distance, and surrounded by a mile-long circus of splendid buildings, is certainly worthy of the capital of the world; and once the young saplings have grown into old giants, it will scarcely find its match anywhere.[2]

Other novelties in garden design were less to his liking. A few days after his arrival he visited Chiswick, which he had looked over with great pleasure during his first stay. This time his feelings were more mixed because of a new formalism in the gardens and pleasure ground, something he saw often enough in other places over the next few months to realise that it constituted a new trend:

> In the garden I found that much had been altered, but not for the better, and what prevails now is a mixture of regularity and irregularity that makes for an unhappy effect. In many other places too the unsightly fashion has caught on of planting almost the whole pleasure ground with single specimens of rare trees arranged more or less in rows, making the lawns look like tree nurseries. In the shrubberies each plant is pruned on all sides to prevent any chance

of it touching its neighbour; the soil around them is carefully worked over every day, and the edges of the lawns are cut in rigid lines, with the result that there is more black earth than green foliage on view, and all natural shapeliness and uncribbed beauty are suppressed.[3]

Also in the early days of his stay he rode to Hampton Court and saw the Palace, the Royal Stud and the Great Vine, which already filled the seventy-five-foot greenhouse built for it. Nearby was the villa where Pückler's former fiancée Lady Lansdowne lived alone. A few years before, in Aachen, he met the husband of one of her daughters: 'He assured me that Lady Lansdowne had only ever spoken positively of me, and that the whole family, including his wife, were still very attached to me.' Emboldened by this he now paid the elderly marchioness a visit and found her delighted to see him. He told her candidly what had brought him to England again and she promised to help if she could, though as she no longer mixed much in society her influence was, she said, diminished. Soon after he ran into her former negotiator Lord Lauderdale, who greeted him just as cordially. Pückler also paid his respects to a third acquaintance from 1814, the Duke of York, and was sad to find him 'much changed'.[4] The sometime hero of bibulous dinners was in the last stages of heart disease and dropsy, and died three months later.

The person he saw most was the Prussian legation secretary Count Lottum. A career diplomat and later ambassador at The Hague, Lottum was an intelligent, bright-eyed young man determined to enjoy London but hard put to do so on his inadequate salary. He became Pückler's best friend in England, and the first of his many good offices was to let him use the diplomatic bag for his correspondence with Lucie. Pückler also got on well with the ambassador Maltzahn, a steady, well-meaning man who kept a fairly low profile, and he was a regular guest at the Prussian Embassy at 4 Carlton House Terrace. Indeed many of his regular companions in England were members of the diplomatic corps, who, unlike the native higher classes, lived in London all year round. Among these were Count Münster of Hanover, Prince Polignac of France, Marquis Palmela of Portugal and

Prince Lieven of Russia. The last was a mere cipher, and Russia's real representative his wife Dorothea, Princess Lieven, the most influential foreigner of either sex in England. This position owed little to her looks—'very thin, very coppery and very ugly', in Pückler's view[5]—but she was a supremely distinguished woman whose alluring manner and intellectual acuity mesmerised British and Continental statesmen alike. She was also an arbiter of fashionable society, and to prosper a visitor had to get on the right side of her.

Austria provided the most flamboyant and best liked of London's diplomats in Prince Paul Anton (Pal Antal) Esterhazy von Galantha, a Hungarian magnate of incalculable wealth. Pückler often attended the epicurean feasts at his residence, Chandos House, and they established a close camaraderie. The Prussian basked in his host's 'Austrian good nature' and found him 'a man of talent, refined manners, skill and tact, and withal cheerful, unpretentious and obliging, although the devil certainly has his part.' The final phrase alludes to Esterhazy's notoriety as a roué, an occupation he pursued with hoggish insatiability. Newspapers joked openly about his illegitimate children and forays into insalubrious districts, and the courtesan Harriette Wilson published an account of his clumsy attempt to secure her services as a procuress. Baron Neumann, his rather fastidious secretary, despised him for his easy-going carnality and felt sorry for his dignified, high-born wife, who despite an understandable coolness towards her husband was a perfect ambassadress.[6] Pückler admired her too, and sometimes visited her in her apartments to play *écarté* or join in the games of her three winsome children.

Another foreign friend was his creditor Nathan Mayer Rothschild, the greatest of that illustrious clan. Born in Frankfurt in 1777, he began working at the age of twelve in his father's commodity trading business. In 1798 he moved to England to act as his commission agent, but later turned to dealing on the London stock exchange, concentrating on foreign bills, government securities and bullion and using the policy of making small profits on large transactions to earn a reputation for caution and reliability. Meanwhile his brothers set up operations in Paris, Vienna, Frankfurt and Naples, and over time the House of Rothschild became established as the banker to monarchs and governments across the Continent. A stocky, bald man and a frank philistine, stern at his counter but jovial away from it, Nathan Mayer Rothschild was one of the City's best-known characters. When Pückler met him he had been in England for nearly three decades but remained an unmistakeably German figure, speaking with a thick accent and routinely using German words when the English ones escaped him.

To Rothschild Pückler's letters of credit must have seemed very small beer, and from the first he treated him in an avuncular spirit. When he drew £150 on his arrival the banker smiled and said he wished he could afford to travel for pleasure rather than having to work for his living; the prince returned the twinkle in the older man's eye and protested that Europe could not function without him. Every few weeks he was invited to dinner parties at Rothschild's house in Piccadilly or his villa near Stoke Newington, at which his host revealed a genial love of display. One day he let himself be persuaded to parade before his guests in his various court uniforms, and on another gave his opinion of those who had bestowed them: 'This people, how do you call them? Yes, the King of France and family—they would have been starving, if I had not given them money, and the Emperor of Russia, and the King of Prussia and the Emperor of Austria, and all that sort of people, what would have become of them without me?'[7] The great man certainly lacked tact, and Pückler wondered how much of his social success was owed to his more refined, English-born wife Hannah.

He had not been in the country long when Lottum got him into the Travellers Club in Pall Mall, established seven years earlier for globe-trotting Englishmen and resident foreigners of note. This, and to a lesser extent the United Services Club, which he joined later, played a central role in Pückler's London life. The sheepskin rugs, the marble fireplaces, the well-stocked library, the journals laid out on a large table, the inviting armchairs, the immense wine cellar: everything appealed to him about these exclusively British institutions. Most of all he was struck by the way even the grandest persons obeyed all the written and unwritten rules framed for general convenience. In the assembly rooms and casinos of Continental Europe someone wanting to play whist had to find his own partners and then wait, often an hour or more, for a table to come free, whereas at the Travellers a man standing by to join a foursome automatically replaced another who had completed two rubbers. The only unfortunate thing about English clubs, according to our observer, was that though they might admit a foreigner, they could never quite treat him as an equal: any complaints he made about the service were taken in bad part; his petty debts were called in more promptly than those of other members; and if he raised his knife to his mouth (normal practice in Germany) he would be met with hard stares.

After a fortnight in London Pückler felt his equestrian enthusiasm stirring within him and set off for Newmarket. The town was crowded with visitors, and he was lucky to find a room in a private house for three guineas a week. Here he chanced to meet his old friend Count Gustav Batthyany, a lively Hungarian who spent most of his time and money in England indulging his passions for the turf and the chase. The two men were up early the next day to watch the afternoon's competitors being gently exercised, and after breakfast they went to Mr Tattersall's auction. At midday the races began and they positioned themselves among the rows of unharnessed carriages that stood three or four deep on either side of the final stretch of the course. It was exciting viewing because almost every contest was close:

> The main skill of the jockeys here is keeping to the shrewd policy of letting their horses show as much of their pace as they need to win, but no more. If they see that they have no chance they fall right back, and there is never very much separating those still in contention at the finish. The grotesque spectacle of a rider a thousand paces behind the field belabouring his mount like a steam-engine with whip and spurs is only seen in France and Germany.[8]

On his first day he picked a winner three times and pocketed a tidy sum, but on the next his judgement deserted him and he lost twice as much.

Pückler found several old acquaintances in Newmarket and made some new ones, including the Tharp family of Chippenham Park, who invited him and Batthyany to dinner. Chippenham was just three miles away, and so after the day's racing they rode straight there and were received by Captain John Tharp, his wife Anna Maria and their son and three daughters. The other guests included a local landowner with his pretty wife and her equally pretty sister; Miss Brummell, a niece of the now exiled Beau; and a City dandy (as opposed to the superior West End sort) called Mr Moseley. Pückler records the experience of dining in a large private house with anthropological precision:

> As in France one leads ladies to the table on one's arm rather than by hand; and here, like there, there are none of the antiquated bows and curtseys still exchanged in the best society in Germany by the gentleman and the lady he has just handed out. On the other hand precedence is scrupulously observed, even as the rank of foreigners is very little understood. I cursed my own today, which caused me to be seated next to the hostess, while my friend sensibly contrived to place himself between the pretty sisters. On entering you find the whole first course, but not the smaller course that follows it, already on the table, and when the covers are removed after the soup you help yourself and your neighbour from the dish before you,* though if you want anything else you must ask across the table or send a servant for it. Because this is so tedious many elegant families that have travelled on the Continent adopt the more convenient German practice of having the servants go round the table with the dishes.
>
> It is not customary to take wine during dinner without draining your glass with someone else: two people raise their glasses, stare at each other, nod slightly, and then gravely drink off their wine. Even some of the more seemingly bizarre customs of the South Sea Islanders are less ridiculous. However, it is a mark of consideration to ask someone to drink with you thus, and often a messenger is sent from one end of the table to the other to tell B that A

---

* 'A good upbringing in England therefore includes instruction in the art of carving, too often neglected in Germany' [Pückler's note].

would like to drink with him, upon which both try to fix their eyes on each other—sometimes quite an effort—and then, like Chinese bonzes, go through the obligatory nodding ritual with all solemnity. If the party is small and you have already drunk with every acquaintance but would still like more wine, you must wait for dessert or else find the courage to break with convention.

After the main course comes an entremets of cheese, salad, raw celery and the like, sometimes served with ale twenty or thirty years old and so strong that it flares up like spirits if thrown on the fire. Then the tablecloth is removed and the dessert set down—on a second, finer tablecloth underneath the first in the best households, and directly on the polished table in others. This consists of all sorts of hothouse fruits, which are of superb quality here, as well as Indian and native compotes, stomachic ginger, ices and so on. Fresh glasses, dessert plates, cutlery and little fringed napkins are placed before each guest, and in front of the master of the house stand three bottles, usually of claret, port and sherry. He passes these to his neighbour on the left, either on their coasters or on a little silver trolley. Each man serves himself and, if she wants anything, the lady sitting next to him, and so on until the bottles are back where they started and a second circuit begins. [. . .] The ladies remain seated for another quarter of an hour, sometimes taking sweet wine provided specially for them, and then rise from the table. The gentlemen stand, and one of them opens the door. Once the ladies have filed out everyone draws together more cosily, the host takes the place of the hostess, and conversation turns to topics of local everyday interest, at which the foreign visitor is pretty much forgotten and must content himself with listening.[9]

Pückler enjoyed his evening at Chippenham, especially the opportunity it gave him to observe social types. During dinner he spoke with Mr Moseley, who had spent a lot of time in Paris, read some German literature and considered himself an *esprit fort*. But a dandy must not be too attentive, so when the party reconvened in the drawing room Moseley ostentatiously sat alone with a book, his delicately shod right foot slung over his left knee. The Tharps themselves belonged to the newly rich. The family had amassed a fortune managing plantations in Jamaica, but now directed their affairs from England and adopted the lifestyle of the landed gentry. Pückler sensed that he and Batthyany had only been invited because of their titles, though foreign noblemen 'are worth only fifty per cent of home-grown ones'. Mrs Tharp asked him if he knew the Queen of Bavaria, to which he replied that he had once had the honour of being presented to her. 'She's a great friend of mine,' the lady continued, and showed him a portrait the queen had given her, while her daughter produced a very personal letter from one of the royal princesses. 'Is it not highly striking,' Pückler observed, 'how our great people in Germany, many of them not exactly devoid of pride and haughtiness towards their compatriots, treat every son and daughter of England, even without any distinction of mind, almost as equals, just because they are English, not making the least enquiry whether their position at home justifies such favour?'[10]

It is interesting in this connection to peep into Captain Tharp's diary of a tour he made with his family to Paris and Baden nine years earlier. On reaching Baden Mrs Tharp 'sent a letter to the Queen of Bavaria announcing her arrival', and they were introduced by that royal personage 'to more Princes, Grandukes & great people'. The Grand Duke of Baden personally handed Mrs Tharp into his residence, while the Prince of Hesse-Darmstadt 'in the most handsome manner' sent them 'his own carriage & four capital horses'. At a ball the Miss Tharps danced with 'three princes & all the first rank'. And so it continues. 'It is therefore a great joy for the English middle classes,' wrote Pückler, who had seen similar cases, 'to travel on the Continent, where they easily make superior connections that they can speak of on their return as intimate friends.'[11] The self-abasing reverence shown by Germans to English visitors had long irked him despite his own admiration for England, and the twinge of national mortification he now felt in talking to Mrs Tharp would grow stronger once he began to feel the awkwardness of his position as a fortune hunter.

As Pückler and Batthyany rode back to Newmarket they could not help laughing heartily as they reviewed their hosts' foibles. It is to

Pückler's credit that he afterwards felt rather guilty at so ill requiting the welcome the Tharps had given him; but human nature is corrupt, he mused, and the two of them were probably faring equally badly in the house they had just left, and 'in any case this is what comes of hospitality that springs from ostentation.'[12] Two days after the dinner at Chippenham Park Pückler headed back to London, while Batthyany made his way to Melton Mowbray to hunt.

5

PARK-HUNTING

'Travelling in England is in truth extremely delightful'

After Pückler's return to London there was a sort of mini-Season occasioned by the new session of Parliament in November, and invitations soon landed on his dressing table at 41 Jermyn Street, where he had moved from the Clarendon just before going to Newmarket. He went to some balls and parties and attended the state opening of Parliament, where he was shocked to see how George IV, the debonair Prince Regent he had known in 1814, had become a livid-faced, monstrously obese man who, though only in his early sixties, could barely stagger to the throne and needed a long pause before reading his speech. At a royal levee a few days later the king, though visibly unwell, was as gracious as ever and touchingly proud of his famous memory, which recalled his German visitor's name and their first meeting. Unfortunately, with most of elegant society still in the country, Pückler had few opportunities to begin his assault on the affections of English womanhood: he met a Miss Elsa, of whom we then hear no more; and a Miss Elliot, a pretty girl but, as he soon ascertained, without a fortune.

One problem in these early months was the language. In French and German he could usually win a smile from beauty's lips, but in English any amusement he provided was probably unintentional. To improve he read newspapers and novels and worked his way through William Fordyce Mavor's *English Spelling-book*, which by this time had gone through over three hundred printings. On the other hand he did not sense that his age—he had just turned forty-one—would be a problem, though it necessitated the hateful business of dyeing his hair, which was very uncomfortable, took many hours and sometimes went wrong, his hair turning red rather than black. The mere prospect of it put him out of humour, but once it was complete he looked and felt rejuvenated. One newspaper complimented him on his 'commanding and graceful' appearance and 'exceedingly pleasing and expressive' countenance, and a writer in the *Literary Gazette* recalled him a few years later as 'a fine-looking fellow'. In a letter to Lucie, who always took pride in her handsome Lou, he summed up his looks: 'Here you have a man whose youth is past but who imagines he is still twenty years old!'[1]

During this autumn of 1826 Pückler established a routine that stayed more or less the same for the duration of his London residence. After getting up late and reading three or four newspapers over breakfast, he consulted his visiting book to see what 'morning calls'—which by convention took place from two o'clock in the afternoon—he had to pay.[2] Once these were over he would ride around the city or the surrounding country until dusk, then dress for the evening, dine at seven or eight and go on to some social or cultural event before returning in the early hours of the morning to write to Lucie.

Despite this outwardly relaxed mode of existence he had plenty of worries, of which the greatest was the cost of living in London. In late November he calculated that at his current rate of spending he would have to go home after six months, and he cursed himself for arriving so long before the Season. But if it sometimes felt like he was wasting time, in fact he was adjusting himself to English society, making useful contacts, and improving his knowledge of the language, so that when the hectic springtime ritual began he would be ready to make the most of it.

In the meantime he decided to spend some weeks in Brighton, where much of society mustered during the winter months. But before that there was something else he wanted to do. On his way back from Newmarket he had stopped to look at Lord Braybrook's property, Audley End, with its enormous park containing five hundred stags and a grotto-and-waterfall-themed flower garden, and this had sharpened his appetite for an extended bout of park-hunting such as he had undertaken in 1814. At the end of November he summoned

Jakob Heinrich Rehder, his head gardener, to join him on a three-week tour of the great properties of the northern Home Counties, Oxfordshire and the Midlands. Five years younger than Pückler, Rehder had been in his employment for nine years and played an important role in the transformation of Muskau. Pückler incurred considerable costs in bringing him to England, but he knew that 'a good gardener can make more progress in his field during a brief stay here than in ten years' study at home.'[3] Rehder arrived in mid-December, and while the prince's travelling carriage was made ready they looked at a few parks in the vicinity of London: Syon House, Wimbledon Park and Kew.

On Christmas Day they set out. The weather would often be miserable, but the great advantage of winter was that the leafless trees allowed for an easier overview of complete park designs than was possible in summer. After Stanmore Park and Bentley Priory in Middlesex their first major stop was Cassiobury Park in Hertfordshire, belonging to the Earl of Essex, who kindly gave Pückler cards of admittance for the rest of the journey. Then he saw the Earl of Bridgewater's property, Ashridge Park, the child of Humphry Repton's old age. At his next stop, the Duke of Bedford's Woburn Abbey, he was shown around various parts of the house and grounds by four or five different servants, who all demanded tips. He seems not to have realised that, in a precursor of the visitor charge, the tips were appropriated by the owners, who thereby profited from their 'generosity' in letting people see their properties.[4]

'By Heaven! Now for the first time I am filled with true and boundless enthusiasm,' Pückler wrote to Lucie on 28 December. 'What I have described so far was smiling nature combined with all that art and money can produce. I left it feeling satisfied and not without admiration, though I have seen similar places before and even own one myself. But what I saw today was more than this—it was an enchanted spot, clothed in the most alluring raiment of poetry and enveloped in all the majesty of history.'[5] The cause of this exhilaration was Warwick Castle. All mighty towers and ramparts without and luxurious home within, it justified its reputation as England's pride. The baronial hall, the armoury, the priceless paintings, the sumptuous grounds with their giant oaks and cedars and the River Avon flanking the castle walls: everything enchanted him, but what really mattered was the unique feeling of a place with eight hundred years of history. Like many intelligent aristocrats of his day, he knew that noble rank was losing its meaningfulness and must in time be swept away with the advance of the money economy. But though a liberal in some things he still believed in the value of his caste, and Warwick embodied what he hoped against hope was an enduring difference between lords who held their lands by birthright and parvenu merchants in their gingerbread palaces.

His next object was Eaton Hall in Cheshire, the property of the fabulously wealthy Grosvenors, later Dukes of Westminster. Unfortunately the gardens and park were the least imaginative he had yet seen, despite their size and reputation, while the house, recently rebuilt in the neo-Gothic style at the greatest possible expense, gave Pückler a lasting aversion to extravagant medievalism in architecture. Then came Hawkstone Park in Shropshire, where the hand of nature had fashioned a dramatic landscape of cliffs, grottoes, tunnels and ravines that was hardly in need of further embellishment. He completed his gardener's binge by taking a different route back to London and saving the best till last: the Duke of Marlborough's Blenheim and the Duke of Buckingham's Stowe, both owing much of their magnificence to Capability Brown. On 15 January 1827 he was back in his quarters in Jermyn Street, and four days later he despatched Rehder with a portfolio of diagrams—'like a bee full of honey'—to Muskau.[6]

Pückler was pleased with his tour. Other than when tramping round towns to see their sights—Birmingham, Chester, Stratford, Oxford—he examined between one and four properties each day. No wonder Rehder sometimes complained of tiredness. The head gardener was also homesick, and his employer found him a less enthusiastic companion than he had hoped. Still, he worked conscientiously on his diagrams and also kept a park-visiting journal. Pückler himself must have spent a good two hours every evening recording his impressions in words and diagrams for Lucie, who was of course directing work at Muskau in his absence—one day he joked that he had written off a quarter of an inch of his fingers. Whenever he learned anything his first wish was to communicate it to her, and if he was sometimes a little peremptory in his instructions, more often he caught himself being high-handed just in time to express confidence in her judgement or respect for her wishes: 'Carry out diligently what I have prescribed,' he wrote, 'and give me the pleasure on my return of seeing the realisation of all my gardening dreams that meet with your approval.'[7]

At Syon House he picked up the ideas of dragging chain-metal nets through ponds and lakes each June to remove unwanted plant growth and of having a small portion of the pleasure ground mown each day rather than employing a large number of people to mow it all at once—invariably creating a great mess in the process—as was customary in Germany. He also made notes on the combination of stone, wrought iron and glass (but not wood) in the construction of hothouses, having already examined the use of steam for heating them at Chippenham Park, where simply turning a valve produced exactly the temperature required. At Woburn Abbey he was delighted by small glasshouses for tender heathers, with plantings of hardier varieties on the outside. Both these glasshouses and a large one specifically for palm trees used mirrors effectively to multiply the displays and create an impression of space.

Warwick Castle was an object lesson in setting a great pile within a sculpted landscape. It was elevated on an artificial hill, its entrance approached from densely wooded ground so that it did not immediately come into full view. Around it on three sides lay flower gardens and paths bordered by exposed stone, and on the fourth the castle walls were skirted by the fast-flowing River Avon, with a waterfall and a picturesque flour mill. The most interesting feature of the park was that, rather than merging with the surrounding countryside, it formed its own horizon with thick belts of trees, 'which gives the imagination so much latitude and in itself also forms a highly romantic view.'[8] Other monuments to the ingenuity of English gardeners were the aviary at Audley End, a huge walled enclosure full of dense, shade-giving trees providing a habitat for a thousand golden and silver pheasants and various other brightly-plumaged exotics; and a walled Chinese garden at Cassiobury Park containing rare dwarf specimens in formal beds bounded by white, blue and red sand and interspersed with benches, fountains and vases on pedestals.

But learning from England was not simply a matter of passive as-similation. In his letters he also described things he disliked, and which prompted him to do otherwise at Muskau. One of these was the ex-tension of the park right up to the house on one side, so that grazing animals together with an absence of human cultivation and, often enough, of visible human beings made these properties look empty and neglected. Pückler strove for a higher level of cultivation all round the high, turreted walls of Muskau, with a garden full of flowerbeds under the windows, and then, receding from the house, a pleasure ground with hothouses, a vegetable garden, a winter garden and an or-angery. Another of his dislikes was standing, algae-filled, often stink-ing bodies of water. A particularly bad example was a long trench dug at a cost of £5,000 at Chippenham Park and intended to look like a stretch of river, but far too stagnant for that illusion. At Muskau he had the luxury of a real river, from which the little lakes he laid out were all fed, but landscapers without this facility were, he thought, in most cases well advised to avoid water features altogether.

Another of Pückler's criticisms, already mentioned in connec-tion with his visit to Chiswick, was of the fussy arrangement of some pleasure grounds and an excess of rare specimens more curious than pleasing. In several places he found a tendency to formality in the pleasure ground such as would be more appropriate for the garden, for example round or oval flowerbeds carved into the lawn and regularly undulating rather than more naturally shaped borders. As for the shrubs, whether in borders or island shrubberies, they should, he thought, be allowed to grow into each other and drape themselves over the lawn, rather than being pruned vigorously so that they sat well back from the sharp-edged lawn and the black earth rising up steeply behind it. Admittedly this looser arrangement meant that shrubberies could not be enlivened with seasonal plantings of flowers, but there were plenty of flowering shrubs to add colour, and in any case the proper place for planting flowers was the garden.

His most common complaint is of the monotonous openness of many parks, with isolated trees ringed by unsightly fencing to protect them from deer and sheep. This contrasted with his practice at Muskau of providing a distant focal point and items of interest in the fore and middle ground, and of giving the observer a sequence of prospects as he traversed an area rather than a gradually changing perspective on the same vista. In his remarks on this subject, and to a degree in what he says about pleasure grounds, Pückler positions himself, implicitly at least, within a long-standing debate in park design. The basic principle of English picturesque landscaping, what differentiates it from the formal 'French' style, is its avoidance of symmetry, geometric forms and straight lines and its use of features such as lakes, meadows and clumps of trees which, by convention at least, make a scene look natural rather than man-made. The label 'picturesque' comes from the inspiration that this tradition drew from the landscape paintings of Claude Lorrain and Nicolas Poussin, particularly the way they synthesise harmonious beauty with naturalistic detail.

This very synthesis was at the heart of what became known as the 'picturesque debate', launched by the garden theorist Sir Uvedale Price in the 1790s and still current at the time of Pückler's second English tour. Price argued that many landscaped parks, especially those of Capability Brown and his disciples, aimed too much at harmony and too little at naturalism. He urged the retention of old trees, textured slopes and rocky outcrops to create a more dramatic and richly detailed effect than Brown had sought. The difference between these two approaches came to be formulated with the opposing terms 'polite picturesque' and 'rustic picturesque'. Humphry Repton, the greatest practising landscaper when the debate began, took Brown's part, though in some ways his own work shows precisely the move away from Classical harmony towards Romantic sublimity that Price advocated.

Pückler never explicitly engages with this debate, but although he was certainly no critic of Brown, whom he called 'the Shakespeare of English garden design', his own preference seems consistently to have been for sublimity, hence his love of the soul-stirring grandeur of Hawkstone Park and indifference to the stately refinement of the broad open spaces at Wentworth House, the Earl of Fitzwilliam's palatial seat in Yorkshire which he saw later in 1827. At Muskau his use of dramatic views like a flooded meadow and of 'rustic' features like a fisherman's hut and the English cottage support the idea that his own landscaping eye was essentially Romantic.[9]

If the endless succession of parks was Pückler's main pleasure in touring the English provinces, the business of moving from place to place also offered much to enjoy. 'Travelling in England is in truth extremely delightful,' he told Lucie.[10] The pretty countryside rolled past like a magic lantern as he skimmed along the excellent roads, which wound their way gently round hills, valleys and even ancient trees rather than following tediously straight lines as in many other parts of Europe. He wondered why the English were always so keen to go abroad when they had so many fine things to see at home. Admittedly the climate could have been better, but what was inconvenient for people was good for plants, and in no other country was the scenery so verdant. When the sun did make an appearance he got out and covered a mile or two on foot to take in the scenery at his leisure, and when it withdrew he got back into the travelling carriage he had brought from Muskau, a large, sturdy vehicle of English manufacture. For each stage of his journey he hired fresh horses at a posting house. The system worked very smoothly, and in one place a foursome was harnessed in a single minute from the cry of 'horses on' being given.

It was also an expensive pastime, with the prices for horses, postilions and repairs many times higher than in Germany. He could have saved a lot of money if he had used the mail coach, but this would have been awkward as the distinction between posting and coaching folk was strict. In any case a private vehicle had obvious advantages: it was far more comfortable, the traveller could start and stop when he wanted, and the nuisance of sharing space with strangers was avoided. With his habitual satisfaction in getting little details right, Pückler had fitted his 'nomad's residence', as he called it, with great care. It had a coal-filled heating pan, an internal lamp for night-time reading, leather blinds so that he could sleep during the day, and a fold-down writing table on which he scrawled long letters home. He was proud of how much he had packed into the small space for luggage and how speedily he could transfer whatever he needed to his room when he stopped at an inn. It was a subject on which he could give a lecture for the edification of other travellers, he told Lucie.[11]

English inns were another source of contentment, especially their clean rooms and comfortable beds, the solicitude of landlords and the efficiency of waiters and chambermaids. Sadly these things did not come cheap, and on top of fixed charges for bed and board the traveller found everyone who had served him waiting by the door on his departure to wish him a pleasant onward journey and collect a small gratuity. For Pückler it was a price worth paying:

Everything is of a higher quality and more plentiful than on the Continent. For example the beds, made up of three mattresses piled on top of one another, are large enough to accommodate two or three people, and when the curtains of the square canopy, resting on stout mahogany columns, are drawn, you find yourself in a small cabinet—a space that a Frenchman might comfortably dwell in. On the washstand you do not just find a miserable bottle of water with a single earthenware or silver jug and basin and a length of towelling, such as are on offer in German and French hotels and even some private houses; rather a proper little Chinese porcelain tub in which you can easily plunge half your body, and above it taps that instantly deliver just the flow of water you desire, as well as half a dozen generously-sized towels, a quantity of large and small crystal bottles, a tall adjustable standing mirror, and a foot-bath, not to mention elegantly designed specimens of the other nameless conveniences of the toilet. It all looks so appealing that on waking you are positively seized with the desire to bathe. And if you need anything else, then a ring of your bell will summon either a very neatly dressed girl, who makes a deep curtsey, or a waiter with the attire and poise of a well-trained valet, who respectfully takes your orders; rather than, as with us, an unkempt lad in a cut-off jacket and green apron, who with stupid brazenness asks: 'What is it, Yuronner?' or 'Was it you as rang 'ere?', and then makes off before you have finished telling him what you want.[12]

Pückler was not the only one to find the contrast with Germany stark. In her *Private Anecdotes of Foreign Courts* of 1827 Catherine Hyde states that at the Red Deer, Munich's principal hotel, 'they bring you, if you ask for a towel in the morning, a piece of linen fit only for a razor-rag; if you require water to wash yourself, a small *wine-glass full* is presented on a saucer!' The Duchess of Dino, accustomed to English comforts by her long residence in London in the 1830s, was shattered by the experience of staying at inns while travelling through Germany: if she remained indoors during the day she had either to shiver in an unheated room or be suffocated by its cast-iron stove. Worst of all were the beds: the equestrian journalist Charles Apperley found during a tour of 1828 that they were 'something like the bottom of an English sofa' and wondered how marital relations were possible in the country; while a few years later the writer and translator Edmund Spencer had to sleep on a straw mattress 'supported on a bedstead five feet long, composed of deal boards nailed together, in form not unlike a packing-box. [. . .] Curtains there are none, and comfort does not exist for any person beyond the height of four feet six inches!'[13]

Where English inns compared less well, perhaps predictably, was in their food. Apart from the excellent breakfasts Pückler found the fare insipid. His loudest complaint was that cooks knew no other way of preparing vegetables than boiling them in water. In one or two places he went into the kitchens himself to teach them how to roast potatoes, apparently without success. The range of dishes was narrow, and the endless repetition of mutton chops, turkey with bread sauce and apple tarts dulled his appetite. But stranger than what the English ate was the way they ate it. Just once he encountered the Continental *table d'hôte* system, whereby travellers all sat at a large table and conversed while eating. Elsewhere the arrangements reflected the nation's famous compartmentalism:

> It is amusing to observe the great uniformity of everyone's behaviour, as if they all issued from the same factory, and this is especially evident in their eating habits. Each person is placed at a separate table, none taking the slightest notice of the others, and yet they all appear to have the same manners and gastronomic tastes. No one takes soup, which is not to be had at all unless specially requested in advance [. . .]. A large roast is taken from one person to the next,

and each carves off as much as he wants, while potatoes boiled in water and other similarly prepared vegetables, as well as a dish full of condiments, are placed on each table, and beer is served. That completes the main course; only a minority indulge in the luxury of a fish course beforehand. But now follows the important second stage of the proceedings. The tablecloth is removed, clean cutlery set down, and wine served in a fresh glass together with a few miserable apples or pears and rock-hard navy biscuits. Only now does the diner seem fully to settle into his chair. He leans back with a contented expression, stares fixedly in front of him as if lost in deep thought, takes deliberative sips from his glass, and breaks the silence only to crunch effortfully on one of the rock-biscuits. Once he has drained his glass, the third stage—digestion—can commence. Now all movement stops, and the sated diner falls into a kind of magnetic sleep, distinguishable from the real thing only by his open eyes. After half an hour or an hour has passed, he suddenly starts up, and like a man possessed shouts out 'Waiter, my slippers', and, taking a light, he wanders solemnly out of the room to his slippers and his night's rest.[14]

Whether his subject was horticulture, the conditions of travel or something else, Pückler found himself deriving ever more pleasure from describing his English experiences to Lucie. He had long known that he was a better writer than talker, and now, with interesting matter to hand, he positively revelled in composing letters. The ones he received were probably of a similar standard, for to judge from her surviving correspondence of later years Lucie was a gifted writer, with a cultivated and witty style and a great facility for telling anecdotes and drawing characters. She was, however, less prolific than he. Sometimes she put down her pen out of jealousy or pique, and it seems that a twenty-two-day silence to which she subjected him after his return to London with Rehder was caused by his too obvious enjoyment of his park tour. She told him he was obviously not missing her, while she was pining away and might even die; to which he replied that he felt this reproach like an axe-blow to the head and would not recover for days.

This was the sentimental hyperbole of the day, of course, and things were soon put to rights. In any case the main reason why she wrote less is that she did not enjoy it as much as he did. He was always cajoling her to write more, telling her repeatedly that hearing from her was his greatest joy, especially if she provided plenty of detail about her life in Muskau. 'Do you know how I read a letter from you?' he asked.

> First I race through it ravenously to gain a total effect. In the mood that *this* gives me I sit at my desk to write an answer and then go though it again point for point [. . .]. Once my answer is complete I read your letter a third time *con amore* for my private pleasure, jumping over the passages that disquiet me or hurt my feelings and savouring the good bits in a slow, deliberate way.

He was still full of gratitude for the sacrifice she had made, and reminded her that even the most splendid fulfilment of his hopes would have no value for him unless she shared his pleasure. It was Lucie's love, he told a cousin at this time, which provided 'the only sure guarantee that I am of some worth'.[15]

6

BRIGHTON AND MISS GIBBINGS

'Dear Lord, she really is not my type'

'Brisk, gay, and gaudy, like a harlequin's jacket' is how Brighton appears to the narrator of *Vanity Fair*. It is here that George and Amelia spend their disastrous honeymoon, Jos Sedley tries out the seductive power of his colourful waistcoats and Rawdon Crawley fleeces him at backgammon, while all four are twisted round the 'pretty little finger covered with the neatest French kid-glove' of the diabolical Becky Sharp. The town's prominence, to which Thackeray pays ironic tribute, was only recently won. In the eighteenth century England's chief watering place, its therapeutic and fashionable capital outside the London Season, was Bath. The first blow for Brighton was struck by Dr Richard Russell, whose renowned seawater cure attracted 'ellegant cases' to bathe in the icy English Channel and drink its contents, supposedly as a way of combating glandular diseases.[1] The resort's real founder was the Prince of Wales, later George IV, who settled there to enjoy the company of his secret wife Maria Fitzherbert at a safe distance from his parents' court. His patronage drew many others and sparked a building frenzy that produced the Assembly Rooms, Fisher's Library, the German Spa and the Royal Pavilion. Later he tired of the place, but high society continued to disport itself there well into the reign of Victoria.

Pückler arrived on 4 February 1827 and put up in the town's best hotel, the hundred-room Royal York. On his first day he walked around the clean, smiling streets and squares, as stately as any in London, saw the Steine and the Marine Parade, and strolled to the end of the Chain Pier to watch families board steamboats for Boulogne, a favoured destination of those whose improvidence called for a period of 'rusticating over the water', as it was known. He also looked in at the Turkish vapour baths of Sheikh Deen Mahomed, which were popular among the resort's invalids and would-be invalids who could not face the rigours of seawater bathing. As for the fantastical Chinese-Indian Pavilion, finally completed after many false starts by John Nash and now, with the king's loss of interest in Brighton, something of a white elephant, Pückler found the building less at fault than its setting. In large gardens stocked with Oriental plants it would have looked good, he said, but 'here in the middle of the town, close by ordinary houses and connected with them on two sides by streets, it looks like the creation of a lunatic.'[2]

Also in Brighton at this time were the Lievens, the Esterhazys and other London friends. The people he saw most over the next few weeks were the Anglo-French couple Count and Countess Flahaut. He had known the countess in 1814 when she was still Margaret Mercer Elphinstone and a sought-after heiress, and now he renewed the acquaintance and passed many evenings in the house she and her husband had taken. It was they who launched him into Brighton society by giving him a ticket to a subscription ball two days after his arrival. This naturally led to other invitations to balls, dinners and card parties, and he felt sure that he was now on the right path: 'I am beginning to make headway here; in other words, although it will take a while I am persuaded that I shall find what I need in England. The time I have already spent was not wasted because I needed to acclimatise myself a little.'[3]

He followed up introductions to young ladies with visits to their families and discreet inquiries into their financial circumstances. The strongest impression on him was made by Miss Wyndham, a niece of the Earl of Egremont. 'With this wife,' he told Lucie,

> I could be sure of being able to do as I pleased; she is one of those charming, naturally graceful creatures, more or less without a thought of their own, and with these qualities she would submit obediently and unreservedly to a superior mind. [. . .] You would soon come to like her and not be jealous for long; she is beauty, innocence, sweetness, and grace incarnate, and no brains—what joy![4]

This is a point to which he often reverts in his letters home: that his future wife must not only be rich, but also docile enough to tolerate his continued relations with Lucie. Miss Wyndham met the latter requirement, but to his regret he soon had to discount her because her income, which he had initially thought large, had not yet been settled—she might become wealthy, but she might get nothing.

Soon Pückler's days took a regular shape. After spending his afternoons riding on the South Downs and watching the sun set over the sea, he went to two or three evening entertainments. Among the most popular of these, much more so in Brighton than in London, were amateur concerts, at which it became clear to him how the English had come by their reputation for cloth ears:

> Every mother with a grown daughter, for whom she has had to pay good money to a music master, is determined to have the satisfaction of seeing the young talent admired. Thus on all sides there is an overpowering screeching and thumping at the piano fit to make you melancholy, for even when an Englishwoman can hit the notes she scarcely ever has any method or voice. The men are far more agreeable dilettanti, for at least their singing offers the entertainment of a comical farce. The matador among the local society singers is one Captain H. With no more voice than a hoarse bulldog, no more musicality than a peasant in church, and no more ear than a mole, his greatest pleasure is singing in public, and he stepped up with more self-assurance than the biblical David. The most extraordinary thing was the manner of his rendition: the way he took his place at the piano and immediately struck his forefinger on what he thought was the aria's first note, emitted a noise like a thunder-clap on what he thought was the same note, but each time was a tone or two lower, then worked his way through the entire aria without pausing and with no other accompaniment than his own wonderful facial contortions, and all this in the presence of at least fifty people—only those who have witnessed it would believe it possible.[5]

As for the daily balls, they were held in rooms far too small for the purpose, so that 'in the space given over to quadrilles it is mathematically impossible to do more than make dance-like gestures.' Though disagreeable in some ways, this squash had the advantage of pressing him up against the good-looking girls who seemed to make up much of Brighton's population. The beauty of Englishwomen was an article of long standing in German travel writing—their swan-like necks, oval faces and lissom figures, but especially their flawless white skin, kept fresh, it was thought, by the damp climate. The reluctance of matrons to give up the pretensions of their maidenhood was under-standable, thought Pückler, for 'nowhere will the admirer of the "middle age" find more well-preserved women.' On the other hand there were some odd sights, like three sisters upstaged by their own mother, 'a fat lady of at least fifty-five, wearing black velvet trimmed with white and a turban decorated with swaying ostrich feathers, who waltzed around like a frenzied bacchante whenever she had enough room to do so.'[6]

Pückler himself rarely danced. This was an odd policy on the face of it, for he thereby missed opportunities to endear himself to young women, not just by gliding them around the floor, but in the con-ventional turn taken arm-in-arm afterwards in an adjoining room. He pretended that by a sentimental vow he had foresworn dancing for a year, hoping that this might pique people's interest and scotch any idea that he was a common fortune hunter. The real reason for his re-luctance, as he admitted to Lucie, was that he was not very good at it. Despite this he was a worthy addition to ballrooms, with his tall figure, handsome features, aristocratic demeanour and the star of his Russian order gleaming on his breast. He was made welcome everywhere, and his doings were recorded together with those of society's more es-tablished ornaments in the 'fashionable movements' columns of the local and national newspapers.[7]

The circle of his acquaintance slowly grew. He acted as escort to Mrs Clifden, a vivacious, attractive woman in her thirties married to a housebound invalid, and she introduced him to her friends. He met the boisterous Mrs Coutts, England's richest woman, who had begun adult life as an obscure Irish actress but after roles as the mistress and then wife of the great banker Thomas Coutts was currently playing the part of merry widow and would soon marry the Duke of St

Albans, a man half her age. Among men he became friendly with the French writer and shadowy government agent Casimir de Montrond, who joined him at the Flahauts, and Alexander Ranaldson, chief of Clan Macdonell of Glengarry and founder of the Society of True Highlanders, who had toured Europe in traditional Highland costume to promote Gaeldom. Pückler's social success was sealed when he was invited to a small party at the home of the former royal consort Mrs Fitzherbert. Now an old lady, she spent most of each year in the town which, in a sense, she had co-founded, and where she was still highly esteemed. He found her a refined, unpretentious woman of great charm 'who keeps a very agreeable house'.[8]

It was a sign of the freedom he enjoyed as a foreign visitor that he could mix with the cream of society at Mrs Fitzherbert's but also with wealthy 'nobodies' who did not dream of being admitted there. One of the latter was Mary Woolley Gibbings, a physician's daughter he met at the Old Ship Assembly Rooms on 19 February. Three evenings later, at another event, they were already on familiar terms: 'Miss Gibbings was so attentive to me that I felt a little ashamed in front of everyone, for it created a strange impression that instead of dancing she waved me over and talked with me incessantly, so that for half an hour we made rather a spectacle of ourselves.' In the following days she invited him home to sing duets with her and attached herself to him visibly in public. The situation was moving along smartly, and he had to decide what he wanted to do. She was 'certainly pretty and would make a brilliant wife', as she was very accomplished and a considerable heiress, but there was something pursed, artificial and rather forceful in her manner that contrasted unfavourably with the gentleness of most English girls. Her parents were worse: the father an ill-bred, ill-dressed man with a ponderous manner, and the mother a fat, blatant woman who spoke of nothing but money.[9]

So much for Pückler's impression. Whether it tallied with the general view is hard to gauge, since the family inhabited the murky shadows outside the temple of fashion and is rarely mentioned in the period's memoirs. Robert Gibbings was born in 1756 as the son of Bartholomew Gibbings of Gibbings Grove, County Cork, and his wife Elizabeth, a daughter of the Anglican Archdeacon of Limerick. He was, in other words, a gentleman by birth, though Pückler and others later assumed him to be a thoroughgoing parvenu. There was probably not much money to share among Robert's many brothers and sisters at Gibbings Grove, so he trained as a doctor and worked for many years at Cork Hospital. He married Barbara Woolley comparatively late, and Mary, their only child, was born in 1799. They moved from Ireland to Cheltenham in 1817, and it was here that he made a very large fortune in a short time, not as a doctor but as an apothecary. In the mid-1820s he retired and settled with his wife and daughter in Brighton.

Here the Gibbingses were allowed to join the social round, not least as they did plenty of entertaining themselves, but the Irish bonhomie of the parents and the earnest musicianship of the daughter were viewed with amusement by those with greater claims to gentility. This comes across in the diary of Thomas Francis Fremantle, later Lord Cottesloe, who met them in 1825:

> Went to Miss Gibbings party in the Evening danced three times—
> not a bad ball, tho but few people. The supper was excellent.
> Tierney much amused with old Gibbings.
> [Miss] Gibbings sang a good deal [. . .]—her execution is quite wonderful, but the performance is by no means pleasing.
> Went at 2 to Miss Gibbings, where there was a sort of morning concert—Miss Lloyd, Escudero and the Gibbings sang—There was an excellent luncheon prepared and the room was quite full [. . .]
> We came away before it was all finished, leaving the Doctor on his knees singing catches and Glees as Mrs G described him quite in his glory.
> Old Gibbings was greater fun than ever and made us laugh amazingly—Tierney and Gordon played him off—came home much pleased with the Evening.[10]

One of the most noticeable things about Mary Gibbings was her devotion to her parents for all that their unpolished manners made her blush, and even Pückler, though not fond of the family, was touched by this trait. Just as apparent was the calibre of her mind. The journalist George Augustus Sala remembers her as 'a handsome lady with flashing eyes and very glossy black hair' who was 'very rich, very clever, and very witty; a brilliant musician, and a delightfully humorous artist'. But it was precisely her intellect and talents that were judged excessive—by Pückler, who preferred the uncomplicated Miss Wyndham; and by Edward Bulwer-Lytton, who wrote to his fiancée, also in February 1827, that at a party 'given by Miss Gibbings, the heiress, that young lady delighted us with her knowledge of 6 languages, her skill in drawing, her knowledge of music and her science in chemistry! I would as soon marry *The Public Advertiser* as an Exhibitor of that sort in spite of the £80,000.'[11]

It seems that hers was the fate of the bluestocking: she was too clever to be popular. At this distance in time it is hard to determine whether she was simply a victim of the prejudices of her day, or whether there was something conceited in her manner that would be unpleasing in any age. Her own view is clear from some verses she wrote much later, which express frustration that a woman must hide her mental powers to avoid denting male complacency, and that unless she does so she will be found less amiable than one who really has nothing to say:

And men prefer weak women of this kind,
To her with intellect and reasoning mind.
For intellect is power, we are told,
And intellect in petticoats may scold.
Then imbecility we know most men adore,
And helplessness they worship even more.
Combined, no male disputes the potent claim,
And till our world end, 'twill be the same.

Elsewhere there is a sentence that she must, one feels, have written with Pückler in mind during a passage on the subservience expected in Englishwomen of the higher class: 'The most obedient wives in the world on this account, foreigners are anxious to secure them, fully reliant on their humble docility.'[12]

To return to 1827, Mary Gibbings knew that her great object must be to marry, and together with a refusal to conceal her talents went a strong desire to find a husband—so strong that it exposed her to unkind remarks. It was the norm for an heiress like her to marry into the aristocracy, gaining a title for her dowry, and the feelings of her parents on this issue may be deduced from their residence in Brighton, opulent entertaining and exclusive mixing with high society. They certainly approved of Pückler, among whose papers is a letter from Robert Gibbings reporting his progress in the self-appointed task of finding him a perfect mount—with its strained affability and display of expertise on horseflesh it plainly shows a man trying too hard.[13] Meanwhile Mary was unmistakeably setting her cap at him, and the imminent need for a decisive step on his part made him feel quite dejected. Brighton came to seem a cheerless place: his many-windowed hotel room was impossible to heat; his manservant Berndt caught a bad cold and took to his bed; his saddle horse developed a sprain and had to be rested; and one of Lucie's letters took a querulous tone, forcing him to remind her again what they should be like. Only the cosy dinners and whist parties at the Flahauts kept up his spirits.

A particularly irksome constraint of his courtship was suppressing his normal habits of gallantry: he hid the fancy he had taken to Miss Wyndham and to Admiral Rolles' alluring daughters, known to society as the 'hot Rolles'. But he could not resist Miss Fremantle, the prettiest girl in Brighton and presumably a relative of the diarist quoted above. She was a sylph of seventeen as lively as quicksilver, and he won her friendship at a ball by giving her a bag of cracker sweets, which despite parental prohibition she threw at unsuspecting colonels and dowagers for the fun of seeing their startled faces. She invited him to ride with her the next day, but as he was already engaged to sing with Miss Gibbings he met her the day after instead. Once a girl was 'out' she enjoyed far more freedom to mix with men than did her Continental sisters, and Miss Fremantle took her admirer on long walks unattended, enjoying her own powers of fascination with a touching artlessness. It was all innocent, and Pückler, who was not without a sentimental streak, quite liked it that way.

However he had to 'sacrifice the agreeable to the useful', as he put it, and concentrate on Miss Gibbings: 'But Dear Lord, she really is not my type.' Could a biddable wife be made of such a spoilt young woman, he wondered. The spectre of her parents haunted him too, as did the social stigma of such an alliance: it would be pretty awkward if it became known in Berlin that his wife was a physician's daughter, or if one of his enemies sneeringly asked him in public what his father-in-law's occupation was. He told himself to banish such thoughts. The family had shown him every courtesy, and the girl herself could scarcely have encouraged him more. In any case after nearly five months in England he had no other prospect in view. On the other hand, he still had £950 to draw on his £1,700 letter of credit, so there was time to try for something better in London. Unable to make up his mind what to do, he placed the matter in the hands of his 'good Schnucke'.[14]

If he hoped that she would direct him he was disappointed: Lucie's approach to problems requiring action was to dither, and she told him to do as he thought best. Just then he learned something that tilted the scales strongly against marriage: Mary Gibbings could only take a husband who was prepared to let her parents join their household. Even now he did not throw in the towel. After all there was the money, by his reckoning at least £50,000 on marriage with more to come later. He weighed up the situation: 'Try as I might, I am over-mastered by my horror at the whole family, and yet when I examine them dispassionately I find no objections that ought to check me given the sad position I am in.' Meanwhile at social events he saw meaningful glances exchanged whenever he and Miss Gibbings were together, and when they were apart he had to keep his countenance as inquisitive remarks and arch allusions were fired at him. 'All in all my pride is suffering terribly with this wife-hunting,' he lamented to Lucie: 'If only you had 150,000 thalers I should marry you again in an instant.'[15]

In the end he decided he could not wed Mary Gibbings with her parents as an appendage, and in the second week of March he told her he was about to leave for London. She was 'visibly shocked' and so deflated that he felt sorry for her.[16] Latterly he had learnt that she had already been obliged to turn away more than one suitor who found the stipulation of residence with her parents unpalatable, and perhaps in him she thought she had found a man who would not mind. Now in her late twenties, she must have worried that she might never marry, a bleak fate at a time when old-maidenhood was considered a personal tragedy. It is hard not to feel the pity of her case: the waving of a dowry in men's faces, the studied flirtation, the endless round of stale entertainments, and parents too selfish to let her go if she did find a mate.

Pückler would see her again, but having decided to discontinue his courtship he now had no reason to stay in Brighton. He spent his last evening playing *écarté* at the Flahauts and was back in Jermyn Street on 14 March.

7

THE LONDON SEASON

'The seventh heaven of the fashionable world'

In William Pitt Scargill's *Rank and Talent* of 1829, as in many of the 'Silver Fork' novels of elegant life, there is a palpable excitement as the characters move to London for the Season: 'New faces were prepared, and old ones repaired, for exhibition. All the world was weary of the country; the ocean was monotonous; and the game all killed. Equipages came in one after another. Saloons were lighted up; and every successive night the noise of wheels and brilliancy of town mansions increased.'[1] The months from April to June that elegant society passed in the capital provide much of the spark of interest that still flickers down the years from the otherwise dead embers of the period's fashionable literature, just as the nostalgic glow that continues to emanate from the Regency as a whole derives in large part from the doings during a quarter of each year of a charmed circle of a mere few thousand persons.

Not that everyone who made the annual migration enjoyed it. Middle-aged gentlemen hated being prised away from their snug manorial life; mothers sighed at the thought of chaperoning their daughters night after night; and horticulturalists of both sexes were sorry to leave their gardens to bloom in their absence. Moreover, many of the Season's pleasures were of a curiously joyless kind, infused as they were by the spirit of competition: wits fought for the limelight, dandies out-dressed one another, and hostesses racked their brains to devise ever more extravagant entertainments. As Stendhal said of the English, 'With them fashion is not a pleasure, but an earnest duty.'[2] The greatest tension was felt by parents with a cargo of grown children to marry. Sons had to be steered towards well-born and well-dowered girls rather than being ruled by their own fancy, and daughters put in the way of first-born noblemen, known as 'desirables', and shielded from their younger brothers, or 'detrimentals', who would inherit neither title nor property. Only the most hawkish attention could prevent the impressionable young things from committing some romantic folly and throwing away their prospects.

To make sure he looked the part Pückler had himself fitted by several different tailors for clothes in the latest style. The sportsman Grantley Berkeley's recollection of him as 'something of a fop' and the novelist Lady Morgan's as 'a most *finished* fop' are borne out by combinations like the following, described in a letter to Lucie: a dark brown coat with a velvet collar, a white cravat, a lapelled outer waistcoat in crimson with golden stars and a gold watch-chain hanging from the pocket, a white satin under-waistcoat decorated with a golden floral pattern, black trousers, black stockings and square-toed shoes. He also needed a carriage to match, and nothing could be better than the cabriolet he had ordered the previous autumn, a super-light, elegant vehicle drawn by a single horse—'a thing without which even a quarter-dandy cannot exist in London.' Pückler's was green and black with his coat of arms in red and sky blue and a fine black leather harness worked with brass. How good it would look with the grey he had selected for it![3]

Many of the people he now mixed with were the celebrities who fill the period's memoirs, especially the great ladies who set the tone for everyone else. The doyenne was the Dowager Lady Salisbury, nearly eighty but still a tireless party-giver. She all but exhausted the vast Cecil fortune with her spending on clothes and other luxuries and a few years later died a horrible death after accidentally setting her headdress alight. At sixty-six the Dowager Lady Hertford, the king's ex-mistress, was, Pückler found, not only beautifully dressed but still a beautiful woman, always covered in diamonds and with the carriage of a queen. Another acquaintance was Countess San Antonio, formerly Miss Johnstone, famous for her musical parties and currently promoting the soprano Giuditta Pasta. The most admirable of the hostesses, he thought, was Sarah Sophia, Countess of Jersey—whom, it must be said, most people found rather imperious—for she alone united the qualities of beauty, refined and obliging manners and perfect aristocratic composure. She was also known as a friend to foreigners, which may have counted for something in his judgement.

'What riches everywhere,' Pückler exclaimed to Lucie early in the Season, 'and how impoverished are we by comparison.' In late March the sixth 'Bachelor' Duke of Devonshire, probably the wealthiest private individual in England, invited him to an entertainment at Devonshire House, which he found to be as magnificent as a court. With his eye for detail and interest in good ideas to implement at home, he noted a practical solution to the problem of catering for a large number of guests:

> In a room dedicated to this purpose there is a long table richly loaded with the choicest refreshments of every kind and placed in such a way that the guests can only approach it from one side. On the opposite side stand serving girls in uniform (albeit the female uniform of a white dress with a black apron), who give everyone what he desires, and have sufficient room to work comfortably. Behind them is a door communicating with the pantry, through which whatever they need is brought unimpeded by the crush of guests. This avoids the irritation of having numerous servants pushing around the room with large trays held aloft, and the danger that they might pour the warm or cold contents thereof over three or four of the guests. Supper is served later in the same way in another room next to the kitchen, this time by male attendants, allowing good and prompt service to be provided with no fuss and a far smaller staff than would otherwise be needed.[4]

Others with less palatial homes invited just as many guests, so that many parties, and especially the aptly named 'routs', were very overcrowded affairs. The aim of the hosts was to have as many distinguished persons pass over their threshold as possible, and the aim of the guests was to let the world know they had been invited. For Pückler such gatherings were more a test of stamina than anything else. It started outside with a long wait in a traffic jam of carriages, as no one covered even the shortest distance to an entertainment on foot. Finally he alighted at the bottom of a staircase and joined the throng trying to get up. Once inside things were often little better, and at one event he saw men put the hats they had removed on entering back on their heads to free both arms for pushing and pulling, their curses mingling with the shrieks of diamond-bedecked ladies as they were shunted round the floor. The din was such that conversation never got beyond shouted pleasantries, and the heat so oppressive that few stayed long, sometimes not even long enough to greet their hosts, before making the journey back downstairs. 'People certainly have very odd ways of pursuing pleasure and happiness in this world,' was Pückler's conclusion.[5]

Such inconveniences were never mentioned in the *Morning Post*, the organ of high society, and Pückler thought it was for the pleasure of reading a lengthy report in its columns that many went to the trouble of opening their houses. The following example shows the gratification even a fairly minor hostess could enjoy:

> The Countess of LISTOWELL's Grand Ball at Kington House, on Thursday night, will long be panegyrised in the fashionable world, for the splendour, liberality, and refined taste displayed throughout. The noble suite of rooms were most splendidly illuminated with wax lights, placed in chandeliers of the most superb designs. The matchless beauty of the decorations were heightened by a conservatory at the end of the ballroom, which contained all the choicest plants of the East, tastefully illuminated with variegated lamps, at the end of which was an elegant transparency, representing an Italian scene by Moonlight. The odour of the plants, wafted in by a gentle breeze from the conservatory to the rooms, kept them in delightful temperature.[6]

Not that Pückler could laugh too hard at such snobbery given his own interest in other people's houses and furniture; indeed his description of the décor at the countess's ball is as long as the *Morning Post*'s. Nor did he deny the pleasure it gave him to find his own name in that organ, and at the height of the Season it was included more days than not, if often only on a list of 'company we noticed' at a particular event.

Some newspapers were less helpful. In March at least four printed the same report: 'Letters from Prussia say, that Prince PUCKLER MUSKAN, who was married to the daughter of the late Prince HARDENBERG, has divorced her, to marry the widow of King Christopher, a negress, of Hayti, who is still young, if we may believe the *German correspondent*'; while a fifth punned that a 'German Prince has divorced his wife to marry a *negress*, the widow of Christophe.— This is hardly *fair*.' The story appealed to a certain cast of mind, and eight years later a writer in *Fraser's Magazine* could recall that Pückler had 'turned his thoughts towards the sable widow of the Emperor of Hayti, who was believed to be immensely rich.' The woman in question was Marie-Louise Christophe, the widow of Henri Christophe, King of Northern Haiti. She was neither rich nor in England. After the overthrow of her husband's government she had fled to London, where the Italian exile Count Pecchio saw her in 1823 'with the two princesses, her daughters, of the true royal blood, "black and all black"'.[7] Without protection or money, she then crossed the Channel and moved from place to place, finally finding refuge in a Franciscan convent in Pisa. There, having outlived her daughters, she died, quite forgotten, in 1851.

Pückler was unperturbed by this report and reassured Lucie that such things did little harm, for the British press was notoriously scurrilous and printed far worse calumnies about others in the public eye: 'An article that would send a Continental into hiding for three months provokes at most a brief smile of malicious pleasure here, and the next day is forgotten.' But who was the 'German correspondent'? He did not know, and nor do we, but suspicion must fall on Lord Clanwilliam, the British ambassador to Prussia, who was Pückler's enemy throughout his time in England and about whom a few words must now be said. Clanwilliam got his Berlin posting in 1823, when he was still only twenty-eight, but although it was an honorific post for a man of his age, and he received 'constant invit[ns] to all Court doings, f[m] wh. my envious colleagues were excluded', he soon grew bored and took to behaving in a haughty, flippant way. Whether it was taking up an officer's hat at a formal assembly and using its cockade to dust a windowsill (or, in another version, his own boots) or riding straight at an artillery detachment on a country road instead of giving way, he displayed a contempt for his hosts that made him thoroughly unpopular.[8]

Why he hated Pückler is not exactly clear. Eliza M. Butler, Pückler's English biographer, asserts that Clanwilliam was 'envious of his popularity with women and of his prowess on horseback'. There is no specific evidence for the first part of this statement, though it could be true; as for the second, both men were indeed dashing equestrians and rivals at events like a steeplechase of 1823, when the earl's courage failed him at the last fence. It is also possible that Pückler poked fun at him, or at least Clanwilliam suspected him of doing so, for his extravagant but unrequited attentions to the soprano Henriette Sontag, which earned him a good deal of ridicule in society generally and a painful lampoon in a much-read comic novel: 'A more warm-blooded man would have called me to account face to face about this supposed wrong,' Pückler reflected. 'But diplomats all too readily develop a fish-blood constitution, and so the noble Lord preferred to carry on a secret intrigue.'[9] When the prince arrived in London in September 1826 his antagonist was there on leave and immediately started spreading rumours about him. He soon learned of this, though not what the gist of the rumours was. If it was also Clanwilliam who relayed the story of Pückler's Caribbean marriage from Berlin the following spring, it was his second, but not his last attempt to damage him.

Pückler's sanguine response to this titbit was vindicated, it seemed, by his flattering reception in society. He was invited everywhere he could possibly wish to go, and even royalty was gracious: the Duchess of Kent invited him to a small party, where he saw her eight-year-old daughter Princess Victoria; the Duke of Sussex shared his cigars with him and spoke in excellent German of his Continental travels; and the Duke and Duchess of Clarence, the future William IV and Queen Adelaide, invited him to parties at the Admiralty. He found the heir presumptive to be a good but unremarkable man, 'very busy without doing much, voluble without saying much, alternately over-familiar and over-distant'.[10] Like other visitors of the period Pückler was surprised at how readily the royal brothers and sisters mixed with others and put off all court etiquette in doing so. Only the king stayed out of sight, for he was now more or less a recluse at Windsor.

Another success came when the all-powerful Princess Lieven, whom he was carefully cultivating, gave him a voucher to attend his first ball at Almack's Assembly Rooms in King Street, St James's. This, society's most prestigious institution, opened its doors every Wednesday during the Season, but no one gained admittance who was not personally known to at least one of the six or seven Lady Patronesses. This should have ensured that City wealth and the new industrial fortunes never intruded on what Captain Gronow called 'the seventh heaven of the fashionable world'. However, according to Pückler this end was not achieved:

> The first Almack's Ball took place this evening, and after everything I had heard about this famous gathering I really had a strong desire to see it, but never were my expectations more disappointed. It was not much better than in Brighton: a large, empty room with bad floorboards and ropes all around like the horses' enclosure in an Arab camp; a few equally bare adjoining rooms in which the most miserable refreshments were served; and, despite the great difficulty in obtaining tickets, a company into which a large number of no-bodies had smuggled themselves to parade their bad deportment and tasteless dress.[11]

The main function of Almack's was as a meeting-place for eligible parties, and many a declaration was made on its tearoom sofas. No one with matrimonial aspirations could afford to spend their Wednesday nights elsewhere, and Pückler put aside his reservations and went almost every week. Fortunately he knew Princess Lieven and Lady Jersey among the patronesses, so obtaining vouchers was never a problem. His attendance was duly reported, for example in a notice in *John Bull* that at an Almack's of early May 'PRINCE PÜCKLER MUSKAU was present, and danced with MISS DUNDAS.' We need not concern ourselves with Miss Dundas, who plays no further part in his story, but it is interesting to see that he had given up his vow not to dance, a development confirmed by a *Morning Post* report a month later that he led off a ball at the French embassy.[12] He must have seen that the standard of English dancing was such that he could happily 'sport a toe', as the saying was.

By mid-July the three months of frenetic West End dissipation were over and it was time for everyone to return to their seats, set off on a round of country house visits or repair to a watering place. Despite his outwardly good reception and the admiration for English customs he had brought with him, Pückler had enjoyed the Season much less than he anticipated. He gradually came to the view, arrived at independently by many other visitors, that, for all their socialising, the English were not really a sociable people. Attending ten or fifteen parties a week was a wearisome duty, an eternal round of late nights, heavy meals and overheated rooms, with very little pleasure mixed in. It was partly the fault of the ladies, Pückler decided, that these experiences were not more agreeable. There were excellent hostesses, but in general it seemed that the very qualities of modesty, equability and domesticity he admired in Englishwomen precluded the different, but also essentially feminine skills required at large social events:

> It is a shame that English ladies, whether of gentle birth or not, as a rule so thoroughly lack the graceful *tournure* and well-chosen words to make such occasions complete. [. . .] In their everyday clothes, at ease in their own homes with familiar faces around them, young Englishwomen often appear very much to advantage, but in full evening dress and at large gatherings almost never, because an unconquerable timidity robs them of all grace and even paralyses their intellectual faculties to such a degree that keeping up a stimulating conversation with them is uphill work.[13]

This was very different from the dazzling quick-wittedness and display of pleasure in powers of attraction that were the delight of female society on the Continent, especially in France.

The men were worse, especially in their mania for discussing politics and steady refusal to speak to anyone to whom they had not been formally introduced. Most harmful to true conviviality were the dandies. In past years it had been Pückler's pride to imitate them, both in dress and in hard-boiled worldliness, but now, observing them at close quarters, he found them odious. He was especially shocked by the sneering undertone they used even when being ostensibly civil and their clever way of affronting people who could not give them the same return. Despite this, and although their only achievements were dressing three times a day, riding around in a cabriolet and gambling at Crockford's Club, they wielded great influence.

> That [a dandy's] conversation consists wholly in trivial private jokes and scandal-mongering; that at large gatherings he whispers into a woman's ear without caring that there are other people in the room; that with other men he talks only of gambling and hunting; that he is unbelievably ignorant of anything beyond a few modish clichés that the shallowest minds most easily retain; that his bearing exhibits the clumsy nonchalance of a country lad stretching himself out on a fireside bench; and that he has as much grace as a bear taught to dance—all this detracts not a jot from the esteem he enjoys.[14]

With its general conversation so ponderous, Pückler reflected, it was hardly surprising that society felt the need to invite recognised wits to add spice to its gatherings. But in his opinion these patented entertainers only made things worse. Their humour consisted to a large degree of malicious, rather trite remarks, and the mirth that these invariably elicited was probably often not truly spontaneous. The society wit was by definition in vogue, his sayings choice and his jokes exquisite, and to appear unamused was not to grasp his meaning and therefore to stand outside the charmed circle; but many who laughed must have wondered what he would say about them once their backs were turned, and the fear this inspired often froze their own conversational powers.

The prince concluded that on close inspection the elegant world in England was every bit as tedious as in Prussia, different though the two cases were. In Prussia the single criterion for membership of this world was rank, which made the question of admittance straightforward but was also rather arbitrary and excluded many clever, talented people who might have provided variety and sparkle. In England rank could not be grounds for the same absolute segregation because the aristocracy, unlike its remarkably pure German counterpart, was full of recently ennobled families, some of illegitimate or plebeian extraction. This assimilation of able and wealthy commoners renewed the vitality of the peerage, but corroded the notion of pedigree without which it could not hold itself aloof as a distinct caste.

Now, Pückler continued his reasoning, any society is hierarchical, and if birth no longer provides a reliable ordering principle, another is sure to replace it. In the present instance what emerged was fashion, 'a goddess who, one might say, rules personally in England, wielding her sceptre with pitiless despotism.'[15] Exclusivity based on fashion maintained itself by shared jokes and references, complex, unspoken rules of dress and deportment, and knowing glances exchanged by initiates, and was all the more rigid for the fact that it was completely artificial—as artificial, in fact, as exclusivity defined by birth alone. And because membership of the privileged group needed to be constantly reasserted (one could fall out of fashion), it was, if anything, even harder than in a purely aristocratic system for people to relax and enjoy themselves at social gatherings. They were, Pückler said, 'too slavish in adhering to all the established usages, too systematic in their pleasures, too shot through with prejudices, and finally too little vivacious to attain to that freedom of spirit which alone forms the basis of agreeable companionship.'[16]

Although there are many other negative verdicts on Regency society from foreign and native observers—one thinks of Gronow's famous denunciation of the dandies of his youth—they of course only hold as much value as such generalisations ever can. Pückler knew this and admitted the existence of 'a hundred honourable exceptions' to the norm as he described it.[17] He was further aware, and we shall presently see, that he also had personal reasons for his antipathy.

8

Four Good Prospects

'There is now a real animosity here towards foreigners suspected of wishing to marry'

With his constant attendance at balls and routs, Pückler felt well placed to raise up the nuptial torch. Moreover, he had two champions to assist him in doing so. The first was his 'good old friend' Lady Lansdowne, who decided to see something of the Season this year and moved to London in March. Though her reputation was a little faded she still stood high in society by rank and fortune, so that his presence at her parties and her visible attachment to him can only have enhanced his position: 'I did not miss the opportunity to show everyone what excellent terms we were on,' he told Lucie after one such event. Equally helpful was the Prussian ambassador Baron Heinrich von Bülow, who took up his post in April. A first-rate diplomat and future foreign minister, Bülow was a more effective representative than his likeable but diffident predecessor Maltzahn, and luckily for Pückler he was one of the few Prussian state officials who had always been well disposed towards him. This partiality continued: 'He is an intelligent man and seems to like me, and he also gives more friendly attention than others to my interests.' Bülow tried hard to bolster his compatriot's reputation and even gave him advice on how best to present himself, though the *Morning Herald*'s claim that he 'chaperoned' him rather overstates the case.[1]

Soon the fortune hunter was making headway, and at the end of May he could announce four good prospects:

1. Miss Gibbings, the doctor's daughter, pretty and accomplished, with at least £50,000;

2. A merchant's daughter, very pretty, good-natured and stupid, with £40,000;
3. A well-born, ugly girl with £100,000;
4. A gentle, intelligent, pretty and well-born girl with only £25,000.

It seems odd to find Mary Gibbings at the head of this list. After his departure from Brighton Pückler wrote to Lucie, 'You are very, very good to approve of the way I have handled things with regard to Miss G.,' which suggests that she had after all needed some cajoling to agree to his giving up that option. He began to reconsider of his own accord when he called on the family in London in April and found the young lady 'very pretty and likeable', her mother 'welcoming', and the house they had taken 'superb', and he decided to do just enough to keep the flirtation warm in case nothing else turned up. To this end he secured admittance for the two Gibbings ladies to their first Almack's ball, a 'favour without parallel' that he was only able to bestow after much fawning on one of the patronesses. They would certainly not have succeeded with a direct application, and were, he said, almost ready to kiss his hands when he gave them their voucher.[2]

Pückler nowhere recorded the name of his second bridal candidate, one of two grown-up daughters of an immensely rich merchant he had met at a soirée two weeks earlier. He decided straight away that both would be ideally suited to the life at Muskau he had in store for his new spouse, and that he would take either if she came with £50,000. According to his informants this sum was the equivalent of just one year's income for the family, but as there were ten sisters in total, most of them still children who would all need to be provided for, it was not clear how much the already marriageable girls would get. His preference was for the younger of the two, who was attractive, straightforward and good-natured, 'in fact not very bright, which I like a great deal', though if the father preferred to find a husband for the elder sister first then he would gladly focus his attention on her.[3]

The third option was an admiral's daughter of seventeen: '[She is] ugly to be sure, and a redhead too, but does not displease me for all that. She is light-hearted and has big, mischievous eyes, a voluptuous little figure, good teeth and pretty manners, which I like to see.' Apart from her fortune, the largest of those under review, she had the advantage of noble birth, which meant that their union would not raise eyebrows in Berlin. Her name was Georgiana Auguste Henrietta Elphinstone and she was the half-sister of Countess Flahaut. Their father Lord Keith had remarried after the countess's mother died, and on his own death in 1823 his second wife was left to supervise their only child's forays into society. Pückler's opinion of her appearance is seconded by the diarist Thomas Creevey, who called her 'an ugly little tit', and, more generously, by the Whig hostess Lady Holland, who is reported to have said 'that tho' her face was not as pretty as it might be, [...] her figure was remarkably so.' Gleanings from various sources suggest a cheerful, frolicsome personality, rather flighty even, with a great love of amateur theatricals. Lady Holland found her 'a very clever, lively little thing', and according to her friend Louisa Smythe she was 'very amusing' and 'a most good-natured little person, remplie de vie et d'intelligence'.[4]

The list was completed by Harriet Kinloch, the only surviving daughter of Sir Alexander Kinloch, Baronet, and his wife Lady Isabella, of Gilmerton House in East Lothian. Her father died in 1813 and, as with Miss Elphinstone, the responsibility for finding her a husband fell to her mother. Though she was probably only about twenty at this time, her health was delicate and she had already travelled in France and Italy with Lady Kinloch to improve it. Pückler played loo with the two ladies a few times in Brighton and the acquaintance blossomed in London, where he joined them in their box at the opera. He rode with Harriet in Regent's Park and, on a fine May afternoon, to Chiswick, having received the Duke of Devonshire's permission to visit the place and look over the grounds; afterwards he referred to her as 'the Scottish girl I once went riding with'. She was a pleasant, conversable companion, and he was chagrined to learn that she only had £25,000, 'though she passes as being richer'.[5]

Of these young women Pückler wrote: 'Unless a powerful enemy intervenes, I think that if I apply myself seriously I need not fear a refusal from any of them.' He now needed to pick a single quarry and chase her down, but instead he divided his attention and scattered his game. Late in the Season he saw all four of his 'fair ones', as he called them, in a single day, and was not enthusiastic about any.[6] Why, he reflected, should he take a bride who did not meet all his criteria? After all, there were plenty of heiresses in the land. So Harriet Kinloch was allowed to return to Scotland and Mary Gibbings to Brighton, both without a proposal of marriage. He made more effort with Georgiana Elphinstone, and as she seemed responsive their names began to be linked. Her diminutive form can be seen next to his heavily whiskered likeness in a satirical print by William Heath—he asks her to dance while her mother stands to one side holding a bloated bag of coins and another girl looks on in vexation.[7] He must have had a fair chance, for it was known that Miss Elphinstone intended to marry a foreigner as her half-sister had done, but he detected an obstinacy and a hint of malice in her character that would not have made for quiet domesticity in Muskau, and so he dropped the courtship.

He did, however, get as far as addressing a letter to the merchant with the attractive daughters, professing an attachment to the younger of the two, who, he had noticed, was unmistakeably keen on him,

> And I added some information on my own situation, which, as you can imagine, I presented in the most advantageous light. Nonetheless his answer, though very courteous, was a straightforward rejection, with the explanation that he (the father) would never reconcile himself to one of his daughters marrying a foreigner, whatever his rank and fortune. He therefore thanked me sincerely for having been so good as to turn to him in the first instance, for if I had begun by trying to win the affections of one of his daughters I should merely have caused her and him unnecessary grief.

Having assumed that the man would be pleased to see his daughter a princess, he had instead been given a thorough 'pawing'. He declared he would discontinue his efforts among the commercial classes, 'because I am too proud to bear their insufferable arrogance, which unfortunately and humiliatingly rests on such a ponderable basis.'[8]

But Pückler was not only too proud to place himself at the feet of the newly moneyed. In the *beau monde* too he hated to give the impression of craving approval. When at ease he was lively and engaging, and one young lady remembered him as 'a very handsome man, who walked with us always at Brighton, and who talked *incessantly.*' However, in unfamiliar company he masked his feeling of constraint behind a self-contained manner and thereby came across as standoffish. In late spring he learned from a good source, probably Bülow or Princess Lieven, that some people found him haughty and tedious, and there are other testimonies of the poor impression he could create: the *Court Journal* said he was reputed to be a 'heavy man'; Louisa Smythe, who met him in Brighton, described him simply as 'uninteresting'; and the diarist Clarissa Trant found him 'a most laughable specimen of a consummate coxcomb'. He was, he realised, his own worst enemy, for 'the fear of appearing ridiculous or of not being sufficiently captivating makes for an awkward manner and a comical facial expression.'[9]

He was also discountenanced by the supercilious attitude the English adopted towards foreigners, a trait noted by countless writers.[10] In particular they were unsure what to make of Continental titles, and in common with many of his ilk Pückler found that he was invited to any number of parties for the esoteric lustre his name added to the guest list, but if he wished to forge closer ties he ran into scepticism about his true status. According to the *Foreign Quarterly Review*, his name 'was conjectured to be an assumed one by some, who imagined that his princehood and estates existed only *in nubibus*'; the *Court Journal* said it was a 'fairy-tale name'; the *Satirist* labelled him a 'titled vagabond'; and Grantley Berkeley recalled that some preferred to call him 'Prince Pickle and Mustard'. This pun, and its variants 'Pickled Mustard', 'Pickling Mustard' or just 'Pickle', were no worse than what others had to put up with, but the attitude that gave rise to them sapped his confidence and thickened the carapace of pride that made him unpopular. How, he asked Lucie, could he succeed in a country where he and those like him were looked upon 'more or less as beggars'?[11]

Such scorn turned to unease if a foreigner showed matrimonial inclinations, and the merchant who would not let any of his ten girls marry one displayed a sentiment increasingly prevalent in the highest ranks too. 'There is now a real animosity here towards foreigners suspected of wishing to marry,' Pückler told Lucie, 'and even in the daily papers strong words are often printed on the subject and English girls enjoined to make loyalty to their country a matter of honour.' He was struck by the vehemence with which a German wooer of the previous Season was denounced in a verse satire as a 'young foreign monkey'. Soon he acquired a nickname of his own: 'The Fortunate Youth'. This may have referred to a sketch performed at the Adelphi Theatre in 1818, in which a maltster's son fools the world into thinking he has a large fortune and courts a rich girl before being exposed as an impostor and fleeing to Paris. Or it may, as Pückler believed, have been the title of a fairy tale about a princess whose suitor, by some form of trickery, appears to embody charm, youth and wealth, but is then revealed to possess none of these qualities—a parallel, he conceded, 'by heaven as accurate as can be'.[12] Either way this moniker showed that at least some people were getting wise to his schemes.

To complete his troubles Pückler lost heavily at the gaming table. Since his arrival in London he had abided by a promise to Lucie to play only for low stakes. Nonetheless his skill at whist and écarté won him small sums in more or less every session at card parties and at his club, providing a useful supplement to the limited funds he had to live on. For the first half-year of his stay his net winnings were £362, and April, May and June 1827, the months of the Season, yielded £425. Then, suddenly, he was gripped by madness and lost £800 in a single week. He was devastated, and could not believe what he had done. He tried to be philosophical, reflecting that 'God has sent me these eight days [. . .] to try and knock some sense into me, and no doubt He has more help of the same kind in store.' For now the chastened prince vowed to give up gambling.[13]

These reversals made the month of July a depressing one. His reputation seemed to be compromised, and his disastrous run at cards was made worse when a remorseful letter home failed to soften his 'good little mother', who, anxious as she ever was about their finances, berated him soundly. In his reply he declared his spirits had never sunk so low; he was, he said, thin and pale, and a few days later apparently quite yellow. But in August he regained his composure. He had probably imagined his stock with English society to have sunk lower than it really had, he decided, and even his financial setback was not as grave as it first appeared. Fortunately he had an ideal creditor in Rothschild, who remained 'trusting and obliging' and also hospitable. And then there were two things to be glad of: first, that he had not proposed to the inadequately dowered Harriet Kinloch 'just to get it over with'; and second, that his aversion had held him back 'from desperate measures with the dreaded Miss G.'.[14]

Aided by such reasoning Pückler watched London empty itself of society with much of his equanimity restored. Yet the seeds of resentment had been sown: he was fair-minded enough to realise that distrust of his motives was justified, but the prejudice and air of superiority with which foreigners were viewed in England made him bitter. A good barometer of his feelings on this matter was his Bonapartism, which waxed strong at this time. Though a former soldier in the Allied cause, he had long thrilled to the grandeur of Napoleon's achievement; and now, confronted daily with the earthbound smugness of the English, he found in him a nobility of spirit that soared above the nation that had finally brought him low and then chained him, like a second Prometheus, to the rock of St Helena. Pückler was therefore incensed at a reconstruction in the Vauxhall Gardens of the Battle of Waterloo, at the end of which Napoleon, who in reality had withdrawn from the battlefield in good order, was shown fleeing back and forth in his carriage with the British cavalry in pursuit before clambering out and making his final escape on horseback, all to the noisy cheers of the crowd. This spectacle left Pückler 'with a painful feeling', but his admiration for his idol only grew.[15]

A less abstract refuge from England's chilly opulence was the light-hearted company of resident foreigners. Apart from Lottum and Esterhazy his main cronies were Count Buol-Schauenstein, subsequently an Austrian foreign minister but now a thirty-year-old bachelor travelling for pleasure; and the Dane Count Danneskiold-Samsøe, a hymeneal speculator who after long endeavours carried off Lady Elizabeth Brudenell-Bruce in 1833.[16] He also frequented London's sizeable population of prostitutes, whom he found prettier than those he had known elsewhere and far more tender and responsive while servicing their clients—'perfect' in fact.[17] It is a sign of the openness of his relationship with Lucie that he could mention such encounters, though he did have to apologise for the following excessively frank account:

As one needs to see everything if one is to travel with profit I decided, begging your pardon, dear Schnucke, to visit a regal personage with a dozen other ladies at her court. The house was almost as splendidly furnished as the Duke of Devonshire's, and the exceptional cleanliness as well as the beauty and freshness of the girls are nowhere else to be found. One could live here as in a hotel: baths, an excellent kitchen, superb wine—everything is available. Among the girls there was one in particular, barely seventeen years old, who lacked nothing except her virginity to make any man fall in love with her. She was utterly beautiful in every way, but also utterly ignorant of the arts of reading and writing and unbelievably stupid. But that suited me very well, for as a consequence she blindly did everything I required. I made her strip naked in a warm and very cosy boudoir and adopt all the poses I could remember from famous statues and paintings. She was especially good as Titian's Venus, lying voluptuously on a couch and appearing to try with her right hand to coax along a pleasurable dream. Bathed in the light of the fire and framed by half-drawn curtains, this creature was lovelier than anything I have ever beheld. Her snow-white body had not a single blemish. Her virginal breasts were firm like marble and her luxuriant dark brown, slightly wavy hair played around them. The picture was completed by tiny hands, the prettiest of feet (undeformed by tight shoes), teeth like pearls, and a soulful look on her pale, finely sculpted face, with closed eyes and softly smiling dark red lips. When she opened her eyes the effect was spoiled by her stupid expression, but as I have described her she was flawless. She fired up my imagination so much that I had her twice, quite an effort for your old Lou. But never fear, I did not forget the c[ondoms], and these helpful articles are in an uncommon state of perfection here. They are like gauze but as tough as leather.[18]

On another occasion he was sitting in a borrowed box at the Haymarket Theatre when he noticed a pair of prettily shod feet and white-stockinged ankles perched on the chair next to him. As he turned round his look was met by two mischievous big brown eyes belonging to a girl of about eighteen in a white dress with a poppy-red sash and an Italian straw hat. Her name was Milly. He was capti-vated by her grace and seeming light-heartedness and took her home, where he enjoyed her 'like a sparrow', as he wrote in French, until his vigour was spent. Instead of then sending her out into the cold morning air he let her sleep through the day, watching with the in-terest that people and their ways always held for him as she made a bivouac on his sofa with her things around her. She had sacrificed so little of her charm on closer acquaintance that when evening came and he needed to go out he was sorry to have to ask her to leave. He almost certainly saw her again, for among his papers is a letter from one Bessy Niles inviting him to join the two of them on a trip to Richmond. He knew that girls like Milly hoped to find a protector who would rent a house for them and visit in his spare time, but he was hardly in a position to do so.[19]

Indeed, he was supposed to be securing money from women, not spending it on them. Where should he take his search now that the Season was over? He had one or two ideas, and, importantly, his con-fidence had returned. His best chances were still ahead of him.

9

CAPITAL OF THE WORLD

*'After a long stay in such a metropolis one really grows a
little less narrow-minded in all things'*

In April 1827 another German, one of his country's greatest poets,
arrived in London. Not for the last time, the satirical vein in
Heinrich Heine's verses had landed him in trouble, and his
journey was partly motivated by the need to place himself beyond the
reach of the law. He found accommodation in a boarding-house off
the Strand, where, apart from brief visits to Brighton, Ramsgate and
Margate, he remained until his departure in August. During his stay he
collected the impressions that form the 'English Fragments' section of
his prose masterpiece, *Pictures of Travel*. These were not happy weeks for
Heine, who had severe money troubles, was in poor health and spoke
hardly any English. He received no invitations, and, other than a brief
notice of his arrival in a few of the papers,[1] there is no evidence that
anyone, including his compatriot in Jermyn Street, was even aware of
his presence.

'In respect of its grandiosity London has exceeded all my expectations,' Heine wrote soon after arriving, 'but I have lost myself.'
Unlike Germany, wrapped in a cloud of philosophy and cheap
tobacco, the British capital appeared to him to possess a culture of en-
terprise and practical achievement; yet this went hand in hand, he said,
with acquisitive habits that forced its inhabitants to run after money
to maintain their lifestyles and service their debts, so that the city re-
sembled a vast stone forest filled with people scurrying about in diabolical haste. A student of human nature might learn more by standing
on the corner of Cheapside than from all the books at the Leipzig
Fair, 'but do not send a poet to London! With its earnestness in all

things, colossal monotony, machine-like movement, and irritability even in pleasure, this exorbitant London will crush his imagination and break his heart.'[2] With these as his impressions, it is no wonder that Heine missed the clay pipes and nightcaps, if not the censors, of home.

Other Germans reacted differently, like the writer and scholar Johann Valentin Adrian, also in London in 1827, who delighted in the colourful equipages, the bustle of commerce, the well-maintained streets and the good-looking women, and declared that for elegance and vitality the city had no equal. All the same, most German travellers over the next two or three decades agreed with Heine. Their main quarrel with London was its extent: with a population of more than 1,500,000 in the late 1820s, it was much larger than Paris and about seven times the size of Berlin. Struggling to describe this urban leviathan, they reached for metaphors of the sea, deserts, forests and monsters. Here was a city with no proper boundaries, pushing its tentacles ever deeper into the surrounding country; which could not be viewed whole from any vantage point, and was full of housing so monotonous that it was hard to know where you were. It violated the immutable law that people must live close to nature and witness its daily workings, and turned individuals whose ancestors had each had an established place in their community into cogs in a vast machine.

It was surely most unhealthy too. The smoke-filled air sapped the tourist's strength, and each day, unless he could afford to ride or drive, he faced the hazards of walking in a confined space with thousands of other people. Oddly the locals were able to avoid collisions, but the visiting German was less adept. Crossing the street was perilous, and even if he strolled along the pavement, perhaps stopping occasionally to look at something, he could easily get in a tangle. All in all, the British capital was rather a harassing place, and made Germany's relative economic backwardness seem like an advantage. This was certainly Heine's view, tinged with affectionate irony, after his stay of 1827: 'How much more cheerful and homely is our dear Germany by comparison! The dreamily unhurried pace of life makes every day seem like Sunday!'[3]

We encounter the same difference of mentality in the testimony of Edmund Spencer, who toured Germany from 1834 to 1836:

> An Englishman, who has been accustomed to see in his own country nearly every consideration sacrificed to the love of gain, feels surprised to find that money will not induce [. . .] a German to put himself out of his way. How heartily will every traveller assent to the truth of this, who has attempted to transact business in Germany, between the hours of twelve and two, when the whole flood of affairs stands still throughout this vast empire.

Spencer calls Germans 'heavy, serious, and thinking', not 'quick in comprehension, quick in action, nor, in short, quick in anything'. Though purposeful once launched on a particular course, they are a meticulous people and, of all things, cannot stand to be rushed. The same distinction is made by the Scotsman Thomas Carlyle, this time with a pro-German slant. While the English are assailed by the din of mercantile life, says Carlyle's adopted persona in his *Sartor Resartus* (1833), 'learned, indefatigable, deep-thinking Germany' shows the way to a more balanced existence. Specifically Carlyle justifies that nation's queasiness about London, 'that monstrous Tuberosity of Civilised Life', with its 'ink-sea of vapour, black, thick, and multifarious' enveloping the 'grinding millions' of its inhabitants.[4]

But what of Pückler? He too grumbled about the pollution, which turned day into night and made him feel unwell. Sometimes he shared his countrymen's sense of being overwhelmed by London, especially in the 'tumultuous City, where you could get lost like an atom' and might easily be run through by the shaft of a cabriolet driving too close to the pavement. Moreover, 'there is something very eerie about the daily crowds in the City and the listlessness painted on the harried, gloomy faces you pass.' This pace of life coarsened people's sensibilities, hence their love of freak shows such as 'the famous German dwarf', 'the fattest girl ever seen' and 'the living skeleton'.[5] London, he thought, had a little of the peepshow about it, and often there was an element of brutality in this sensationalism: prize fighting was hugely popular, as were blood sports like rat baiting, and thousands were happy to get up in the small hours to watch a hanging. Even the street *Punch and Judy* shows, harmless in themselves, partook of this violent spirit.

On balance, though, his view of London was positive. He called it 'the capital of the world' and stated that 'after a long stay in such a metropolis one really grows a little less narrow-minded in all things.' In particular he loved the shops, which offered 'quantities of new and useful items that it would be hard to find in such profusion or so well designed on the Continent,' and despite his shortage of money he was easily tempted to buy things for himself and especially for Lucie, whose presents included Chinese vases, Persian rugs and engravings of butterflies. He also attended auctions of the property of bankrupt nabobs and noblemen, and noted down the patter the auctioneers used to cajole bidders: 'At one time he doubtless had more money than sense, and now he's just as certainly got more sense than money.'[6]

He found getting around the foggy metropolis easier than on his last visit as there was now gas lighting in the streets, many of which were newly macadamised. The pavements too were excellent, and despite his unease about the heavy traffic it was on foot that he explored the City: the Guildhall, the Royal Exchange and the Bank of England, where, he said, a poor German could only marvel at the great piles of gold and silver ingots. He toured King's Bench and Newgate Prisons, the first for debtors and the second for hardened criminals; and the Bethlehem Royal Hospital, known as 'Bedlam', a lunatic asylum whose inmates were kept in surpassingly clean, comfortable conditions. He beheld London's technical and commercial prowess in Barclay's Brewery on Bankside, the world's largest, where steam-powered machinery produced up to 1,500 barrels of beer each day; and at the West India Docks, where huge blocks of mahogany were unloaded effortlessly by winches and hoists and stored in vast warehouses with other goods worth millions of pounds. And he sank in a diving bell to the bed of the Thames to observe repair work on the tunnel being built between Wapping and Rotherhithe—'a gigantic undertaking, only realisable here, where people simply do not know what to spend all their money on.'[7]

There were very few museums and galleries he did not visit at least once. He saw the British Museum's collection of antiquities, still crammed into the 'completely unworthy setting' of Montagu House, though work had begun on a large neo-Classical building to replace it. At India House he found a strange miscellany of artefacts from around the world, all spoils of empire, and at Exeter Change in the Strand a menagerie of exotic animals—leopards, hyenas, zebras, apes, condors—of which the star attraction was an old lion named Nero, who had sired six generations of cubs for the English market 'but is now resting on his laurels, and sleeps almost the whole day'.[8] He went to the popular 'cosmoramas', a series of partly animated views: the coronation of Charles X in Rheims Cathedral, the ruins of the ancient Syrian city of Palmyra and the Edinburgh Great Fire of 1824. The antiquarian Thomas Hope let him see the paintings and sculptures in his home in Piccadilly; the Earl Grosvenor admitted him to the newly hung collection at his Park Lane mansion; and the Duke of Northumberland showed him the treasures of Northumberland House. At Somerset House he viewed portraits by Sir Thomas Lawrence, the most successful British artist of the day, but disliked his technique, in which, he said, the faces of the sitters were carefully done but the rest daubed over in the manner of a theatre scene-painter.[9]

Pückler's favourite evening pastime was the theatre. His fare included comedic sketches, pantomimes and 'melodramas' (lightweight pieces with musical interludes), but what really mattered was Shakespeare, and like other German visitors he approached the experience of his plays on their native stage with great seriousness. He saw *The Merchant of Venice, Richard III, The Merry Wives of Windsor*, William Macready in the title role of *Macbeth* and, on one memorable evening at Drury Lane, 'the ruling triumvirate of the English stage' in *Othello*—Edmund Kean as the Moor, Charles Kemble as Cassio and Charles Young as Iago. Only Desdemona, the role in which he had admired Eliza O'Neill in 1814, was poorly taken. After some performances he penned lengthy appraisals: 'I write as if I had a review to supply to the *Morgenblatt*,' he joked one day to Lucie.[10] He rejected the common German view that Shakespeare is better on the printed page than in the theatre, and claimed that Kemble's Falstaff and

Young's Iago made him understand those characters as never before. He also said that whereas German actors were often uneducated and stood fairly low on the social scale, their best English counterparts were men and women of culture who, given the less rigid class distinctions, could mix with good society and acquire the refined bearing they often needed to reproduce on stage and which German performers struggled to convey.

Another difference between the two nations, this time not in England's favour, was in their audiences. In German capitals the theatre was the habitat of the well-born, but even those in cheap seats acted as if they were in church. The London playhouses, on the other hand, were little patronised by royalty or aristocracy, which preferred the visiting French companies; and they were also spurned by portions of the respectable middle class, who wished to avoid encounters with the crowds of prostitutes in the foyers. Without these civilising influences, audiences were very rowdy. Pückler could hardly believe his eyes when men stood up to crack jokes in the middle of a performance, threw food around the auditorium or even got into brawls. But this was nothing new, and his astonishment echoes that of German tourists of the eighteenth century, whose accounts of London's theatres are full of drunken carousing, fisticuffs and hails of orange peel.[11] What surprised him most was that amid such scenes the actors carried on as if unperturbed, and that, however uncouth, an audience always knew when fine things were happening on stage. Kean's Othello won respect effortlessly, and at his smothering of the innocent Desdemona everyone was as if struck by lightning.

More decorous was the behaviour of audiences at the opera; here the problem was the performance. At the King's Theatre operas were at least given more or less as the composer wrote them, if rarely well, but at Drury Lane things were very different, as he discovered when he saw *The Marriage of Figaro* there. The parts of the Count, Susanna and Cherubino were taken by actors who spoke rather than sang their lines, while other characters rendered some of the missing music as well as English songs interpolated at random: 'Every opera is, as the bill announces, "adapted for the English stage", in other words totally disfigured, by a local composer (normally Mr Bishop).' Henry

Rowley Bishop's well-documented mutilation of operatic master-pieces seems incredible to later generations, but his contemporaries were so pleased with his efforts that he was knighted and given the chair of music at Oxford University. 'There is no nation in Europe that pays more for its music and understands and enjoys it less' was Pückler's judgement.[12]

It would take too long to recount his impressions of all the eminent men and women he met. The most interesting, certainly to his mind, was John Nash, an affable septuagenarian who invited him to his home in Regent Street several times to examine plans of the projects he was working on. Born to Welsh parents in Lambeth in 1752, Nash had begun his career as a speculative builder and surveyor. In the 1770s he built some of the first houses in London to be clad in stucco, a material associated with his name for the rest of his career. In the next decades he extended himself from the neo-Classicism universal in his youth to neo-Gothic, 'Old English' (neo-Tudor) and Italianate idioms, and developed a 'picturesque' style in which the scenic beauty of a site and the building placed there enhance each other. From the mid-1790s he began erecting villas in landscaped surroundings before graduating to larger country houses and finally being employed by the Regent to design the Royal Lodge at Windsor, complete the Pavilion in Brighton, and rebuild Buckingham House as a palace. He is of course best known for remodelling parts of London's West End—Portland Place, Regent Street, Haymarket, Carlton House Terrace—and laying out Regent's Park.

Pückler could not make up his mind about Nash's architecture. He admired the grand conception of his work in central London, which he thought gave the city the character of a royal residence that it did not previously have. However, many of the individual buildings and their detailing appeared to him shoddy or tasteless, for example All Souls, Langham Place, with its curious spike atop a circular colonnade; and the new Buckingham Palace, hopelessly confused and undignified with a dome that looked like a powder puff. Nash's unique talent, he believed, was in arranging a cluster of buildings to striking effect and in matching their style with an often 'improved' setting. Indeed, Pückler felt that he might put posterity more decisively in his debt if he worked more as a landscaper and less as an architect. He was the only man who had yet succeeded in giving standing bodies of water a natural appearance, especially in Regent's Park and, to a lesser extent, in St James's Park, though in the latter case the tiny space available made the result even more splendid. As a creator of evocative spaces he considered Nash a genius, and told Lucie he had picked up several technical hints along these lines by studying the plans for St James's Park.

Pückler disagreed with the many foreign observers who declared London to be more impressive by size than beauty. The scene of his fortune-hunting travails, it nonetheless offered plenty to compensate a man whose strongest sensations were visual:

> The night was quite Italian, and I stayed within the well-lit area, riding round the town and its suburbs for several hours. From Westminster Bridge an amazing view unfurled before me. The lamps of the skiffs danced on the Thames like friar's lanterns, and the bridges spanning the river from one mass of houses to another resembled vast flaming garlands. Only Westminster Abbey was unilluminated, but the mystic moon, that old intimate of ruins and Gothic piles, caressed the stone pinnacles and carvings with her pale rays, sank them yearningly into the dark recesses, and silvered the tall, glinting windows; while, higher up, the black roof and towers of the lofty edifice turned away from the teeming, light-flecked town beneath them and rose in tenebrous majesty—sombre, silent and rigid—towards the star-filled sky above.[13]

He often rode out into the country around London and loved its combination of natural landscape and garden-like cultivation, unlike anything elsewhere in Europe. One evening he made an excursion to Greenwich to watch the setting of the sun:

> I stopped at the Ship Tavern, handed my horse to the ostler [. . .], and was shown to a very pretty room with a bay window projecting over the Thames. Underneath it swam the fish that I, as a merciless human predator, would soon devour. The river was enlivened

by a hundred barques and the music and singing that sounded across the water from the passing steam ships, and above this cheerful scene the sun descended, blood red in its light veil of mist, towards the horizon. Seated at the window, I gave a lengthy audience to my private thoughts, until the arrival of eels, flounders and sole, all variously prepared, summoned me to more material pleasures. Iced champagne and Lord Chesterfield's letters, which I had brought with me, added to the savour of my meal. After a brief siesta as night was closing in I mounted my horse and rode the one and a half German miles back to my rooms.[14]

London also fascinated Pückler as a seat of power where statesmen directed the affairs of their nation and influenced those of the world. Though he deplored the English habit of talking politics at social gatherings he was himself very interested in the subject and enjoyed the rambunctiously independent reporting of the London press. He tracked the fortunes of prominent parliamentarians, followed debates on the Corn Laws, the slave trade, rotten boroughs and the Catholic question, and collected satirical prints on political themes. In February 1827 the long-serving Tory prime minister Lord Liverpool resigned after suffering a heavy stroke, and George Canning, latterly the dominant figure in his cabinet, was expected to succeed him. Yet this outcome was not certain, despite Canning's brilliance, for many of his colleagues objected to his liberal leanings, and seven 'High Tories', including the Duke of Wellington and Robert Peel, refused to serve under him. The stalemate was broken only when Canning forged a coalition of fellow liberal Tories and moderate Whigs.

During this tense period Pückler attended several debates in Parliament. In the Lords he heard Wellington, never a good orator, 'stammering and muddled like a schoolboy', and was sad to see Europe's greatest soldier so easily bested in verbal combat. In the Commons he heard Peel, 'a skilled, but not a stirring speaker' and more liberal than his 'High' affiliation suggested—not a bad insight given Peel's subsequent career; and Henry Brougham, later a Whig lord chancellor, who spoke with exceptional clarity and fluency but also pedantry and poor taste, making him 'dangerous as an enemy, but not capable of feeling great enthusiasm or awakening it in others'. This last ability belonged pre-eminently to Canning, whom Pückler heard speak on Portuguese affairs and on the hybrid government he had just formed: 'It was only he who could thrill his audience and fill their hearts and minds with the intoxication that gives a great speaker an incomparable power over people.'[15]

Canning died a few months later, in August, aged fifty-seven and at the peak of his powers and achievement. His replacement, Lord Goderich, was an indecisive man weighed down by private grief, and his ministry, like its predecessor a mix of Canningite Tories and Whigs, did not last long. But the advantage of mature political structures like Britain's, Pückler mused, was that they could function even without a great figure at the helm. Moreover, the ruling class was judicious and pragmatic enough to enact reforms demanded by changing realities and then integrate them into a narrative of continuity, steering clear of the absolutism of German despots and the violence of revolution. There appeared to be deep wells of talent and devotion to duty in both Houses, men whose social advantages came with a sense of obligation, who worked selflessly for the good of their country and, regardless of any differences of opinion, treated each other with dignity and respect.

It seemed curious to Pückler that a social elite which brought forth so many frivolous devotees of fashion also produced such worthy figures. And, like the former, the latter too had no exact equivalent abroad. In seeking to understand the nature of the English governing class, he made a connection between their feeling of responsibility for their inherited acres and for the country as a whole. Whereas many Continental noblemen idled away their time as courtiers or cosmopolites, treating their properties as sources of income to be managed by a steward, English landowners resided on their estates for much of the year and took an interest in their cultivation. By creating parks, improving their houses and patronising the arts, they provided employment and cultural enrichment. In the same spirit they were generous in giving money to subscriptions, and, above all, active in politics, yielding successive generations of public servants with a capacity for leadership and a calm, decorous way of conducting the nation's affairs.

The members of this public-spirited group were by no means all peers. Canning and many other parliamentarians were of good but not titled families, as were countless senior military officers and lawyers. With the hierarchy in any case fairly fluid, someone's precise rank mattered less than his ability and inclination to contribute to the public good. It was, Pückler believed, this body of men, conscious of a calling to lead but open to new talent, that made Britain a dynamic, advanced country. What a contrast with Prussia, run like a cadet school by a cadre of faceless bureaucrats! He never forgot the vexations he endured when Muskau became a part of Prussia, and hatred for its state machinery was a lifelong passion. Functionaries called themselves crown servants, he wrote, but were the true power in the land, while landowners were taxed to the hilt and had their rights curtailed by complex laws; no wonder many were glad to fill a decorative post at court if it came with a stipend, or enter the bureaucracy themselves.

How much better, thought Pückler, if Prussia could regenerate its ruling class along English lines, with constitutional privileges, low taxation and freedom from stifling regulations offset by the moral duty to make itself socially and politically useful. There would be points of entry for new talent and money, thereby avoiding both the destabilising effects of pure egalitarianism and the rigidity of a caste defined by birth alone. This aristocracy would wield power alongside an English-style constitutional monarchy, replacing Prussia's absolute monarchy, which in practice meant absolute rule by state officials. The idea of establishing a powerful nobility may seem to run counter to Pückler's desire for greater civil liberties, but he did not think so. In England, he claimed, the advantages enjoyed by the landed class co-existed with the conviction that, before the law, everyone was equal; property was sacrosanct, but so were individual rights. Most important of all, newspapers could print what they liked, and despite the rough handling he sometimes received he was sure that here too England was lighting the way to the future: 'That Jesuitical principles will no longer rule the world, and that freedom of the press, once attained, will and must work incalculable wonders—of this I am quite convinced.'[16]

10

THE BONHAMS OF TITNESS PARK

*'If I could only send you her picture you would be
astonished at her beauty'*

Pückler hoped that when society quitted London at the end of
the 1827 Season he would be invited by new acquaintances to
their country houses. This did not happen, and had it not been
for Esterhazy, who sent a letter of recommendation to the Harcourts
of St Leonard's Hill near Windsor, he would have had nowhere to go.
As it was he set out with Count Lottum on a beautiful August day.
They put up in Salt Hill, near Slough, at an inn as elegant as a private
villa and approached through a veranda of rose bushes. Pückler's room
to the rear looked out onto a garden and pleasure ground, the radiant
countryside beyond and, in the distance, framed by two chestnut trees,
the gigantic proportions of Windsor Castle. It was already evening
when they arrived and there was only time for a short walk while
their dinner was prepared, but the next day they spent riding around
the charmed corner of England where eastern Berkshire is bounded
by Buckinghamshire to the north and Surrey to the south. Among
other things they saw Stoke Park, which had belonged to William
Penn, the founder of Pennsylvania, and was famous for its rare species
of deer; and Dropmore House, built by Samuel Wyatt, with its gardens
brimful of hollyhocks, dahlias and geraniums, and an arboretum of
rare conifers.

At Windsor Castle they were turned away because the king had
just driven himself over in his tiny pony-drawn phaeton from the
nearby Royal Lodge, where he lived with his mistress Lady
Conyngham. Fortunately by the time they returned after looking
round Eton College the king had left again and they were shown

around by Sir Jeffry Wyatville, the architect who had been rebuilding the castle since 1823. Pückler found some of the internal decoration over-sumptuous, did not like the wallpaper in the guest apartments and wondered why even the grandest buildings in England always had plain floorboards rather than parquetry. He also had his view of the general tastelessness of English monuments confirmed by the tomb of Princess Charlotte and her still-born son in St George's Chapel. Despite all this, and his usual reservations about Gothic Revival architecture, he could not help being dazzled by the castle and called it the most splendid residence of any European monarch. He returned more than once over the following days, and made use of the professional guides who already operated there.

Meanwhile Lottum was unexpectedly called away, and so Pückler went on to St Leonard's Hill and the Harcourts alone. At eighty-three Field Marshal William Harcourt, the third earl of that name, could look back on a distinguished if not brilliant career fighting the Americans and the French. He and his wife Mary, about ten years younger, lived in perfect conjugal happiness in their hilltop home near the village of Clewer, surrounded by flower gardens and a delightful park. The continuing fine weather and the friendliness of his hosts made Pückler's stay there extremely pleasant. Lady Harcourt took him in her carriage to see the park, from which five counties were visible, and each time they reached a vantage point they alighted and a servant thrust a huge parasol into the grass and opened the canopy for them to sit under (something he must get for Muskau, he decided). When he expressed admiration for the enormous oaks and beeches, the countess proudly told him that she had planted them all forty years earlier to frame seven 'pictures' of the surrounding country, and had calculated their height and density so well that only two had since needed to be removed.

Early one morning Lord Harcourt took him on a tour of Windsor Great Park, of which he was head ranger. The king, now so self-conscious about his size and infirmities that he hated to be seen there, would not be about till later. First they drove to the stables, where the famous 'camelopard', or giraffe, a gift from the Egyptian pasha Mehmet Ali, was led out to them by its Nubian keepers. For Pückler, who loved all animals, it was a fascinating sight, especially its eyes, 'something midway between those of the finest Arabian horse and the loveliest Mediterranean girl'.[1] It was known to like visitors, and though unsteady on its legs it walked over in excellent humour and plucked his umbrella with its bright blue tongue. Just then Lord Harcourt spotted the royal phaeton ready harnessed in the stable yard and said they must hurry on. As they drove the punctilious old man stood up with some effort in his landau several times to make sure his master was not yet around, and it was not until the park gates closed behind them that he relaxed. Before that they saw Virginia Water, where the king fished in the afternoons in the company of a bored Lady Conyngham—like the giraffe a favourite subject for caricaturists. Unlike most observers Pückler admired the miniature junk and the lakeside Moorish and Chinese temples, but the best effect, he felt, was achieved by the combination of black and white swans on the water.

Two days later he was invited by Captain Bulkeley, a London acquaintance, to dine with the officers of the Royal Horse Guards, garrisoned in Windsor. Having already noticed that British soldiers on parade, though quite as martial as Prussians, exhibited less stickling precision and swank, he now found a corresponding lack of ostentatious formality in the mess:

> Although the service itself is far from neglected, there is not a trace of our pedantry, and when they are off duty not the slightest distinction is made between a colonel and the youngest lieutenant. Everyone takes as uninhibited a part in the conversation as he would elsewhere. In the country the officers all eat in uniform, whereas in London only those on duty that day do so; but after dinner every man takes his ease, and today I saw one of the young lieutenants sitting down in his dressing gown and slippers to a game of whist with his colonel, who was still in full dress.[2]

A few days later he witnessed an example of soldierly conduct 'that characterises manners here too well to leave unrecorded'. This occurred during a midnight walk in Windsor Great Park with a

handful of uniformed officers and some ladies of the local gentry who
wished to see the castle by moonlight. As they all well knew, it was for-
bidden to enter the park at that hour, and after a while the party was
discovered by a ranger, who berated the men for disgracing their
uniform and took two of them into custody. In Prussia, where the
army was everything, no officer would have tolerated such abuse from
a lowly official, and might well have resorted to violence, but 'in the
land of law and liberty [they] obeyed the civilian authority with
perfect calmness—lions at Waterloo, lambs in their peaceful home-
land.'[3]

What Pückler hoped for most in coming to this part of the
country was to find Lady Garvagh, the most beautiful woman he had
yet seen in England. Two months earlier, in June, he had briefly left
London with a Captain Rose to see the Ascot races. There Lady
Garvagh, an acquaintance of Rose's, had invited them to dine the
same evening at Titness Park, near Sunninghill. They accepted, and
when the day's racing ended they rode over:

> We arrived before the family itself and found the house open, but
> without a servant or any other living creature within. It was like
> the enchanted home of a fairy, for a more magical place there
> cannot be. If only you could have seen it! Standing on a rise, half
> hidden under the most magnificent ancient trees, the house has
> been added to on all sides at different times and was studded around
> with shrubs, so that one could not see the whole of it from any
> angle. A rose bower in the form of a gallery, abundant with hun-
> dreds of flowers, led straight into the hall, from which a sequence
> of rooms and a corridor took us through the house to the dining
> room, where the table was richly laid, but still not a soul could be
> seen. Before us lay the garden, a veritable paradise bathed in the
> warm evening sun. Along this side of the house, projecting and re-
> ceding by turns, was a series of variously shaped interconnecting
> verandas covered with an array of blossoming climbers and bor-
> dering a brightly coloured flower garden that sloped away from us
> as far as the eye could see. Beyond this lay a deep, narrow meadow
> valley, and on the other side the land, covered with ancient beeches,

rose up again to a higher line of hills. At the end of the valley to the left the view extended at ground level as far as a body of water, while above the treetops in the distance we could see the Round Tower of Windsor Castle, with the gigantic Royal Standard planted on top of it, reaching upwards into the blue sky.[4]

At last Pückler and Rose found Lady Garvagh, who immediately saw to it that they were given rooms to change in. Although the invitation had come from her, the hosts properly speaking were her parents Mr and Mrs Bonham, for Titness was their home. Most of her seven siblings, some still children, were also present, as were a few of the local gentry, but her husband was elsewhere.

After an excellent dinner with iced champagne Pückler and Rose had their self-control put to the test when Mrs Bonham entertained the company with an aria. '*Je t'aimerai toujours*' was its refrain, and each time she sang it she larded the first 'ai' with a long trill that sounded like a lamb's bleat. The captain grimaced behind his moustache in an effort to contain his mirth, while Pückler sought strength by thinking how Lucie never lost her composure in such situations. He implored God to make Mrs Bonham cease her singing, for the family had been so kind that he would rather cry tears of blood than laugh, but on and on it went. Eventually she fell silent and soon afterwards the evening came to an end. The two visitors said goodbye, and Pückler shook Lady Garvagh's hand, a strange English custom, he thought, and no way of parting from such a lovely woman.

His hopes that he would see her on returning to the area in August were soon fulfilled, and this time she asked him to come to Titness for a few days. He did not hesitate, and was soon dining 'with a heap of pretty women, of whom Lady Garvagh is the most charming'. Again there was singing afterwards, 'but without any trilling, thank God'.[5] As in June most of the family were present, Lady Garvagh still without her spouse. Titness was the Bonhams' main home, but they were only tenants or sub-lessees, their own properties being Rochetts, near Romford in Essex, and a house in Portland Place. Henry Bonham was an East India Company stockholder, a director of the West Middlesex Waterworks, and the MP for Rye. Now in his early sixties, he had all but retired from business and was a very inactive politician. His wife Charlotte Elizabeth, a Kentish clergyman's daughter, was considerably younger. Both were affable people with the leisurely habits of the landed gentry.

Although its lawns were now baked by the sun Titness still felt like an idyll in its hundred acres of partly wooded grounds, and Pückler would have endorsed the words 'beautiful and fanciful retreat' applied to it in a contemporary topographical survey.[6] A few times he rode into the surrounding country with Lady Garvagh, of whom he was now a most decided admirer. 'If I could only send you her picture,' he told Lucie, 'you would be astonished at her beauty and her indescribably gentle, calm, kind expression, with a slight touch of melancholy transfigured by a heavenly smile.' The physical features that appealed to his unfailingly conventional taste in women were cherry-red lips, perfect teeth, dark brown wavy hair, the fairest English complexion, soulful blue eyes, a slender figure and delicate white hands.

> I deeply lament not having seen this angelic woman earlier when she was still free, for she had £40,000 and every quality one could wish for: she is gentle and good and loving. Her sisters may get as much, but what a difference, even though they are quite pretty. The sun obscures the stars! [...] I see I shall have to make do, and that fate is not disposed to give me such *great* happiness—indeed, who am I to demand it?[7]

Rosabella Charlotte Isabella, known to her family as Rosabel, was twenty-two years old, considerably less than half the age of the widower she had married in 1824. They were an ill-matched couple, and already spent much of their time apart. Lord Garvagh was the cousin and namesake of the famous George Canning, and in 1818, despite only being a backbench MP, he was granted an Irish barony, no doubt thanks to his connection with Lord Castlereagh, whose half-sister he had married. Despite its newness Garvagh's peerage acted like a charm on the Bonhams, who strongly encouraged his interest in their daughter. He also had a respectable fortune, partly from his first wife, and his Portman Square home contained a Raphael and a

Veronese. Pückler learned that for eighteen months Rosabel had resisted his suit before giving way to her parents' entreaties. If only she
had held out for longer, he mused, she might have been his: 'Maybe
she now thinks the same thing, but it matters not—I must forget her.'[8]

And so he turned his attentions to her younger sister Harriet, in
his account an unspoilt girl with a playful, impulsive streak. At only
sixteen she was not yet 'out', but no one seemed to mind when they
went on long walks together. She obviously liked him, as he ascertained during a stroll in some woodland: 'Here and there things happened that would not have been fit for her parents' eyes, but I was
careful not to go too far.'[9] The Bonhams certainly saw nothing unto-
ward in their guest's behaviour, and took him along to dinners with
local families and a county ball in Egham. After four days at Titness
Pückler, who was usually restless after a short while in other people's
homes, found himself wishing he could stay for months. This hospitable, easy-going family was, he reflected, very different from the
haughty aristocrats and self-important plutocrats he had known in
London. For their part the Bonhams enjoyed his company and, with
their weakness for titles, were probably gratified to have a prince under
their roof.

Paying court to one sister but irresistibly drawn to another,
Pückler found an odd expedient for blending duty and inclination.
He told Lady Garvagh that he wished to marry Harriet out of love for
herself, and she, finding the idea compellingly romantic, promised to
promote the match and act as his confidante. This talk took place on
the morning of 1 September, and after it the young baroness kept to
her room with a feigned indisposition so that she would not distract
him for the rest of the day. He spent it with Harriet, her sister
Marianne and her cousin Henrietta on a walk to some local beauty
spots. Well-born women on the Continent rarely went any distance on
foot, and Pückler was one of many visitors to be astounded by the
pedestrianism of Englishwomen: 'Good Schnucke, your old Lou
managed to hold his own, but to keep up with the boisterous creatures
he had to jog up hill and down dale and through vegetation thick and
thin.' Harriet and Henrietta had developed a crush on him, and while
Marianne rested they took him to a copse, carved three intertwined

'H's' and 'Sept. 1' into a tree trunk and then each gave him a kiss.[10]

During this flirtation he did not neglect the fair Rosabel. After dinner one evening Mr Bonham plied him and a local landowner with claret until midnight: 'The ladies became quite impatient waiting for us to join them. My blood had been warmed and I was more forward with Lady Garvagh than before. On the stairs I kissed her, a misdemeanour that offended her English virtue to high degree.' But by morning all was forgiven; indeed, he was a favourite with the whole family, and they delayed a planned visit to keep him a little longer. He finally left Titness Park a week after arriving. On the day of his departure the Bonham girls took him on a three-hour walk and then accompanied him to his waiting carriage, where he presented them with some forget-me-nots he had picked and made a pretty speech. Harriet had picked some for him too, and her heart was obviously full, but he could hardly take his eyes off her sister, and after saying goodbye he drove off 'feeling quite despondent'.[11]

He only went as far as Windsor, where he rejoined Captain Bulkeley and was again entertained by the Royal Horse Guards officers. He found his new idol's image at the bottom of each glass: 'I can see that it was high time for me to leave Rosabel, for her absence is troubling me even more than I expected.' As he returned to London he knew he must master these feelings, 'at least for now, when anything resembling love would be completely *hors de saison*. Good Schnucke, only my love for you remains constant; it is the gold ground painted around my life.' In fact he resumed contact with Lady Garvagh just days later when she too moved to London, once again without her husband. Soon he was writing her 'very beautiful and passionate letters', as he thought them, and they frequently met out of doors, she not being allowed to receive at home in Lord Garvagh's absence.[12] She never went beyond a few minor infringements of marital fidelity, but Pückler knew how to cherish a romantically tinged friendship with a beautiful woman, and told Lucie that too many men, thinking they must play the lover with increasing animation, scare off the object of their affections.

The ostensible, and in part the real purpose of these furtive meetings was to promote his courtship of Harriet. After his tender passages

Be gar. I am de Baron Von Strong e noff. de gran Sausage Bearer
to Her Majesty : aha! by gar I vil live in Angleterre like de Prince.
and vil shew all de pritty lady demoselle all my fine Curiosity from Wertemburg
aha! by gar I vil kiss dem all. aha! and get de money
and Beuf rost.

GERMAN

SAUSAGE

WELCOME HOME.

1. Baron von Strongenoff, the preening and whiskered German fortune hunter of the popular imagination. In this caricature on the visit of George IV's sister the Queen of Württemberg to her native country in 1827, Strongenoff, her Grand Sausage Bearer, declares in a strange German and French accented English that he will impress the ladies with his 'fine Curiosity from Wirtemburg' and 'get de money and Beuf rost'.

2. The Dandy in Germany

3. The Artist

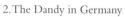

5. The Dandy in England

4. The Soldier

6. Princess Lucie von Pückler-Muskau. She sent this portrait to Pückler in London in April 1828, and he placed it on his writing desk. In a letter he poked fun at her for the diaphanous lace cap and ringlets, 'which nonetheless do not suit you badly at all, I must admit.' (*Briefwechsel*,VI, 393) (*above*)

7. Muskau: a view of the house and part of the town and park in 1825. (*below*)

8. London from near the New Custom House, Lower Thames Street. This is the view that greeted Pückler on his arrival from Rotterdam in September 1826. (*above*)

9. Greenwich, with London in the distance. Pückler visited Greenwich twice: the first time alone, the second time with Henriette Sontag. (*below*)

10. The Marchioness of Lansdowne. A wealthy dowager, Lady Lansdowne became engaged to Pückler during his first visit to England in 1814. Her family then prevailed on her to change her mind, but she and Pückler remained friends and she did what she could to advance his prospects of finding a bride when he returned in 1826.

A View from the Royal Exchange.

Three Influential Foreigners

11. Nathan Mayer Rothschild: 'This is the lion of the Royal Exchange. A curious man, and in his way a conqueror.' (EB 1/30) (*left*)

12. Prince Esterhazy. Pückler thought he looked younger and more handsome than in this portrait. (*bottom left*)

13. Princess Lieven. A flattering likeness, in Pückler's opinion. (*bottom right*)

Two Enemies

14. The Earl of Clanwilliam. From 1823 to 1827 Clanwilliam was Britain's ambassador to Prussia. During this time he clashed with Pückler, and to avenge himself he sought to frustrate his matrimonial schemes in England a few years later. (*above*)

15. The Duke of Cumberland. Always a dangerous man to cross, Cumberland probably never forgave a dressing-down he got from Pückler in Berlin in 1823. In London he spread gossip about him so as to undermine his credit in high society.

16. The Chain Pier, Brighton: 'This is a very pretty promenade, and well-conceived—for as Brighton is only visited in winter the sun is more welcome than the shade.' (EB 1/122) Pückler stayed in Brighton in early 1827 and again in early 1828.

17. Harriet Kinloch: 'The Scottish girl I once went riding with.' (VS 164/78/20/69)

18. Georgiana Elphinstone. Of the four prospective brides Pückler described to Lucie in May 1827, she was the wealthiest.

Frontispiece to the Illustrations to Almacks.

Two Caricatures in Pückler's Travel Album

19. Though he does not identify himself in his remarks underneath, it is likely that the two figures stepping out in the foreground are Pückler and Miss Elphinstone. (*above*)

20. 'This is no more and no less than a caricature of myself and Miss Elphinstone, of whom it was said that I wanted to marry her, though I never thought of doing so.' (EB 3/20r) (*below*)

AN ELECTION BALL

21. Heinrich Heine

22. Lady Morgan

23. Karl August Varnhagen

24. Sarah Austin

25. Windsor Castle. Pückler visited the castle and Windsor Great Park several times in summer 1827. (*above*)

26. Titness Park: 'I shall never forget its delightful sylvan solitude or its kind-hearted owners.' (EB 2/57) (*below*)

27. Thomas Hamlet (right) and his daughter Elizabeth: 'The fortune is immense, and if I obtain it [. . .] I shall be in clover.' (*Briefwechsel*, VI, 374) (*above*)

28. Letitia Bonaparte-Wyse. Pückler's embarrassing tangle with her provided ammunition for his enemies in London. (*right*)

29. Among the cartoons in Alexander von Sternberg's satirical work *Tutu* of 1846 is this one of 'the red-haired barbarians' showing Pückler the door. (*below*)

13

30. Henriette Sontag. Worshipped for her beauty as well as her voice, the young soprano caused a sensation in Berlin and Paris and then conquered London in the spring of 1828. Pückler was introduced to her at the Prussian Embassy and almost immediately fell in love.

31. This aquatint of Muskau appeared in *Ackermann's Repository* on 1 June 1828, showing the chateau in a planned remodelling by Karl Friedrich Schinkel that was never carried out. Pückler hoped the image and the laudatory text that accompanied it would improve his standing in London. (*above*)

32. The dandy at eighty. Pückler in 1865. (*right*)

33. Muskau: the fully restored south façade of the chateau. (*above*)

34. Branitz: the east façade viewed from the pergola garden. (*below*)

16

with her at Titness she had, according to Rosabel, fallen in love, and it was clear that her parents would not reject him. He received conflicting reports about her likely dowry, a subject he could not broach directly with her sister, and decided he could only take her with £50,000, the minimum for a financial rehabilitation of Muskau. He was fond of Harriet, but felt apprehensive about committing himself, and in letters home he mulled over her character ('good-hearted and very likeable') and looks ('pretty rather than not, and as healthy as a doe').[13] Having made up his mind, he wrote to Mrs Bonham asking for her daughter's hand and stating his conditions for accepting it. Her response of 9 September says much about that well-meaning but socially ambitious lady:

> How shall I attempt to express to You, my dear Prince, the various sentiments with which my heart has been filled on receiving the letter entrusted by You to Lady Garvagh to deliver to me—my first emotions were of gratitude and joy for the distinguished honor conferred upon me by your kind and flattering expressions towards my dear Harriet—my next feeling was the deepest regret arising from my consciousness of the utter impossibility of our wishes ever being fulfilled.—persuaded of this sad truth, I at first resolved to spare Mr Bonham the pain of knowing the happiness he must of necessity relinquish—but I felt that I could not deny him the pleasure of all others the dearest to the heart of a father—of hearing the praises of his Child, and I have accordingly laid Your Highness Letter before him—he most deeply laments with me his absolute inability to meet the exigency under which You have been placed—he desires me to express to You the deep sense he entertains of the High honor and distinction which such an Alliance would have conferred upon his Family.—he begs to offer You his sincere thanks for the unbounded confidence You have reposed in him by the frankness and candour with which You have laid open the circumstances of your Estates—which be assured will be ever held *most sacred*—and he desires me also to present to You his very grateful acknowledgements for the noble and elevated delicacy with which every part of Your conduct has been marked during the whole of

this transaction from the time we had first the happiness of seeing You here.—had it pleased Heaven to have placed You under different circumstances where—Oh! where could I have found the Person to whom I should with such joy have entrusted my beloved Child—to You in whom every virtue and every accomplishment seem united—with what gratitude to Heaven would our joyful consent have been given.[14]

Perceiving her disappointment, he returned to the charge with a second letter in his now quite good, but still unidiomatic English:

My dearest Mistress Bonham,

I feard Your kind but nearly hopeless answer would be as it is, still I am most wretched to see it now in reality before me! *Le mal, en effet, parait sans remède*—and notwithstanding all that, I cannot make my mind up to loose all my dream of happiness at once, and for such a paltry reason too! I have turned over and over in my mind every probability to get out of so desoling a dilemma, I invoked dear Harriet's and her gentle sisters spirits to assist me, but all my thoughts gave me but very little consolation. Your noble minded letter still encreases those feelings. If I was only seeking a wife with a large fortune, many opportunities for this purpose would present themselves, but I am seeking for more—a loving and beloved friend for life, domestic happiness in all her extent, and both I was satisfied I would have found in Your lovely daughter.[15]

He refused to give up hope, he continued, and 'if Mr Bonham is only able for our sake to *approach* in any way that unfortunate sum' all might be well. Meanwhile he would ask his mother to relinquish assets that must in any case fall to him after her death, and with this addition to what Harriet would bring him he could perhaps pay off his mortgages. Mrs Bonham's response was encouraging and so he laid the case before Countess Seydewitz, who replied that she was not in a position to help him as he wished, though she was prepared to release a small property she controlled for sale.

This demarche became irrelevant when Pückler discovered that

Harriet would not even get the £30,000 his informants had led him to expect, rather a mere £10,000, while Lady Garvagh, who was thought to have married with £40,000, had in fact only had £8,000. Mr Bonham was not quite as wealthy as people supposed, and still had four daughters to marry. As the negotiations limped on Pückler received some sad lines in French from Harriet: 'I tried in vain to enclose something for you in mama's letter, but I was too deeply afflicted. In any case what was left for me to say? I believed everything was finished, and for good.' Soon it was, but we may hope that at sixteen she did not nurse her sorrow for too long. Certainly Pückler was less disappointed than he might have been. The Bonhams had given him a delicious week and treated him gratifyingly, a balm for his pride after the battering it had received during the Season. Months later Mrs Bonham sent a sketch Lady Garvagh had made for him of Titness Park, and under it he wrote: 'One of the most charming country houses near London, where I spent a few very happy days. I shall never forget its delightful sylvan solitude or its kind-hearted owners.'[16]

11

THE JEWELLER'S DAUGHTER

*'O, would that I could send you some happy news at
long last!'*

During the summer of 1827 Pückler decided to send his
manservant home. He had thought to reduce his expenses
by bringing the moody but reliable Berndt from Muskau
rather than hiring a local man, but it proved to be a false economy.
Berndt failed to adapt to life in England, never learned the language,
could not get used to the food and was a constant victim of the leg-
pulling of English domestics. The only pleasure he seems to have experienced was the ghoulish one of watching a public hanging early
one July morning. He grew homesick and sullen, grumbled about his
master's nocturnal routine and one day refused to fetch provisions
from the Travellers Club, a short walk from their lodgings. Having
long admired the reserved efficiency of English servants, Pückler
engaged one on a temporary basis in early September and packed
Berndt off home with some new park plans for Lucie. And now,
before resuming his matrimonial toils, he went on a short tour of
Yorkshire.

He had funds for the trip thanks to Rothschild, who sent letters
to a number of provincial bankers guaranteeing credit for £800 and
telling them that 'as the Prince is travelling for amusement to see the
Country and all objects worthy of notice you will greatly oblige me by
rendering him such assistance as may be best calculated to obtain his
wishes.'[1] He set off on 16 September and reached Doncaster in time
for the St Leger Stakes two days later. There he found the leaders of
fashion he had not seen since July, and despite himself rejoiced to
behold so many well-dressed people and fine equipages. His next des-

tination was York, where he admired the Minster, the ruins of St Mary's Abbey, the remains of the Roman ramparts and Micklegate Bar, the city's southern gateway. He walked to Clifford's Tower, where Robert Aske was hanged for leading the anti-Reformation Pilgrimage of Grace in 1537, and visited the Guildhall, from which the merchant guilds ran York's affairs in the Middle Ages.

Then he explored the parks of the county's great showplaces: Castle Howard, Harewood House, Wentworth House, Temple Newsam: 'The number of magnificent properties in England is almost beyond counting.'[2] He spent a night in Scarborough, where he rode for miles along the white sand and climbed up to the ruins of Scarborough Castle; and stood on the chalk cliffs at Flamborough Head, looking out at the waves that had claimed so many seamen's lives. Next he saw the small shipbuilding town of Whitby, which offered a fine granite pier, a museum with a collection of fossils and the ruins of a thirteenth-century abbey, though the narrow streets were none too clean. He remarked that in general Yorkshire presented a less scrubbed appearance than southern England, but that its population was friendlier—making it more like Germany on both counts. More ruins awaited his romantic soul at Fountains Abbey, and then it was on to Ripon, to see the Minster, and Harrogate, the great spa town of the North—not fashionable like Brighton and pleasanter for it. He visited factories in Leeds, Rotherham and Sheffield, picking up small gifts for Lucie from display rooms as he went,[3] and then headed south, with many more stops to see the important parks and gardens on his way. On 6 October, after an absence of three weeks, he was back in London and ready to resume his search for a bride.

Almost immediately a new quarry came into range, far richer than any before her. 'I am now taking steps to make the acquaintance of the jeweller's daughter,' he told Lucie just four days after his return, 'and we shall see if any success is to be had. I do what I must faithfully, but with the greatest reluctance, and feel exactly as I did when as a child I was forced at all costs to consume the onion soup I so hated.'[4] Despite this lack of enthusiasm he approached his task, perhaps for the first time, with real resolve. The amount to be secured was a staggering £200,000, nearly three times what he needed to pay off Muskau's debts. He had put out feelers before leaving for his northern tour, and now, to make sure he did not blunder, he hired a matrimonial agent. It would be a month before he set eyes on Elizabeth Hamlet, who was resting in the country after an illness; for now it was to her father that he paid his addresses.

Immortalised as Mr Polonius in Thackeray's *Great Hoggarty Diamond*, the retail jeweller and goldsmith Thomas Hamlet was one of the richest tradesmen in the West End.[5] He was born in obscure circumstances in about 1770 and assumed to be the illegitimate son of Sir Francis Dashwood, the notorious rake and founder of the Hellfire Club. As a young man he walked from his native Cheshire to London and found work as a jeweller's assistant. A few years later he set up on his own, and by the time Pückler met him his affairs had flourished for three decades. Some said he was a millionaire. As Captain Gronow recalled:

> His shop at the corner of Cranbourne Alley [off Leicester Square] exhibited a profuse display of gold and silver plate, whilst in the jewel room sparkled diamonds, amethysts, rubies, and other precious stones, in every variety of setting. He was constantly called on to advance money upon such objects, which were left in pawn, only to be taken out on the occasion of a great banquet, or when a court dress was to be worn. His gains were enormous, though it was necessary to give long credit; and his bills for twenty or thirty thousand pounds were eagerly discounted. In fact, he was looked upon as a second Croesus.[6]

In appearance Hamlet, or the 'Prince of Denmark' as his clients facetiously called him, was plain and unpretending, in Grantley Berkeley's recollection a 'stout, old, churchwarden-looking personage in a brown suit, with gaiters, and a powdered head with a pig-tail'.[7] But behind this bluff exterior was a sharp man of business. One day he called on Mr and Mrs Coutts to show them a diamond cross of particularly exquisite manufacture. Seeing his young wife marvelling at its beauty the elderly banker immediately drew a cheque for £15,000 and pinned it to her bosom, though his feelings towards his

visitor at that moment are anyone's guess. Hamlet also made a spe-
ciality of selling trinkets at inflated prices and on extended credit to
callow youths keen to impress their paramours, usually actresses, who
often sold their gifts back to the jeweller for half the original price
once love had run its course.

Hamlet was a fifty-seven-year-old widower, and Elizabeth his
only child. Because of her father's illegitimate birth she had no pedigree, but qualms about the origins of rich brides were fast disappear-
ing as landed families laboured under shrinking rent-rolls and their
own profligacy, and she had already refused more than one peer. She
was also chased by the writer and politician Horace Twiss, who wrote
some excruciating verses proclaiming that her beauty outshone her
fortune—'for there glitter'd/Ten thousand diamonds in her eyes!'—
which humiliatingly found their way into the columns of the *Age*.[8] At
thirty-one she was still single, and her father determined to find her
a husband. At the same time he was very protective, and she seems to
have led a secluded life, hardly going into society at all.

Hamlet too was a man of private habits, and for a while Pückler
did not know how best to approach him. 'There is no progress with
the jeweller's lady,' he reported to Lucie on 16 October. Then he, or
his agent, hit on the idea that he should ask permission to look at the
art collection in Hamlet's Portman Square home. This flattering
request was granted, and afterwards he professed such lively admiration for what he had seen that he was allowed a second viewing. Now
for the next move:

> Prince Pückler-Muskau presents his compliments to Mr. Hamlet,
> and is very thankful for the pleasure he enjoyed in examining at
> leisure Mr. Hamlet's beautiful pictures. They really appear so the
> more you see them. Still Prince Pückler was this time more at-
> tracted by a little portrait, which he did not observe at all the last
> time. He supposes it to represent Miss Hamlet, and indeed he never
> saw a more amiable expression.
>
> Though very fond of fine works of art, he is not less sensible to
> so fine a work of nature, and hopes Mr. Hamlet will one day or
> other procure him the satisfaction to be introduced to his family.[9]

This had the desired effect, and the two men met soon after. The jeweller was pleased with the prince and hinted strongly that he would introduce him to his daughter. A few days later this warmth suddenly turned to ice; Hamlet must have made enquiries and not liked what he heard. Pückler tried to restore himself to favour, but without success: 'The situation is unchanged,' he wrote disconsolately on 28 October. Two days later was his forty-second birthday, which he celebrated with a dinner at Esterhazy's. He was still a child, he told Lucie, and she his 'good little mama', but it was a depressing milestone for a man pursuing much younger women, and the wet, chilly autumn weather did nothing to make him feel better.[10]

Then, just as suddenly, he was back in Mr Hamlet's good books. This was the fruit, he said, of his and his agent's mighty exertions, but he cautioned that 'these English are such a peculiar race that one never knows where one stands with them.' In fact everything about the courtship was odd, from the fact that the suitor had not yet seen his lady to the way his agent dealt directly with her father instead of operating behind the scenes. On 8 November the three men met: 'Dear Nucke, I have just returned from a dinner tête-à-tête with my future father-in-law and my man of business. Things look highly favourable, and there is every hope of imminent success if only the devil does not have his sport with us.' Now he would be expected to give Miss Hamlet some presents—in particular he wished to buy a pearl necklace—and he urged Lucie to do everything in her power to raise money and send it to him, just as he was working hard for their future well-being: 'My man of business and I have been sweating beads, and God in Heaven give us His blessing! The fortune is immense, and if I obtain it (which is of course not certain) I shall be in clover.'[11]

Two days later came the moment he had been waiting for. Hamlet called to invite him to his house in the country to meet his daughter: 'It is an important point gained, and I very much look forward to finally seeing the heroine of the piece.' If he found her basically tolerable and she liked him ('the trickiest point!'), he hoped to wrap things up quickly: 'O, would that I could send you some happy news at long last!' On the day of the meeting he was too busy to write, but on 12 November he took up his pen and in his excitement lopped five years off Miss Hamlet's age:

> I have just come back, and I must say very satisfied. The lady is twenty-six years old, no beauty, but passably pretty (she looks a little like you, Schnucke), with beautiful teeth, arms and hands almost as good (also formed exactly like my Schnucke's), and the prettiest feet. She cannot be called tall (your height), and inclines somewhat to fullness of figure.[12]

She was well educated and intelligent, but not excessively so, and had a natural if rather earnest manner. As to accomplishments, she could sing, play the piano and sketch with the best of them. Her behaviour, while not positively encouraging, was friendly and polite, and her father made it obvious that he favoured the match. The scale of the wealth being dangled in front of him struck Pückler with awe, and if he still squirmed at the thought of marriage he was now even more afraid of failure. But that now seemed unlikely.

He told Lucie that as long as she was sensible they would cap their struggles with happiness. She must show proper consideration for his bride, who would be their financial saviour, and could do so knowing that he would never love another woman as he loved her. Moreover, she must not doubt that, whatever short-term arrangements might be called for, he meant to re-establish her in Muskau as soon as possible. After readying Lucie for the step he was about to take, he planned how best to take it. He could not decently propose to Miss Hamlet straight away, and so resolved to wait a fortnight, during which time he would write her tender letters and pay regular visits to her father, who had returned to London with him. Lucie sent all the money she could, and though it was never enough for a pearl necklace his books and other gifts seemed to go down well. Before long the heiress was back from the country, and almost every day he went a-wooing to Portman Square. To bring things to a crisis he played the sulky lover; in an undated note he complained, 'When in taking leave of Miss Hamlet on Monday last, I ventured to express to her the humble wish, not to be entirely forgotten—I did not meet with a very encouraging look—so little encouraging indeed, that the remembrance of it has made my own look rather melancholic ever since.'[13]

She was warming to him, assured her father, but was not a demonstrative woman. Of course Mr Hamlet, though he liked him too, would need full disclosure of his circumstances before giving his formal consent, and so Pückler composed a long letter setting out everything he needed to know. First of all he insisted that it was 'the goodness of her heart', 'her charming ingenuity' and 'her amiable temper' that prompted him to seek Elizabeth's hand.[14] Then he turned to practical matters. He stated that he was one of the first noblemen of Prussia, and gave accurate figures for the annual incomes from his estates of Muskau (£14,000) and Branitz (£1,500), pointing out that in Germany these sums bought three times as much as in England. The mortgages weighing on Muskau he put somewhat conservatively at £50,000 (really £75,000). This sum might not seem so very burdensome to a landed family in England, he explained, but in Prussia servicing debts of that size was punitively expensive. In writing this Pückler calculated that he could admit to being seriously in debt because, unlike many foreigners seeking English wives, he really possessed considerable assets.

Though of the same class, Hamlet was very different from the merchant who had refused to have a foreigner as a son-in-law, whatever his fortune and rank. He expressed himself satisfied with the information he had received, gave his consent and offered to take up the matter directly with his daughter. He did so, and then went to Pückler's lodgings to inform him of the result. This was 19 November, and a letter to Lucie that evening warned that clouds were forming. Elizabeth had told her father that she liked her suitor and could not see him again without a pang, but that his divorce made marriage to him impossible. Pückler persuaded the crestfallen jeweller of the folly of this objection and he undertook to try and change her mind. Next evening he called again, but with the same bad news. He had tried everything, he said, but she had burst into tears and begged him to cause her no more pain. From having been so promising, things now looked rather bleak. Pückler still hoped he could win her round, and to this end he produced a twelve-page epistle in a beautiful hand, very unlike his usual scrawl. 'I have written a first-rate letter to Miss H.!' he told Lucie. 'I believe it is the best one I have written in my life, especially in English.'[15]

It begins, after some flowery pleas for indulgence, with an account of his divorce, cleaving far less closely to the truth than his earlier letter about his finances. It was to please his family, he claims, that he took his first wife, and though they got on well she was so grieved by her inability to bear him children that she released him from his bond. He came to England, 'where the fair sex is indeed fairer and, I don't hesitate to say, better than anywhere else,' though he had a 'prejudice against, and even some dread of heiresses', who are 'very often full of pretensions'. Then he met her and found 'an exterior the most pleasing' and 'a mind and person equally fit for the representation of a court and the delight of a cottage'. How she had moved him when she spoke of her illness, and how she had bewitched him with her sense of fun. The final section is a prospectus of life at Muskau, where she would enjoy 'the comfort of an english Nobleman's seat, combined with the pomp of feudal times'. He closes with an appeal to her heart: 'I can not bear the idea that I should have seen You once to loose You for ever!'[16]

He had to wait a few days for an answer. To escape the anguish of displeasing her father and spurning a man to whom she had taken a genuine fancy, Elizabeth left London to stay with a friend, and so Mr Hamlet, feeling he must make one last try, had to travel there with the 'first-rate letter' in his pocket. He handed it to her, but, as he reported to Pückler after his return on 1 December, she refused to open it!

> She explained again that my person had made a very agreeable impression on her, that I had everything to make me a desirable party, and that my divorce itself would not scare her off if there had been fault on my wife's side, but that the idea of a divorce by consent seemed to her to do such violence to the law and to her feelings that she must declare it an insurmountable obstacle, and that as no letter in the world could change this she did not want to crush her heart to no purpose by reading it.

What, Pückler asked, did Lucie make of this? The gods themselves would strive in vain against such principles, for 'the asinine morality of the English when it comes to their preconceived notions is completely unconquerable.'[17]

In fact he knew perfectly well what Miss Hamlet's objections were. Unlike Prussia, where the institution was not uncommon in the higher classes, and least of all in his own family, divorce was exceedingly rare in England. No-fault divorces did not exist, and as no woman dreamed of seeking legal redress for her husband's adultery, the tiny number of cases involved unfaithful wives. A divorce could only be procured by Act of Parliament after hugely expensive hearings, always reported blow by blow in the press, and all the more embarrassing for the fact that the evidential hurdles were high. Couples who could no longer stand each other simply separated. Pückler could not claim to be ignorant of this, because soon after his arrival in England a year earlier his former fiancée Lady Lansdowne had said: 'My dear prince, you will not find a wife here—according to our laws the only possible cause of divorce is infidelity; no other sort is recognised, and an English girl marrying a man in such a second marriage would consider herself a sort of mistress.'[18] At the time he had pooh-poohed this—it seemed too preposterous—but now he realised how truly she had spoken.

In his letter to Miss Hamlet he had taken up this thorny question directly. His divorce was neither immoral nor dishonourable, he insisted, and as it was valid in Prussia, where royal sanction carried the same weight as an Act of Parliament in England, nothing else mattered. Moreover, surely it would be worse if his marriage had ended because of his wife's adultery rather than for the reasons he had given:

> If abroad a divorce takes place occasioned by faithlessness on the wifes side, some prejudice allways is entertained against the husband, and I think by a very good reason, because no wife indeed being beloved and well treated by her husband will, if she had any sense of honour before, leave and betray him. It is, when such a thing occurs, almost allways more or less his own fault—and he scarcely therefore can escape the judgement of beeing either a bad or a weak man.[19]

She never read this argument, and in any case it would not have changed her mind. What stuck in his gullet was the fact that had he presented himself as a cuckold all would have been well. There were humiliations he was ready to endure, he said, 'but at that price even the Great Mogul's daughter would be too dearly bought.'[20]

Was this impasse caused by a mere technicality of divorce law, or, as Pückler clearly thought, by more general cultural barriers between England and Germany? Or perhaps, unbeknownst to him, the difference was not so much between two countries as between two classes and even two eras. The prince inhabited an urbane, amoral eighteenth-century world that lived on in the fashionable society of Regency England and in Germany's still Gallicised aristocracy; while the jeweller's daughter, with her lachrymose tendencies and her rigid notions of duty, gives us a glimpse of the bourgeois values that made Victorian Britain turn in revulsion from the cynicism of the preceding age. And in the middle, as it were, stood the sorry figure of Mr Hamlet, who had thought that at long last he was about to launch his daughter into the married state. He and Pückler had a sad farewell: 'With tears in his eyes the papa took his leave of me, and I of his £200,000.'[21]

12

FADING HOPES

'Bülow says it is astonishing how people here know every last detail about me'

'Very awkward' is how Pückler described Elizabeth Hamlet's rebuff.[1] So it was: he was unlikely to find another woman with such a splendid marriage portion, and his controversial divorce might prove a sticking-point even with less well-endowed parties. So far he had assumed that if he really applied himself to his task he was bound to succeed, but now he wondered if this view was too sanguine. At the same time he was galled by the prospect of going home empty-handed. It would not even save money, for in Muskau his rank as the first man of his district obliged him to live and entertain in high style, whereas Lucie had all but withdrawn from society and pared their household right down. Passing his time abroad, even in an expensive country like England, actually cost less than residing on his estate. Moreover, he did not want Lucie, who took the failure of his efforts with Miss Hamlet hard, to think that her sacrifice had been in vain; and so he promised her he would remain for a second Season and, like a latter-day Sisyphus, roll his rock up the hill again.

The months before it began were the most cheerless of his stay. On his return from Yorkshire he discovered that his rooms at 41 Jermyn Street had been let to someone else, and he had to live in a hotel for a few weeks before finding affordable accommodation above a modiste's shop at 35 Albemarle Street.[2] He was slowly descending the scale of gentility, and financing his existence as a man about town grew ever more difficult. In October he kept Rothschild waiting for his latest letter of credit, and a month later still owed him £600. The banker gave him a few gentle prods, and in January 1828 there was a palpable chill in their relations, though this soon passed. It may have been whist that kept Pückler afloat during the latter part of his sojourn. In the summer he had forsworn it after recklessly losing £800, but in December he took it up again, sticking to small stakes this time and using his winnings to meet day-to-day expenses. As he wrote to his sister Bianca, both of his clubs contained throngs of rich young men who played an appalling hand: 'Such an opportunity for getting money is not to be found anywhere else, and it has the advantage that those who lose it could not care less.'[3]

London's climate and polluted air had never been good for his health, and as the wet autumn turned into a harsh winter he caught a series of colds that were heavy enough to keep him at home. In any case he had been in the city too long to derive much interest from its sights and sounds now. All his life he went in fear of boredom, and now he felt it daily. Worst of all were the Sundays, when activity of almost any sort was frowned upon and nothing was open. This rigid Sabbatarianism was not new to England, but its power was growing, reflecting the way the middle-class piety embodied by Elizabeth Hamlet was slowly changing the country. It was one of many things that got on Pückler's nerves, and, with little to report, the focus of his letters turned increasingly from London to his beloved Muskau—park improvements, the estate's revenues and staff and the local acquaintances whose doings filled Lucie's letters to him.

To help pass the time he immersed himself in a new project. Ever since his arrival in England he had amassed visual material—prints of people and places, social and political caricatures, newspaper illustrations, pamphlets and sketches—relating to his impressions and experiences. A year or so later he purchased the first of what became four folio albums from the print-seller Rudolph Ackermann, and it became one of his chief occupations to paste in his collection of images and append his own, often lengthy remarks. By capturing his responses to his environment in more or less chronological order these colourful volumes, which were recently rediscovered in a state of perfect preservation, complement his letters to Lucie and form a subjective but well-informed record of England in the latter part of George IV's reign: its actors and musicians, dandies and great ladies, exhibitions and showplaces, political events and public scandals. Pückler indulged his taste for the striking and the bizarre, so that English life appears as a sort of cabinet of curiosities. He called the albums his 'Pictorial Reminiscences', and they are one of the main sources for the present book.

Not all his pastimes were so innocent. Some almost were, like his continuing outdoor trysts with the sentimental but virtuous Lady Garvagh, but he also spent many evenings with the loose-living diplomats. Esterhazy was a blatant libertine, and others pursued the same pleasures more discreetly, either singly or in small groups. Pückler's companion in debauchery was Count Lottum, and together they philandered at the theatre and had late-night dinners with girls acquired who knows where. One evening he invited Lottum and some other friends to Albemarle Street together with a bevy of young English, French and Italian milliners who worked in his landlady's business. He decorated his main room with lights and artificial flowers and ordered food from his landlady's kitchen. After dining the more musical guests sang to the company, and there was dancing till two in the morning, the girls pretending to be the belles of a society ball and the men playfully treating them as such.

With one of these girls, a sixteen-year-old from France called Julie, Pückler began a 'positive intrigue', as he informed Lucie in his usual frank way: 'The little thing went at it with such a fury that she must really like it—or else like me. I was also amazed to hear from a young girl's lips such paeans to my handsome (old) face and moustaches. At least that is one pleasure I have not had to pay for.' He could not boast of taking her virginity, which she had felt honour-bound to lose before leaving France, but he was pleased with his 'very pretty and amusing' conquest.[4] His only concern was that he might have picked up a venereal infection. In Leeds the same fear had checked him at the last moment with a girl he met at his inn, but latterly he had become a little careless.

Sure enough, just before Christmas he experienced *la chaude pisse*, as he called it. Fortunately this and his other symptoms—genital sores, feverishness and headaches—were less severe than they might have been, and he was spared the stomach pains he expected. This mishap brought his romance with Julie to an abrupt end, much to her bewilderment:

> She finds my conduct abominable and horrid, and swears I shall never have another bout with her in my life (which is all I ask). It is true that in the meantime I have had four or five other girls. I developed a real passion for them, and I must say that nowhere are they more beautiful and more emotionally engaged while bestowing their favours than here—but all the same I have quite got over this little whim now.[5]

It was tedious to spend hours each day in a hot bath, but he knew his illness would not last long, and reflected that the catalogue of his bad luck must now be complete and he could reasonably hope for better things. He was also amused to discover a fellow sufferer in Lottum—at a Christmas dinner given by Esterhazy both of them felt too delicate to join in the drinking. The young diplomat soon recovered, and by the New Year Pückler too was well again apart from a pressure in his bowels that his doctor said would soon clear up.

In mid-January, hale once more, he went to Brighton to resume his labours. This time he could not afford the Royal York Hotel and instead took lodgings at 5 Kings Road. Some people he knew from last year were in town, as was Captain Bulkeley, the companion of his trip to Berkshire, but the most familiar face was that of Mary Gibbings, 'the first and last to present herself on my nuptial hunting party, like a kind of destiny'. She was still pretty, still rich and, with her parents hanging like albatrosses round her neck, still single. She was no less pushy and over-accomplished than before, and her parents no less vulgar, but he was now faced with the imperative 'eat, bird, or die!' and so resumed his old courtship. He accompanied her to balls and listened to her sing, and then, after a decent interval, wrote a letter of proposal. In it he praised her looks, her charm and her kind heart, 'which shines with the greatest brilliance in your daughterly conduct.' His main qualifications were his good character and his lineage, for she should not confuse him 'with the so-called Princes of Siberia and the Caucasus, whom we do not even consider noble.' He asked her to weigh up his merits, knowing that he awaited her response 'with much emotion'.[6] But he could not go through with it. In late February, without having sent his letter, he said goodbye and left for London and his last push.

If he was to succeed this time he needed to counter the notion that he was an impecunious opportunist. To this end he asked Rudolph Ackermann, a long-time resident in London but like him a son of Saxony, to place an illustrated article on Muskau in the popular *Ackermann's Repository* using information he would provide. The print-seller agreed, and by March text and engraving were ready. The engraving, an aquatint, shows the chateau in the guise of a Greek temple, 'its present, but yet unfinished, form' according to the text—in reality a design by the architect Karl Friedrich Schinkel that never got beyond the drawing-board. The building and its contents are magnificently written up, the park poetically evoked and particular emphasis laid on Lucie's spa, 'one of the most efficacious watering-places in Prussia, provided with every requisite for the convenience and comfort of visitors'. It is an impressive exercise in self-promotion, and the first foreign property to feature in the *Repository*'s prestigious 'Views of Country Seats' series. However, because of various delays it did not appear until 1 June, rather late for its intended purpose.

Even without this boost Pückler's reception in London gave him grounds for hope: he was invited to the best parties, received vouchers for Almack's, and was noticed in the *Morning Post*. As his fluency in English increased, so did his ability to shine in society. He still had awkward moments, and at a dinner party in April was unable to defend himself against a mordant sally from the society wit Henry Luttrell; but in more congenial company he was very much at his ease. His favourite hostess was the Duchess of St Albans, whom he had known the previous year as Mrs Coutts. Pilloried in the press as 'Her Grease', a showy, overweight Irish parvenue, she was nonetheless influential by her vast wealth and the hunger for tickets to her sumptuous outdoor parties at Holly Lodge in Highgate. At one of these he was placed next to Sir Walter Scott, whose broad accent, homely anecdotes and unassuming manner made him seem like an ordinary country gentleman on a rare visit to London rather than the most successful writer of the day. In this convivial atmosphere Pückler ventured an anecdote of his own—a ghost story Lucie had told him— and was delighted at the response it got. While they were talking the duchess made a quick sketch of Scott for him, and he enclosed it in his next letter home.

He could be forgiven for thinking that his standing in high society was as good as ever despite the bad publicity of the previous year. But while his outward success continued, the rumour-mill began to grind again, this time to much more destructive effect. First there was the Travellers Club incident. Because he was not domiciled in England Pückler was classed as a 'distinguished visitor' rather than a full member of the club, and as such he had to renew his status every quarter. When he did so at the end of 1827 he made the mistake of applying to a member of the committee rather than the committee as a whole, and after his term had expired rather than before. The matter was soon cleared up, but word of the mistake spread and spawned a number of livelier stories: that he had thrown plates or loaves of bread at servants; that he had spat on the carpet; that he would have been expelled for not settling a gambling debt if Bülow had not intervened. Pückler was so incensed by these calumnies that he later extracted a formal rebuttal of them from the club.[7]

Another annoying contretemps was his falling-out with the Marchioness of Londonderry, a moderately influential hostess though much ridiculed for her vanity and obsessive desire to be a dominant force in fashionable life. She sent him an invitation and received a clumsily flirtatious reply that so scandalised her (a woman who had openly welcomed the attentions of Tsar Alexander and had portraits of him all over her house) that she showed it to her friends and prevailed on them to give him the cold shoulder. More worryingly, he lost the good graces of Princess Lieven, the 'non plus ultra of fashion', as he heard her called.[8] He admired her peerless breeding and poise, but not her love of power and use of feminine wiles for political ends, and he may not have taken enough care to hide the latter feelings, as he learned through his diplomatic channels that she was defaming him in society. Then, just as she gave signs of warming to him, he thoroughly blotted his copybook. At a dinner at Ashburnham House, her husband's residence, he noticed a bottle of dark liquid by her setting and playfully asked if she had grown so English as to fortify her wine. What he had not known, but soon did, was that the princess was very self-conscious about her red nose, which was wrongly claimed by some to be caused by secret drinking.

An older foe, acquired at the same time as Clanwilliam, was the Duke of Cumberland, a younger brother of George IV and a man with the blackest of reputations. Well earned it was too, for the subsequently much-disbelieved stories that he knifed his manservant to death and fathered a child on his own sister have recently been shown to be quite true.[9] For various reasons, not least his extreme unpopularity at home, Cumberland spent the years from 1818 to 1828 mainly in Berlin, where, aided by his excellent German and ability to entertain lavishly, he played his natural role of political schemer. He was addicted to intrigue in personal matters too, and at his frequent dinner parties he indulged his heavy, bullying humour and love of gossip. One evening he targeted Pückler by joking that Lucie was old enough to be his mother. The duke cannot have expected a retort alluding to his own wife's colourful past, but this is precisely what he got: 'As you please, my Lord. The fact is that I have married a woman of good conduct [...] and not every man in the room may make the same boast.' As everyone looked down in agonies of embarrassment, their host got up and left the room.[10] When Cumberland returned to England in April 1828 he treated Pückler with bantering affability, but spoke ill of him behind his back and awaited an opportunity to avenge himself fully.

These influential figures added fuel to the flames of innuendo, so that even a well-informed man like the publisher John Murray came to think that Pückler was an adventurer '*not worth a shilling*'. Some even believed him to be an impostor. The most extravagant claim was that he had conducted an affair with a married woman and afterwards threatened to publish her letters, extorting £2,000 for his silence.[11] His marriage with Lucie was also a subject of speculation, as in the following version of events that came to his ears and he then passed on to her:

He is a man of pleasing exterior, noble rank and some fortune—but intolerably proud and arrogant and moreover the wickedest man in existence. It is said that he maltreated his unhappy wife in an abominable fashion. He shut her up in his castle in the middle of a forest for six years in complete solitude. *He beat her several times* and filled her life with bitterness, until at last he forced her to divorce him. Woe to the unhappy creature who succeeds her in his toils. In a word, he is a complete Bluebeard.[12]

To scotch this rumour Pückler wrote candidly to Frederick William III that he was in England to marry money and needed all the help he could get. He reminded him that his forbear Frederick the Great had heaped decorations on Count Reuss, a lieutenant in a Guards regiment, to help him win the hand of a fabulously rich Dutchwoman whose wealth had then financed the building of the Palais Reuss in Berlin. Muskau was also a national treasure, he said, and its future depended on the success of his English mission: 'If the London newspapers were to carry an article stating that Your Majesty had, on his own exalted initiative, appointed me a general or awarded me the Order of the Red Eagle, first class, the effect on society here would be electric.'[13] A desperate, not to say impertinent appeal, it went without reply.

Bülow was much more helpful, taking every opportunity to defend him in public, but despite his high standing in England there was little he could do to stem the tide. Eventually the fiction of the prince's cruelty to his ex-wife was supplanted by the—probably even more damaging—fact of his undiminished attachment to her, and all in all he now held few secrets for high society: 'Bülow says it is astonishing how people here know every last detail about me.' The ambassador also confirmed his suspicion that Clanwilliam was working against him and had ensured that everyone of consequence was aware of Lucie's continued residence at Muskau.[14] At the end of 1827 Clanwilliam resigned his Berlin post and joined the swelling ranks of Pückler's antagonists in London for the following Season.

Then, just as his troubles threatened to engulf him, something happened that made them all seem quite unimportant. The fortune hunter fell in love.

13

SURPRISED BY LOVE

*'German feeling and German words awaken the sweet
sensation of home'*

On 27 April 1828, with the Season in full swing, Bülow asked Pückler to a reception at the Prussian Embassy in honour of the latest musical celebrity to cross the Channel, the soprano Henriette Sontag. Pückler had already met her in Berlin in the dying days of 1825, when he was trying to ingratiate himself at court and hurry along his divorce. He had not much cared for her singing, which he found rather lacking in expression, but liked her well enough as a woman, albeit in a fairly detached way: 'She dances like an angel, is exceptionally fresh and pretty, and at the same time gentle, full of enthusiasm and of the best *ton*. With these qualities it would not surprise me if she ensnared some well-born ninny as a husband.'[1]

Born in the Rhineland town of Coblenz in 1806 to a singer and an actress, Henriette Sontag was always destined for the stage. After mastering parts of the Queen of the Night's music in Mozart's *Magic Flute* at the age of five, she trod the boards as a child-actress until her mature debut at fifteen. At seventeen she created the title role in Carl Maria von Weber's *Euryanthe* in Vienna, and at nineteen she was engaged for a season by Karl von Holtei, director of Berlin's Königstädter Theater. In Berlin her first performances, as Isabella in Rossini's *Italian Girl in Algiers*, elicited gasps of wonder. 'Making her appearance descending from a ship,' remembered the astronomer Felix Eberty half a century later, 'she seemed to float down to the ground like a miraculous, enchanting fairy. Such a combination of beauty, grace and flawless singing has not been seen since.'[2] From wine-sellers, fishmongers and greengrocers to the highest nobility, she was praised by all in the most extravagant language. People fought for tickets at inflated prices to hear her, and her distinctive red carriage, an admirer's gift, was mobbed in the streets.

The voice that aroused such excitement was a high soprano, not large but well-projected, with astonishingly accurate trills and runs and a combination of clarity and sweetness throughout its range. In other words Sontag was a 'nightingale', perhaps the first of that breed. As an actress her best genres were maidenly joy and the restrained distress of an innocent victim. Pückler was not alone in finding her artistry a little mechanical, and there is no doubt that the dramatic intensity of her peers Giuditta Pasta and Maria Malibran was beyond her, but many, including Berlioz, praised her demure style for its musical integrity and feminine decorum. She was also exceptionally beautiful, with soft blue eyes, chestnut-coloured hair, a perfectly oval face and a slender, small-boned figure just under the middle height. The poet Théophile Gautier, who became her first biographer, said her looks were 'so far elevated above common mortality, that reason was the slave of sensation.'[3]

Sontag's popularity was enhanced by her cheerful, unpretentious character and playful sense of humour. She had none of the grandeur of most prima donnas, and took an unaffected delight in applause and adulation. Also unusual among theatrical ladies was her spotless reputation, though she was not free from coquetry. Her most avid worshipper was Clanwilliam, and Holtei joked that his frequent visits to her rooms in the Kaiserstrasse were 'a primary function of his embassy'. She offered him only friendship, but in society there were whisperings of more. Varnhagen's diary records the general conviction that they were to marry, and that 'the elegant world is in turmoil over it.' The London press took up this rumour with gusto, with one newspaper embroidering it with speculation that because of her guardian's opposition 'a royal rescript was necessary to enable the fair actress to give her hand to a British nobleman.'[4] Partly to escape this tittle-tattle, Henriette went in 1826 to Paris, where she triumphed resoundingly. She returned there at the beginning of 1828, and during this second stint was pursued by Count Carlo Rossi, secretary to the Sardinian Legation, a well-made young man with a pleasing countenance and a good though unremarkable character. For some reason he succeeded where others had failed, and within a short time they were lovers.

After just three months of this new romance Henriette travelled to London, tempted, like many before her, by the enormous fees. For months beforehand British newspapers had whipped up expectations with breathless accounts of her voice and appearance, as well as gossip about her supposed entanglements, and by the time she arrived in early April curiosity was at a high pitch. A week later she gave a private concert, at which, said the *Morning Chronicle*, her 'naturally sweet, silvery, light, and brilliant' voice and the 'fascinating simplicity of her manners' were much admired. Her public debut was at the King's Theatre a few days later, as Rosina in Rossini's *Barber of Seville*. 'Her reception,' wrote the *Morning Herald*, 'was as gratifying as she could possibly wish. We never saw any Lady welcomed on these boards in a more enthusiastic manner.' After hearing her the *Athenaeum* decreed that 'no person of the least pretensions to taste, within one hundred miles of the capital, can be excused for omitting to pay the homage of one visit, at least, to this most fascinating of all the wonders of the day.'[5] London, like Paris before it, was at her feet.

Night after night the doors of the King's Theatre were thronged. Her next role was Donna Anna in Mozart's *Don Giovanni*, and she subsequently sang in Rossini's *Lady of the Lake*, *Othello*, *Thieving Magpie* and *Cinderella*, and in Meyerbeer's *Crusade in Egypt*. She was in great demand for private concerts, new prints of her were published, and a horse with her name was entered at Newmarket. The modesty she showed on stage was found to be even more winsome at the exclusive parties she so easily penetrated. On one memorable evening she danced with the Duke of Devonshire dressed in a diaphanous white crepe dress bordered with gold, displaying the stunning perfection of her arms and throat. Clanwilliam, now back in England, was as sedulous as ever, but had to compete for her attention with a clutch of other admirers, including Esterhazy and the music-loving Prince Leopold, subsequently King of the Belgians. After a few weeks Sir Walter Scott presented her with a morocco-bound volume full of tributes in prose and verse from writers, artists, musicians and society lions. On the front cover Scott had written 'Souvenir de Londres', and on the back 'Forget me not'.[6]

Despite this reception Henriette was not happy in England. To be sure, there was much to admire: 'There is luxury and wealth here down to the tiniest details,' she wrote to a friend in Berlin. 'We on the Continent have absolutely no notion of such splendid equipages, such heavenly horses, and such elegant servants.' But like many visitors she found the food bad and the weather worse: 'Now that I know the climate I can very well understand why so many Englishmen suffer from so-called spleen. I almost fear I shall get it myself, for I now often suffer from bad moods and irritable thoughts.'[7] She also wore herself out by singing too much, often twice a day. In any case she had recently enjoyed her celebrity less than before, even in Berlin, feeling it to be a sort of slavery to the public. In London her novelty, like that of any imported performer, gradually faded, and though the newspapers continued to be full of her not all the publicity was positive: there were false reports that she demanded a gratuity to sing at another artist's benefit and that she wanted £1,600 to appear at the Manchester Music Festival. Then there was Richard Becke's satire *The Prima Donna*, published to coincide with her arrival. Becke is much harder on Clanwilliam, who as Earl Rainbow boasts of imaginary sexual conquests, and Esterhazy, unmistakeable as the lustful Prince Caprione, than he is on her, but still she found such portrayals hurtful.

When Pückler renewed his acquaintance with Henriette Sontag at the Prussian embassy, she was with her professional chaperone Frau von Lämmers, coincidentally a former companion of Lucie's. Like many compatriots who meet abroad, they were invigorated by the sudden release from the strain of attuning themselves to a foreign language and ways. They fell into an animated conversation that lasted all evening, and before entering her carriage Henriette invited Pückler to join her and Frau von Lämmers the next day to see *Richard III*. He did so, and for once was quite oblivious to Shakespeare, chatting non-stop with the ladies about familiar places and people and growing quite nostalgic: 'German feeling and German words awaken the sweet sensation of home,' he told Lucie.[8]

So enlivened was he that ploughing his matrimonial furrow at a ball later that night seemed lighter work than usual. After this he went to see Henriette perform three evenings in succession. Previously indifferent to her singing, he now developed a taste for it. On the third evening, a private concert, she wore as her corsage a rose from a bouquet he had sent hours earlier; as she sang she glanced at it and then, mischievously, at him.

Emboldened, he asked her to join him the following day for a ride in Richmond Park, and in a clear sign of regard she cancelled her appointments to do so. Given how jealously she guarded her reputation this was not without risk, and to reduce the likelihood of being seen together they drove separately to an agreed spot, where he had arranged for two saddle horses to be waiting. They rode for the whole afternoon; she was as frisky as a deer, he wrote to Lucie, delighting in her temporary freedom from theatres and drawing rooms, and as he watched her trot along beside him he realised why he so disliked courting women he cared nothing for. She said the next day would be her last without engagements for some time, and immediately he asked her to spend it with him: they could ride out to Greenwich and eat by the river. Her consent, given after a token resistance, filled him with a joy that took him by surprise. He told Lucie that an angel had crossed his path: 'Good night, my little Schnucke, I kiss your portrait, which loves me too much to begrudge me a short, short rest, a little draught of sweetness amidst all this melancholy. I am not neglecting business, I assure you, but there are many moments, indeed many full days, when I have no opportunity to advance it.'[9]

For their excursion to Greenwich Pückler again sent horses to a pre-arranged location, which he then reached late in the morning. The sky was cloudless, and it already felt like summer. For what seemed like a long time she did not come and he feared she might have changed her mind, but at last she drove up with Frau von Lämmers. He mounted one horse and lifted her from her carriage onto the second, leaving the indulgent chaperone to return alone to their hotel in St James's Street. Henriette was an excellent horsewoman and rode off briskly. When he caught up she slackened her pace and they resumed their flushed, eager talking of yesterday, 'like a pair of little birds chirruping in the beautiful May sunshine'.[10] She was late, she said, because as she was getting ready Clanwilliam had called with his own plans to spend the day with her, and to put him off she had invented a prior appointment with a lady out of town. Pückler exulted at this victory over his tormentor.

All day they rode around Greenwich and its environs, seeing the sights and searching for the most rewarding vantage points. At sunset he took her to dine in the private room at the Ship Tavern, with its bay window overhanging the Thames, where he had already passed a solitary evening reading Lord Chesterfield's letters. At midnight they returned to London in a darkened carriage. 'You know,' he confided to Lucie, 'it is not my way to let such opportunities go begging, even though here I was afraid of seeming indelicate. At first she was shy and angry, but eventually gave a little ground, and by the time we reached home, although nothing *indecent* had happened, all that tenderness can inspire had passed between us.' He promised he would not try to take things further, partly because it would be wrong to do so, and partly because it would harm his marital schemes: 'But this I must say, because it is true: a lovelier creature, a more adorable nature I have never found, quite different from what I expected. She is a flower in the thorny bush of my present life.'[11]

This was 4 May. What happened next is uncertain as Pückler stopped writing to Lucie about Henriette, and then, for several days, stopped writing altogether. The newspapers inform us that he heard her sing on three of the four following evenings. They must also have met privately, though all we know is that on the 8th he was seated next to an affable, rather tipsy Viennese man at a dinner and was so desperate to get away to her that he could hardly sit still. Things had gone well beyond flirtation, but because of his promise to Lucie he was unwilling to admit his infatuation and wrote vaguely that he was 'very unwell without being ill'. Finally, on 10 May, he confessed that he was in love. His mind was so agitated that he had hardly eaten in eight days, he said. He was sick of hunting for money, which, even if he won it, would bring him no joy: 'I believe all I lack is love—the motherly love of my Schnucke and that of a precious being who would, like me, be your child. Why should that not be?'[12] Would it not be best, he asked the next day, to marry a girl who could make him truly happy, even if she had neither title nor fortune?

While he was contemplating a marriage that would wipe out any chance of saving Muskau, Henriette's thoughts took a different turn, and three days after telling Lucie he was in love he had the nastiest shock of his life. For four days he wrote nothing, and when he took up his pen on 17 May it was in real despair:

> If ever a springtime brought me sadness, Schnucke of my heart, and to all the cares and woes of outward circumstances added the deepest, most annihilating agonies of the soul I have yet experienced, then it is this terrible May. Fate wills it that I should drain every cup of bitter poison, and then slowly, painfully die of the effects. But enough—my wounds are too raw for me to speak of my state. Soon, my faithful Schnucke, my only constant friend through life, we shall see each other again, and when we do I shall tell you how I found an angel in this world who made my own personal dreams of perfection come true, how I quickly conceived a passion for her unlike anything I have previously felt, and then was *compelled, compelled irrevocably* by forces beyond my control to leave her for good.[13]

After this he fell silent for another three days, and not until nearly a month later could he bring himself to say what had happened:

> If I had the whole female sex to choose from she would be the wife I should take—but before I had the chance to say what I had in mind she declared its impossibility from her point of view with unshakeable firmness. She broke off the swelling torrent of our relationship with a resolve and a magnanimity that astonished me, and gave me the *strength* to do likewise. In the prevailing circumstances I should eventually have been obliged to take the same step myself, but God only knows what would have ensued if she had not behaved so admirably. For *never, never* have I experienced anything like what this girl has made me feel [. . .]. She herself said to me, 'I have let myself get carried away by a feeling that has blinded me to

a strange degree—for a moment I forgot that duty binds me indis-
solubly to another man, whom I love truly and deeply even if the
first passion has passed. I have awoken from a dream, and nothing
can now draw me back into it. From this moment we must forever
forget what has happened . . .' Those were her words and plenty
more besides—and as she spoke she was pale, cold as ice, with an
almost eerie calm and majesty about her.[14]

Pückler's letters home were always candid, and there is no reason
to doubt his account. What he suffered after this harrowing exchange
was the desolation of a man no longer young who falls in love for the
first time and then finds his happiness brutally cut short. Racked with
sorrow, he hardly ate or slept, and later he shuddered to recall his 'love
fever' and the sensation of being close to insanity that went with it.[15]
In time the little distractions of everyday life began their slow work
of diluting his grief. After the unprecedented gaps in his diary-letters
he set down a few words each day to reassure Lucie that he was well
in body and that his febrile state had given way to a feeling of numb-
ness. To aid his recovery he applied his rational faculties to what had
happened, blaming himself for chasing soap bubbles all his life and
understanding his grand passion at the age of forty-two as a punishment for earlier frivolity. On 31 May Henriette gave her final performance in the *Barber* with the flower of London society in
attendance; he wished her well, but could not bear to go along.

A month after Henriette dashed his hopes Pückler described her
conduct as mysterious, but at the time he was so stunned that he did
not even wonder who her established lover was. Her explanation for
her change of heart, which so awed him with its invocation of duty
and will, omitted another factor that would have surprised him still
more—she was pregnant. Exactly when she became aware of this is
unclear, but the father could only be Rossi. The distress of the episode
with Pückler and the anxiety of her unplanned pregnancy exacerbated the strain of her hectic schedule, and her drooping looks were
increasingly remarked upon. Her greatest worry must have been that
Rossi, whom she had not seen since March, would not be in a position to marry her. He wanted to, and they may have become engaged

before she left Paris, but he faced opposition from the Sardinian court, and the certainty that if he wed a commoner who sang for a living he would lose his post and with it his only source of income. In early July Henriette wrote despondently to a friend that her lucky star had forsaken her, and towards the end of the month she felt so exhausted and overwrought that she curtailed her stay in London and spent three weeks recuperating in Boulogne. In mid-August she returned to Paris to take up her engagements there.

Then, in September, French newspapers carried a notice that Mademoiselle Sontag had slipped on a peach stone and injured her knee so badly that she was forced to cancel her autumn performances. This could only mean one thing, and Parisians revelled in the scandal. Her rival Maria Malibran affected to be disconsolate: 'She has dropped in public favour like a fallen soufflé. I am very angry about this, but very angry, for she was very nice.' A few days before Christmas Henriette gave birth to a daughter in a secret location, and only five weeks later she returned to the Paris stage to quieten the scandal. The gossipy Lady Granville saw her perform the following May and found her 'thinner than anybody I ever saw, looking as if she had cried her eyes out'.[16] In the summer her daughter died of scarlet fever. At some point (the date is uncertain) she and Rossi married in secret, and in 1830 his monarch grudgingly accepted the *fait accompli* on the strict condition of her retirement. At the age of twenty-four, with a glittering future ahead of her, she gave up her career to become a diplomatic wife.

As for Pückler, he could not forget her. In 1848, twenty years after the torment of his love, he built a shrine to her in his pleasure ground at Branitz: a gilded bust of Henriette mounted on a granite plinth and set within a bower of slender blue-painted iron columns twined around with flowers. It is still there today.

14

Napoleon's Niece

'What the devil have you done to make poor Madame Buonaparte drown herself because of you?'

As Henriette Sontag began to fill his thoughts Pückler assured Lucie that he would not neglect his search for a wife; in fact the whole of May was sacrificed to his emotional turmoil. Once he had sufficient composure he resumed his social activities, and to counter the now generally entertained suspicion that he was still close to his ex-wife he asked her to leave Muskau for a while and tell everyone the move was permanent. This she did, but in a fury. She had sold her last horses and silverware to raise money for him, and had been sympathetic during his unhappy love affair, but being bundled out of her own home was too much. She lashed out in a sentence that he paraphrased back to her: '*I now think I have no further use for you*, and because I delude myself that it would be better if Muskau stood empty I am *sending you into a miserable exile*.'[1] As always when she was angry, even if it seemed unreasonable, he felt he must have done wrong. His attachment was passive, even narcissistic, while hers was generous and intense, and his awareness of this gave him a deep sense of gratitude and guilty obligation. He took her reproaches to heart and answered them in detail: the move was just a charade, he reminded her, and in the long term she was to live with him and his future wife, if he ever found one. Fortunately her temper soon cooled.

Meanwhile he carried gamely on with his matrimonial endeavours, though he had now lowered his sights: if he could not fell a stag, he told Lucie, he would at least try to bag a hare. Still among his friends were Lady Kinloch and her daughter Harriet, 'the Scottish girl I once went riding with'. After spending the winter at their East

Lothian seat they returned to London for the 1828 Season, and he went to the theatre with them and visited their house. Earlier Harriet's £25,000 had seemed paltry, but now this sum, together with an attractive, affectionate person, seemed a good proposition, and so he put his best foot forward:

> I felt sure she would not make any difficulties, and after having paid court to her all this time, and having been treated most favourably by her, I took the opportunity today of a *tête-à-tête* to bring up the subject in a roundabout but still fairly clear way—and by heaven she refused out of hand, with considerable calm, sympathy and friendliness, for the same reason as the goldsmith's daughter, and showed herself so well informed about everything that I was quite deflated. It seems the Duke of Cumberland has made everyone thoroughly *au fait*.[2]

He was also still on excellent terms with the Bonhams of Titness Park. By spring his flirtation with Lady Garvagh had petered out, but he kept in contact with her and the rest of the family. In February he reminded Lucie that little Harriet Bonham was still an option; although she had a bare £10,000, even this would stave off the necessity of selling Muskau for a while. In April he dined with the whole family while they were in London, and he felt rather sad at seeing Harriet again—she was so very charming. There was talk that a relative might be able to double her dowry, and at least it did not look like his divorce would be a hindrance in this case. He kept up his negotiations with the Bonhams until the middle of June, but the extra sum did not materialise and he decided it would be madness to marry for so little.

Still on the market too was Georgiana Elphinstone, the wealthiest of the four potential brides he had listed a year earlier. As in the previous Season they were often seen together, and it was widely thought that there was something between them. But he found her no more likeable than before, and as she was close to the centre of fashionable life she would probably have known what was being said about him. She was not especially encouraging and he sensed that his chances were slim. If he had acted a year earlier, he told Lucie, he might have succeeded: '*This one* I think I could have had as she wished to marry a foreigner, but I should never have resolved to make the attempt (at least I think not), although once or twice I had a vague impulse to do so. It makes me shudder every time I seriously think about it, and I hope you will not reproach me for having missed this opportunity.'[3]

There was one last glimmer of hope when he was befriended by the Countess of Shrewsbury, an enthusiastic matchmaker with a preference for uniting English girls with Continental men. She told him she wished to find foreign husbands for her own two daughters, each worth £150,000, and he cursed his luck that they were only eleven and twelve years old (both later married Italian princes). Lady Shrewsbury did what she could to be helpful, inviting him to dinner and introducing him to her circle, but to no avail. His reputation was past mending and his inactivity during the middle month of the Season little short of calamitous. A few more young women flickered before his weary eyes, but he did not get beyond preliminaries with any of them. Then, in early July, the curtain was so decisively rung down on his aspirations that there could be no thought of raising it up again. Paradoxically, the heroine of this episode, more farce than tragedy, was a sprig of the dynasty that he admired above all others.

Letitia Bonaparte was born in 1804 as the second of ten children of Napoleon's younger brother Lucien, Prince of Canino. She grew up with her family in Italy, and when she was fifteen a Grand Tourist, the twenty-nine-year-old Thomas Wyse of Waterford, saw and fell in love with her. Two years later they married, but the domestic life of the earthbound Irishman and his headstrong, profligate bride was a disaster from the start. After a spell in Italy they moved to Waterford and then Dublin, where Letitia's impetuosity and scorn for etiquette soon threatened to scupper her husband's parliamentary ambitions. She outraged the Protestant Orange Order by attending balls in slippers trimmed with orange ribbons that were then symbolically shredded as she danced, and she repeatedly made herself conspicuous with the dashing Waterford MP Henry Villiers Stuart. In January 1828, fed up with her marriage, she ran away to London, accompanied by her father-in-law's prediction that once there she would be ensnared by a 'multitude of suitors, attracted by and doing homage to her superior Beauty'.[4]

In London Letitia became a common sight in her landau with her tiny footman perched outside. There was a smacking of lips in the press, with reports of 'some interruption to the domestic harmony of this lady and her husband' and of her residence in a hotel 'where it is said, a certain Hon. Member [i.e. Villiers Stuart] is also domesticated.' Despite this whiff of scandal society was glad of such an exotic acquisition and she was invited almost everywhere. The diarist Mrs Calvert, who did not approve, saw her at a ball looking 'like a painted doll, tossing herself about, and waltzing a great deal'.[5] Pückler was among those who enjoyed her company, less for her looks, which were too strongly contoured for his taste, than for the flirtatious verve he missed in Englishwomen. He takes up the story in a letter of 21 June, in which he relates that he had, at her request, procured her a ticket to a fête given by the Horticultural Society of London in Chiswick:

When I brought her the ticket this morning she asked if I would also drive there with her. I told her in a perfectly good-natured way that if we went together people might talk (nowhere is society more parochial than here) and that we risked getting our names in the papers. Instead of replying she broke down in tears, and then said she did not care as she would probably not live to see tomorrow. At this she showed me a vial full of opium, which, as she added, she was resolved to drain this very night. She is considered a beauty and has a very good figure, but is a type I do not much like, with an aquiline nose, big eyes, and a more masculine than feminine expression. I was not a little astonished, as you can imagine, and did my best to calm her. Meanwhile the carriage arrived and we got in, with her repeating that she was only going to this fête because the torment of loneliness had become intolerable. I could see love must be to blame and confess that my own painful experiences in a like case aroused my strongest sympathy. During the drive, amidst many tears, she told me her secret.

For three years a well-born Englishman, Mr Villers [*sic*] Stuart, has been her lover. Her passion for him has made her separate from her husband (full divorce being impossible as they are Catholics), and now that she has thrown off all her former ties and is about to travel with her lover to Italy, she finds that he has cooled towards her. She suspects he has fallen in love with another, and if this proves true she is determined not to survive her misfortune, for her whole life revolves around him. While I sought to still my fair friend's sobs, I could not help thinking inwardly how strange are the workings of fate, and how even stranger are the ways we come to terms with them. Next to me sat a niece of Napoleon, the former master of almost the entire civilised world, a woman whose uncles and aunts until very recently occupied Europe's oldest thrones, only to be thrust down by the most tremendous events into the common run of mortals—and all this makes not the slightest impression on the individual sitting next to me, or gives her any pain; but the despair caused by the infidelity of a silly English dandy drives her to the decision to take her own life!!! With genuine indignation I bade her remember whose name she bore and follow the example of endurance in real adversity that her uncle offered to her and to the world. But like a true woman she took no notice of this tirade, and replied, 'O, if I could choose now, I should far rather be the happy mistress of my lover than Queen of England and the Indies.'[6]

Nonetheless the distractions of the fête and the champagne he pressed her to drink seemed to diminish Letitia's grief. At six o'clock he left her, sure that the opium would remain untouched and pleased with the aplomb he had shown in a delicate situation. What happened next was reported in the *Sphynx* three days later:

A singular circumstance took place on Saturday evening, which has not been noticed in any of the daily papers. On the morning of that day Madame Buonaparte Wyse, who is at present residing in an hotel at the west end of the town, ordered her carriage early, and proceeded to the Horticultural Society's Gardens. There she met Prince Puckler Muskau, with whom she walked about for some time, and appeared to enjoy every thing with great zest. At seven o'clock Madame Wyse left the gardens, and proceeded direct to London. On alighting from her carriage she dismissed the coachman for the night, saying she would not go out any more. About nine o'clock, however, the servants were surprised at a hackney-coach being ordered, into which the lady got, ordering the coachman to drive to the Green Park. Arrived at the gate, the coachman was paid his fare; and the lady entered into the Park, and forthwith flung herself into the river. Providentially however, a gentleman who was passing on the instant, heard the splash, and seeing a cloak on the bank, plunged in, and rescued the lady, in all probability, from a watery grave. She now soon became sensible; and on declaring her name and address, she was conveyed in safety home.[7]

The day this story appeared Pückler rushed round to see if she was out of danger. She was, and he decided the whole thing had almost certainly been a stunt, a view shared by her husband's sister-in-law Winifred Wyse, who said that there were carriages about when Letitia made her 'pretended attempt at suicide', which was therefore sure to be halted. Her rescuer, a Captain Hodgson, afterwards showed the quick thinking of an indigent military man by bringing her together with his patron the Duke of Buckingham. Over the next few years Buckingham visited her whenever he could while employing the gallant captain as her visible companion.[8]

Pückler thought no more about the matter until an assembly on 5 July, when he succumbed to what looked like a calculated double thrust from two royal brothers. First the Duke of Cambridge, whom he hardly knew, shouted to him in several people's earshot, 'So, you've left all your estates in the princess's hands.' Ignoring a gestured plea that he drop his voice, the duke continued, 'Well, well, I hear she's an excellent administrator.' Still reeling from this, Pückler was accosted equally loudly by the Duke of Cumberland: 'What the devil have you done to make poor Madame Buonaparte drown herself because of you?' 'Because of me? What a fairy tale.' 'Not at all, I saw you in a carriage with her myself two days before, pressing her hand and so on. It's quite clear, everyone is informed, and I've already written to the king in Berlin about it. You're performing some fine tricks here!'[9] Next day the *Age* noted 'a very ugly story current just now in the higher circles, respecting a foreign Prince', and Bülow told him he was universally blamed for the incident.

After this final blow, Pückler admitted defeat and decided to leave London. As he makes ready to depart we must ask why his plans miscarried so badly. His divorce was a great impediment, of course, but a greater one was his attitude of mind: he was too shy, or too proud, to seem eager for favours that might be bestowed or withheld, and too fastidious to take the dowries of Mary Gibbings or Georgiana Elphinstone despite not liking their persons. He was also uncomfortable professing an attachment he did not feel. As he later wrote to Count Heinrich von Redern, another wife-hunting German he met in London at this time: 'In England my soul was sick, because I had to pursue a goal from which my heart recoiled.'[10] This repugnance makes it hard to see him as a villain, as does his incompetence, which turned what might have been a tale of deceit and blighted young life into a comedy of errors. It is therefore pleasing to note that, tarnished though his reputation became, the parents of the girls he wooed never shunned him. At the close of the 1828 Season Dr Gibbings sent him a cheerful letter wishing him well, Lady Kinloch invited him to her June ball and Mrs Bonham asked him to stay for a few days at the family's Essex seat. Later there was a friendly exchange of letters with Mr Hamlet.

Where should he now go? The obvious answer was Muskau, but he could not face it: 'I shall come home like the Prodigal Son, blushing in front of you and my own servants, for to fail is to be guilty,' he told Lucie.[11] He suggested they meet elsewhere, and tried to accustom her to the idea that the estate must be sold. But, having returned there after her brief exile, she was not about to leave again. By now Muskau was almost more her project than his, and while he felt a resigned indifference to everything, she was defiant that the park—their creation—should stay in their hands. It seems from his letters that there was an impasse between them on this point, and to avoid bringing matters to a head he chose to travel for a while before going home.

After sending Lucie a few last presents and attending a farewell dinner given by Esterhazy, he departed from London on 11 July.

Over the next months he meandered through southern England, Wales and Ireland, and as he did so he drew up a balance sheet of his fortune-hunting adventure: it was of course depressing that he had not achieved his goal, but his experiences had strengthened his character, he had learnt a great deal, grown nearly fluent in English and increased his mastery of landscaping—albeit without the means to put his ideas into practice. In December, with the shame of his failure to find a wife less fresh and his disagreement with Lucie over Muskau resolved, at least for the moment, he prepared to go home. On New Year's Day 1829 he crossed to Calais, where he saw the sad figure of Beau Brummell, decaying in genteel poverty and, twelve years after fleeing his creditors, still clinging to vain hopes of being recalled to the stage of his former glory. Just over a month later he was reunited with Lucie at Muskau. They embraced on their knees and in tears for a long time before speaking, which we know because the next morning he was arranging some gifts he had bought in France and took up his pen to write her yet another short note even though they were now under the same roof. It was a habit he would never break, but the letter-diary of his English voyage, the 'great correspondence' as he jestingly called it, was at an end.[12]

15

SUCCESS AFTER ALL

'Your odious book has set the Metropolis in a ferment'

In mid-July 1828, seven months before Pückler's return to Muskau, Karl August and Rahel Varnhagen went there from Berlin to visit his lonely ex-wife. After a tedious drive through flat, unremarkable country to the west they came upon a scene which, as Varnhagen wrote in his diary, was 'uniquely beautiful, magnificent and rich, everything kept up with the utmost care, cheery and delightful [. . .]. This creation is entirely the work of Prince Pückler; it reflects great honour on him and shows a quite new, respectable side to his character.' That there was more to the prince than the likeable man of pleasure he had known in Berlin was confirmed for Varnhagen when Lucie read out extracts from his English letters. They were entertaining and vivid, and their charm was heightened by Lucie's evident pride, for 'although divorced, she is passionately attached to Pückler, and thinks only of his advantage and well-being.'[1]

From Muskau Varnhagen sent its absent owner a letter extolling the beauty of the park. The two men were mere acquaintances, but Pückler was so delighted by this gesture that he wrote a heartfelt reply and thereby cemented a lifelong friendship. His exact contemporary, Varnhagen could scarcely have been less like him in temperament. He combined regular habits and a taste for hard work with a reserved, slightly starchy manner, giving the impression of a man who had never been young. At times he was a little conceited, and his diaries show a tendency to despair of others, but in person he was always obliging, and his promotion of talented writers was selfless and unstinting. The praise of such an important literary arbiter for Pückler's letters, which

Lucie passed on to him, was decisive in making him do something he had already considered: revise them for publication.[2]

It is unclear when the seed of this idea was sown in his mind, but it must have germinated after he gave up looking for a wife. Back home he edited the letters, cutting out references to his courtships, his finances and other personal matters, as well as passages on Muskau and responses to Lucie's news, while most names he removed entirely or reduced to initials. He excised over half of the original in this way and rewrote the remainder, polishing the style, adding passages from the travel albums and giving unified treatment to topics addressed fragmentarily. He decided to publish the book anonymously under the pretence that its author was dead, and so there are prefaces and footnotes by a fictional editor. Finally, Lucie becomes 'Julie'.

The chief gain from this process is greater elegance in descriptive passages, which is why these are quoted from the published text here. All in all, though, this version is an impoverishment, as a historical document and as autobiography. Together with anecdotes and pen-portraits too lurid even with the names left out, we lose the sense of the shape and material reality of Pückler's life in England, accreted from bulletins on his daily round, health and spirits. And while the letters to Lucie are spontaneous and candid, the book has a patina of literary stylisation, most obviously in its replacement of the fortune hunter's labours with the bland fiction of a man travelling for pleasure. Having said that, it would of course have been impossible to give the letters to the public without bowdlerising them to some degree.

The final text filled four volumes in the first edition, of which, rather bizarrely, the two covering the latter part of the journey appeared first. The publisher was Franckh of Munich, the date was August 1830, and the unremarkable title was *Briefe eines Verstorbenen* (*Posthumous Letters*). The book sold well despite its high price of three thalers and eighteen groschen, and in late 1831 Hallberger of Stuttgart, which had meanwhile acquired Franckh, brought out volumes three and four, describing the earlier part of the journey. In preparing the first two volumes Pückler worked alone or with Lucie, but he sent his manuscript of the rest to Varnhagen, asking him to make any changes he deemed necessary and sending him pineapples from Muskau's hothouses and a new copying device ordered from London to thank him for his efforts.

As well as his editor, Varnhagen became Pückler's literary sponsor, and in this capacity he wrote to Goethe, the octogenarian patriarch of German letters, to solicit a review. Goethe usually held himself aloof from new writing, but was glad to oblige Varnhagen, a fervent admirer who had performed all manner of services for him. 'A significant work for Germany's literature' are the opening words of his review, and he goes on to present the author, whose identity was unknown to him, as an intrepid traveller with masterly descriptive powers, the easy refinement of high rank and a scintillating way of telling stories. Such an accolade from the great man was a rare honour, and Pückler was beside himself when he read it. It amounted, he told Lucie, to a 'winning draw in the lottery of happiness'.[3]

Varnhagen further wrote to Heinrich Heine, the most talented writer of the younger generation, saying how highly the author had spoken of him and how much a good puff would be appreciated. Heine had not seen the book, but good-naturedly worked an endorsement into the final part of his *Pictures of Travel*, and when he got hold of a copy was relieved to find himself fully in agreement with his own praise. Finally Varnhagen wrote a long review of his own, in which he stated that the letters reveal the 'invaluable gifts of a sympathetic, fresh mind, unprejudiced insight and a sound, measured judgement'. After reading Varnhagen's review Goethe told him jovially that the two of them had given the work a powerful launch: 'Author and publisher may be content, for who will not read the book now?'[4]

Varnhagen was the first to note the work's most original feature: whereas France had a Madame de Sévigné, a Prince de Ligne and many more, Germany had no modern tradition of high-born writers who conveyed the spirit and manners of their own class, not least because the aristocracy tended to consider literary pursuits as beneath its dignity. No other German travel writers of the day attended glittering balls, chatted with royalty or entered great ladies' boudoirs. No one described conversations at diplomatic dinners, the décor of town mansions or the elegance of his own dress. And yet the author was not vainglorious; instead he seemed merely to make the most of the lifestyle his rank afforded him and to invite his readers to enjoy it vicariously. The book's anonymity, it hardly need be said, was a transparent garment, for everyone knew who the princely traveller was, and by welcoming readers into his world he became the first German writer to do what some of the Silver Fork novelists had done in England: he commodified his noble birth.

Also working in the book's favour was the strong interest in England, which explains the quantity of travel literature on that country published in Germany in the mid-nineteenth century.[5] It is fair to say that Pückler's letters hold a special place in this tradition; indeed, no German work of any sort on England, before or since, has ever made such an impact. He learned soon after it appeared that it was the opening topic of conversation in courtly, commercial and literary circles in Berlin. Never, he told Lucie, had anything given him so much pleasure. When Hallberger published the second part he reissued the first, and the whole was reprinted throughout the 1830s. Varnhagen declared he knew of 'no literary event in Germany for many a long year that from its inception has been carried forth so splendidly and then continued its course under such a favourable star.'[6] The book was quite simply the publishing sensation of the decade, and launched Pückler on a career that would see him, at least by his own account, earning fees larger than those of any previous German writer except Goethe at the end of his life. The wheel of fortune had turned at last, and England, after all, had given him the financial relief he so badly needed.

In late 1830 this runaway success came to the attention of the London publisher John Murray. He got hold of a copy and asked Sarah Austin, a translator and expert on German literature, for her opinion as to its suitability for the British market. Without knowing who had written it, she was instantly won over. The book's charm, she told Murray, lay in the 'peculiar and interesting mind of the author, the philanthropy, freedom from all prejudice, and the gentle and somewhat melancholy philosophizing mingled with a strong sense of the ludicrous and a great power of describing it'.[7] It was this last point, however, that began to trouble the publisher, who did not wish to jeopardise his good relations with high society. For a while he wavered, and in March

1831 Sarah Austin gave him an ultimatum: either he commit himself or she would take the book and her services elsewhere. After further vacillation Murray's caution got the better of him, leaving her free to sign a contract with Effingham Wilson, who had made his name with radical tracts and was not afraid of controversy.

At some point during her labours Mrs Austin discovered who the author was and began corresponding with him on the question of alterations to his text. She wanted to exclude accounts of places already very familiar to English readers, observations she judged to be excessively disobliging and passages that 'a woman's pen could not gracefully touch'.[8] The last point refers less to the narrative of Pückler's doings, already largely cleansed of impropriety, than to some dinner-table anecdotes and sexually charged descriptions of paintings. The first two of four volumes went on sale for eighteen shillings in time for the 1831 Christmas trade, but with an 1832 imprint. The title was *Tour in England, Ireland and France, in the Years 1828 & 1829; with Remarks on the Manners and Customs of the Inhabitants, and Anecdotes of Distinguished Public Characters. In a Series of Letters. By a German Prince*— thereafter always shortened to *Tour of a German Prince*.

On receiving his copies Pückler was horrified at the devastation wrought by Mrs Austin's blue pencil. Varnhagen assured him that this was normal practice among translators (as indeed it was), but he was not satisfied and wrote her a stinging letter:

> Really Signora, your womanly fear to offend one or the other insignificant person, and still more the consciousness [of] your sex being known to the public, makes you such a little coward that you are taking away almost every 'sel' [spice] of my book. But a translator ought to be of no sex at all. The German letters offered a consommé to the public, and you think of course that you ought to change it in[to] a breadsauce for your English. I am in a rage and should quarrel most furiously with you if I could reach you.

This angered Mrs Austin, who had expurgated a book she sincerely admired to make it palatable to a readership she knew better than he. She told him he was welcome to find a more faithful translator for the remaining volumes if he wished to give himself up 'to all the rage, scorn and vituperation of the whole press of England'.[9]

There was much hot air blowing both ways in this exchange, which continued until Pückler was given a compelling reason to cease his lamentations: his book was a best-seller. Thanks to Mrs Austin's exceptional work-rate, the concluding volumes came out in February 1832, with the title *Tour in Germany, Holland and England, in the Years 1826, 1827, & 1828 etc.* and priced more steeply at twenty-one shillings, by which time the first part was already in its second edition. There were several reports in the press of the waves the book was making. The *Atlas* could not recall 'any similar pro-duction that, in so short a time, took so strong a hold of the public mind'; the *Courier* thought that 'perhaps no work of the present century has excited more speculative interest'; and the *Morning Chronicle* stated that a large first impression of the final volumes was exhausted on the first day of publication and that the new technol-ogy of steam printing was being used round the clock to keep pace with demand.[10] The *Tour* was reviewed in almost every newspaper and periodical of note, and the passages extracted from it are beyond counting.

All the reviewers identified the 'German Prince' as Pückler, and, alongside the natural curiosity to know how England appeared to an intelligent foreigner, they relished the prospect that a man of his rank would have more credible stories to tell of the *beau monde* than the muckrakers of the yellow press. If the book had been too indiscreet they would have felt obliged to castigate it, but Mrs Austin seems to have measured the dose to perfection, provoking outrage and amuse-ment in equal proportions. One point of general agreement was the excellence of her prose, which, though sometimes rather free with the original (the reason her version is not used here), does indeed read very well. Her reputation was made: Thomas Carlyle called her the 'celebrated Translatress of Puckler Muskau', and she later told Varnhagen that as a result of her efforts she was 'instantly crowned Queen of English translators'.[11]

Reviewers were similarly united in endorsing Pückler's praise for much of what he saw during his visit. He was quite right, they said, to admire the excellence of English institutions, the quality of English manufactures, the beauty of English showplaces and the pre-eminence of the English art of living. Many were impressed by his tableaux of urban and rural life, his keen eye for the telling detail and his fluent, limpid style. The way he made himself an object of interest in his narrative also pleased several critics: in the words of the *Westminster Review*, 'It is our friend, our warm-hearted, noble-minded, imaginative, though somewhat wayward, friend, who is wandering from society to society, from land to land; and, by the aid of his individuality, we take as much pleasure in his letters, as if we had had the satisfaction of having them addressed solely to ourselves.'[12]

Those well disposed to him did not mind his fault-finding, especially if they had the same axes to grind. Progressive reviewers wholeheartedly echoed his verdicts on the uncharitable severity of English piety and the snobbery of those just outside the best circles. The book's main butt, the tyranny of fashion, was kicked again several times, and even the *Court Journal* felt 'compelled to admit that he has laid bare the hollowness of fashionable society, and exposed in its utmost flagrancy the cold artificiality of the London world.'[13] Some, however, claimed that he was too tendentious on this score, or accused him of hypocrisy for abusing society while frequenting it so much (the elision of his fortune-hunting makes his constant presence at balls and routs inexplicable). None of the critics seems to have known that he was in England to find a wife, but many discerned that he wrote under the effects of wounded vanity.

Harsher terms were used for his remarks on those who had received him in their homes. No one identified the Tharps of Chippenham Park, but elsewhere dashes and initials failed to prevent reviewers guessing his hosts' names and disapprovingly but eagerly passing them on to their readers. *Fraser's Magazine* thought he could never set foot in the country again without risking a horsewhipping, and the *Quarterly Review* hoped that 'the Lady Janes and Lady Marys, who waltzed and gallopaded with this "thoroughly illustrious" prince—their fathers, whose wines he drank—and their brothers, whose horses he rode' would all know better in future. Readers were reminded that Continental noblemen were too numerous and too poor to be considered as equals of the holders of literally equivalent titles in England, and the *Metropolitan* asserted that German princes, like hob-nails, could be had by the hundred. That such a man should presume to speak slightingly of the British elite, especially its female component, disgusted the *Edinburgh Review*: 'The ignorance and the audacity of it, (from a German, too, of all people) are inconceivable.'[14]

It is hard to generalise about attitudes to the author's nationality, not least because there was a palpable uncertainty about how 'German' he actually was. The *Foreign Quarterly Review* said 'he thinks and feels throughout as none but a German would', the *Monthly Repository* detected 'a good deal of true German expansiveness' in his style, and some considered his flowery compliments to 'Julie' and poetic sketches of scenery to be typically Teutonic. Others, however, found it hard to contain such a shimmering figure within the stereotype of deep-thinking stolidity: 'There is nothing of that darkness in his nature which popular prejudice assigns to the German constitution,' admitted the *Atlas*, while the *Metropolitan* was surprised 'that German phlegm should put on an air of vivacity'.[15] For those who disliked him, foreignness in general rather than Germanness in particular was the stick to beat him with.

From Muskau Pückler watched with glee as this ding-dong battle generated publicity and sales. He read the English reviews Sarah Austin sent him avidly and then forwarded them to Varnhagen, who was following his progress with avuncular pride. Effingham Wilson wrote that he would be 'highly honoured' to publish any future work and use his 'best endeavours to render it as successful as "the Tour"'. Among private opinions, the cosmopolitan Lady Shrewsbury said she had never seen so many truths in a single book; the Whig political wife Lady Lyttelton found it pleasant but lightweight; the Unitarian radical Harriet Taylor thought the author a coxcomb but cheered his freethinking views; a friend of the novelist Lady Blessington dismissed him as an impertinent gossip with a poor knowledge of English society; and an elderly guide at Windsor Castle was so appalled to find his royal anecdotes in print, albeit unattributed, that when a notebook-wielding German sightseer presented himself soon afterwards he was too scared to talk to him.[16]

The most irate reader may have been the novelist Lady Morgan, with whom Pückler had quarrelled in Dublin and whose unflattering portrait, easily identifiable as 'Lady M', is included in the book. She avenged herself by representing him in her novel *The Princess; or, The Beguine* as Count Katzenellenbogen (cat's-elbow), a preposterous mountebank who tries to ensnare the wealthy heroine.

> [T]he Count, as hero, author, wit, cavalier, and mediatized Prince of the *ci-devant* absolute sovereignty of the Cat's-elbow, was, in his own estimation, an object to fix the world's attention, whether he figured in the *salons* of Stutgard, Paris, or London; or withdrew from their distractions, to his own castle and domains, in—he was not very certain where [. . .].
>
> There was in his gait and gesture a mobility, which almost tempted the beholder to believe that 'his whiskers thought'. His well-turned *moustaches* bristled like the brindled cat's; and his svelte and serpentining figure had all the elasticity of youth; though 'the damning witness' of time, which crowded round the corners of his small and feline eyes, bore testimony against his juvenile assumptions.

Katzenellenbogen fails to impress the princess, and at the end of the novel an old chestnut is reheated when he is seen at the feet of 'the black Empress'.[17]

Equally hostile was the Tory polemicist Theodore Hook, who wrote the damning *Quarterly Review* article cited above and followed it up with caricatures that are probably partly based on Pückler in two of his novels. The first is Count Stickinmeyer in *Gilbert Gurney*, 'a very distinguished person in his way' with a reputation as a duellist and gambler and a comical style of speaking English. The second is an unnamed German visitor in *Jack Brag*,

> who beat anything I had ever seen out of a travelling caravan,—an animal which certainly talked, and was therefore human, otherwise I should have taken it for an astounding cross in the breed between an ape and a horse-jockey: he affronted half the party, after having

disgusted all of it, and made his escape from a pelting of decanters and wine-glasses.[18]

There is a gentler treatment of Pückler as Count Smorltork in Charles Dickens's *Pickwick Papers*. A 'well-whiskered individual in a foreign uniform', Smorltork flits about noting down whatever he hears people say in his 'tablets'. Mr Pickwick tells him he will have his work cut out to gather all the materials he needs for his planned book on England:

> 'Eh, they are gathered,' said the Count.
> 'Indeed!' said Mr. Pickwick.
> 'They are here,' added the Count, tapping his forehead significantly.
> 'Large book at home—full of notes—music, picture, science, poetry, poltic; all tings.'
> 'The word politics, sir,' said Mr. Pickwick, 'comprises, in itself, a difficult study of no inconsiderable magnitude.'
> 'Ah!' said the Count, drawing out the tablets again, 'ver good—fine words to begin a chapter. Chapter forty-seven. Poltics. The word poltic surprises by himself—' And down went Mr. Pickwick's remark, in Count Smorltork's tablets, with such variations and additions as the Count's exuberant fancy suggested, or his imperfect knowledge of the language, occasioned.[19]

In his *Adventures of a King's Page* Charles White, one of the lesser Silver Forkists, borrows traits from Pückler and Esterhazy for Baron von Spritzenrauch, a reputed lady-killer with, inevitably, 'a large pair of whiskers'. During a conversation in a London drawing room about the German singer Mademoiselle Trillenheim—Henriette Sontag, of course—Spritzenrauch insists that she merits her reputation for virtue while 'smirking as if he wished to be disbelieved'. There follows a debate about the appreciation of musical excellence, in which the baron says it is sincere in Germany but only a 'fashionable caprice' in England. Piqued by remarks on the greed of visiting performers, he then tartly observes that their fees have to be high considering the risks to which London's fogs expose their voices.[20]

Further down the literary scale, Lord Francis Leveson Gower puts our hero on a minor London stage in 1832 in *The German Prince*, of which the plot, according to Mrs Austin, is that a Jewish pedlar passes himself off as the eponymous personage and cheats everybody. In the same year a fictitious correspondence of Pückler's is printed in the *Court Journal*. 'Your odious book has set the Metropolis in a ferment,' an unnamed countess tells him in the first letter, before mocking his failure to find an English wife (the only published allusion to this during the book's initial reception). There is more of the same in a second letter, and then the belaboured prince does his best to frame a saucy reply. This idea is rehashed in the *New Monthly Magazine*'s 'Miss-Directed Letters' of 1834. These, the preamble explains, are sent by one 'Pickle and Mustard' to his 'dear Henriette' but mistakenly delivered to the periodical's offices. The aim of these cumbersome attempts at humour was to present Pückler as an insufferable fool while also skewering various native notables.[21]

Even such undignified afterpieces had the benefit of keeping the *Tour of a German Prince* in the public eye. Meanwhile there were translations into other languages, including Swedish and Dutch. Jean Cohen's French volumes appeared in 1832, having already been serialised in the *Revue des deux mondes*, and the publisher Fournier wrote to tell Pückler that copies were selling like hot cakes. In the United States the first part of the Austin translation was offered by the Philadelphia firm Carey & Lea in January 1833, followed in February 1834 by an abridged, one-volume edition of the whole work. It got a strong if unintended boost from the publication in New York just a few months earlier of Frances Trollope's *Domestic Manners of the Americans*, which gravely offended the nation it described. The *North American Review* called Pückler 'the best possible answer to Mrs Trollope', and his book was lapped up by that lady's victims, achieving eight editions in just a few months.[22]

80

The German Prince's final conquest—a curious coda to his other successes—was of his English translator. Despite the testiness of their first letters he and Sarah Austin were soon writing regularly, and discussion of his book gave way to more general, and more personal, topics. An attractive and much-admired woman of thirty-eight, Mrs Austin was trapped in an unhappy marriage with a legal philosopher whose great intellect was hobbled by hypochondria and severe depression. John Austin's posthumous reputation as a pioneer in the field of jurisprudence is secure, but during his lifetime he published almost nothing and was considered a failure by everyone, including himself. His inability or refusal to work forced his wife to turn breadwinner by translating and editing books and teaching English to refugees, as well as nursing him, running their household and educating their daughter.

Amidst all this domestic gloom and drudgery, Mrs Austin's mental image of Pückler began to shine in a beguiling light. Here was a different sort of man from her husband: no great thinker perhaps, but a writer with wide interests, an unmistakeable charm, a great zest for life and at the same time a vulnerable streak that made its own appeal to the capable woman in her. Soon she was responding in kind to the bantering, flirtatious style of his letters. In late 1831 she inquired about his reputation as a sensualist, to which he conceded that his morals were not of the strictest, and asked her to take a lenient view: 'I am really a spoiled child and have been so the greatest part of my life, perpetrating colossal follies but always more or less getting by in the world.' He teased her by saying that her translation showed she must be typical of her strait-laced countrywomen, provoking the indignant reply that 'in vivacity, passion and energy I am very little like an Englishwoman.'[23]

Unfortunately most of Pückler's letters to her are lost, but they must have had a powerfully suggestive effect. Late in life he reflected that when crafting letters to women he was in his 'true element' as a writer, which may seem an odd statement given his clumsy missives to English heiresses, but when addressing a woman was a pleasure rather than a duty he was a different man, and many of his love affairs were preceded by well-conducted epistolary campaigns. After eliciting Sarah Austin's rejection of the charge that she was a prude, he began telling her of the vivid dreams he was having of her. She responded that he was in all her thoughts too and the portrait he had sent her a most cherished companion. Though fearful of what he was unlocking, she found her will to resist it broken by sexual frustration. Her husband's love-making was, she admitted, 'a torture, not from any personal disgust, but for want of preliminary commotion de coeur'.[24] She would not leave him, but nor would she give up her own chance of happiness.

Indeed, she fairly ran after it. After a few months she told her 'secret and unknown idol' that she loved him, and promised to respond eagerly to his foot-worship and other fantasies. She even provided an enticing physical description:

> I am exactly 5 feet 6 inches. [. . .] My throat is too small and always was so, my shoulders are wide and well formed and my waist extremely slender in proportion to the expanse above and below. My bosom is not extremely large and prominent but round and firm. But I tell you the rilevati fianchi [the hips] and all below them are singularly handsome, I believe I might say perfect. [. . .] From my usual good health too I have a remarkably fine elastic muscle, '*clean-limbed*' as jockies say, knee and ankle sharply turned, and calf and thigh firm, round and accurately formed.[25]

As well as yearning for sexual fulfilment she envisioned calmer moments of domestic bliss: she saw herself living in the English cottage at Muskau and tending its roses, and even imagined having his child. Meanwhile they planned how they could meet. In early summer 1832 there was talk of the Austins moving to Germany, perhaps Berlin, to benefit from the low cost of living, and it would be easy for her to pay surreptitious visits to Muskau without her self-absorbed husband thinking anything was amiss.

This plan fell through later that summer when John decided to stay in England after all. Still Sarah did not give up hope of being united with her lover, but with the failure of this scheme Pückler's enthusiasm cooled. He let her down gently, blaming himself for his waning interest, but she was deeply disappointed. It now dawned on her that his attachment had never matched hers, indeed that he had carried on a postal affair with her partly to satisfy an interest in female romantic psychology. Slowly she recovered her equanimity, and as she did so her sorrow turned to fear that he would be indiscreet. He promised secrecy, and was true to his word, for while he loved cat-and-mouse games he also observed the code of chivalry and never endangered a woman's reputation. Though Sarah's name was safe, however, her conscience troubled her, and until her husband's death in 1859 she threw herself into the wifely duty of alleviating his sufferings and anxieties. She and Pückler exchanged occasional letters, but when they finally met, in Berlin in 1842, the embers were cold.

16

A EUROPEAN PERSONALITY

*'Throughout my long life, I have practised art, according to
my abilities, in the realm of nature'*

T he sales of his book spared Pückler the grim necessity of
selling Muskau, but if this was to be more than a reprieve he
was obliged to exploit his literary fame to the full. His next
production was *Tutti Frutti*, published in 1834, a medley of reflections,
anecdotes, essays and fiction. In it he lampoons religious hypocrisy
and invasive officialdom in Prussia, takes aim at various follies of the
day, advocates full emancipation of the Jews and has his say on various
prominent writers. It is a ragged parade of hobbyhorses, but there
were good reviews—again encouraged by Varnhagen—and the book-
buying public played its part as before. Hard on the heels of the
German publication came a French translation and Edmund Spencer's
version for the British and American markets, which received about
a dozen reviews in the London press.

Even while he was writing his main endeavour remained the park
at Muskau, on which he now worked with increased confidence.
England had, he said, turned him into a 'perfect gardener',[1] and lapses
of taste like bearded old men dressed as hermits were a thing of the
past. When he had money he worked tirelessly; when it ran out he
groaned with impatience. His draining and earthworks were carried
on at a frenetic pace, and to hurry things along he transplanted adult
trees rather than grow new ones. He pulled down a village and rebuilt
it on another spot, gave the orangery a new façade, incorporated areas
previously given over to agriculture and created an ornamental farm
and a tree nursery. As the estate was the sole provider of employment
for its inhabitants he devoted great care to combining beauty with

practical purpose, and his landscapes accommodated an alum mine, a grist mill, farmland and a glassworks.

No one in Germany was now better versed in the gardener's art, and it was time to set down what he had learnt for posterity. Before leaving for England he had begun a small brochure on Muskau, which he had then expanded while he was there. Now he rewrote it, commissioned nearly fifty colour illustrations and published the result as *Andeutungen über Landschaftsgärtnerei* (*Hints on Landscape Gardening*), still today the best-known title on its subject in German. Like some English garden theorists Pückler sees landscaping in painterly terms and claims a place for it alongside painting as an art form. As artists, he says, both painter and landscaper take the harmony that exists in nature, but over too large an area to be discerned, and make it discernible by recreating it on a smaller scale. However, unlike a painter, who captures his subject on canvas with brush and paint, the landscaper has as his materials the capricious elements of nature itself, so that for him art as imitation of nature and nature as imitation of art are in unique combination.

Technical details make up the bulk of the book. The author acknowledges his debt to Brown and Repton but advises against slavishly copying English models. Instead German park designers should draw their inspiration from local topography, vegetation and crafts. The topics he covers include the progression from house to garden to pleasure ground to park; closed and open spaces and the play of light and shadow; the planting and tending of trees; the selection of grass seed and preparation of lawns; laying paths that lead the observer as if by chance to the best vantage points; and the use of ha-has (fences concealed in ditches) and creeper-covered walls to mask boundaries. Almost lyrical is the section on the calming beauty of water. Rather than see an entire lake or stream, the observer must have his view half obscured by islands or curtains of trees, prompting his imagination to fill in what lies beyond. Indeed, in all aspects of park design partial concealment is better, if harder to achieve, than open display:

> If people, finding a view remarkably beautiful, look at it awhile and
> say, 'What a shame that big tree is standing in the foreground, and

how much more splendid everything would look if only it were removed'—then you have very likely hit the mark; and if you really did their bidding and felled the condemned tree, they would be astonished to find that suddenly there was no picture left to admire—for a garden in the grand style is but a picture gallery, and every picture needs a frame.[2]

In Germany the book's reputation was immediate and lasting, and its influence spread to France with a translation of 1847. In England the founder-editor of the *Gardener's Magazine*, John Claudius Loudon, wanted to translate it for his 'Library of Landscape Gardening', but he died before the idea could be realised, and, as no one else took it up, Pückler never became known as a gardener in the country that had inspired him. Starkly contrasting with this was his impact on the landscaping tradition that emerged mid-century in the United States. One of its best exponents, Charles Eliot, thought Muskau the most impressive park he saw during a tour of Continental Europe in 1886, not least because it transcended traditional design by integrating living and working space with sculpted parkland. In 1906 Muskau was visited by Samuel Parsons, a founder of the American Society of Landscape Architects, who wrote that nothing of his own day surpassed Pückler's achievement. And it was in the United States, in 1917, that his book was finally put into English, with a laudatory introduction by Parsons and another by John Nolen, the pioneer of American city and regional planning, who wrote that the author was 'not only one of the best interpreters of the landscape art of his time, he was also a prophet of city-planning'.[3]

By the end of 1834 *Tutti Frutti* and *Hints on Landscape Gardening* were in print, and Pückler had also dug out the journal of his early pedestrian tour of France and Italy, which appeared the following year. He needed fresh material, and the success of his book on England convinced him that travel writing must be his genre. In any case he loved journeys, which provided his readily stimulated but easily bored mind with a constant stream of new impressions. After a delay caused by the need to fight a duel with a Prussian officer who mistakenly thought his wife's family had been slighted in *Tutti Frutti* (from which Pückler emerged unscathed and his opponent with a grazed neck), he began what became a five-year odyssey. A few months in France were followed in January 1835 by a steamboat crossing from Toulon to the chalk-white city of Algiers, colonised just a few years earlier by the French, and from there he travelled on by land and sea to Tunis, Malta, Greece, Egypt, Sudan, Palestine, the Lebanon, Syria and Turkey. His literary renown served him well, as everywhere he went he was laden with gifts by potentates eager for a good write-up, and much of his journey cost him nothing. His most honorific reception was by Egypt's ruler Mehmet Ali Pasha, who lodged him in a palace with twenty servants and gave him firmans valid throughout his domains.

Throughout his Oriental voyage Pückler wrote hard, often in uncongenial surroundings, and sent his manuscripts to be edited by Varnhagen, Lucie and Leopold Schefer. The yield of these labours was six books in eighteen volumes. None has the vitality of his account of England, based as it is on real letters to a real person, but they are full of evocative passages and spirited anecdotes. The appearance of each title was a major literary event. All subsequently appeared in French, and in Britain all were reviewed and about half translated. His fame was bolstered by dozens of works by other hands that referred to him or his books or used the nonchalant aristocratic style, known as the *Kavaliersperspektive*, which he had made popular. Pückler enjoyed his success to the full, especially the opportunity it gave him to help other writers with recommendations and financial assistance. However, by the mid-1840s his novelty had passed and he put down his pen. Vain but not conceited, he had enjoyed his time in the limelight without ever fancying himself a great writer. He was flattered when Byron's half-sister Augusta Leigh requested an autograph, but in a letter to a friend he dismissed his books as 'tattered old stuff' written for money.[4]

Pückler's homecoming in 1840 was marred by turbulence in his relations with Lucie, who was hurt that he had been willing to spend years away from her, and, even more so, that he now wished to bring home Machbuba, his teenaged Abyssinian concubine. He had purchased her, still half a child, at a Sudanese slave market three years before, and in his Egyptian travelogue he recalls her classic East African beauty as she was displayed naked by the slave trader, dwelling pleasurably on her flawless copper-brown skin, firm, perfectly-formed breasts and pearly-white teeth. He became her lord and master, but treated her gently, communicating with her in the Italian he taught her and respecting her privacy. Before long his fond amusement at her playful spontaneity, wilfulness and untaught grace grew into a stronger feeling, and his biographers are agreed that she was the only woman he ever loved fully and lastingly. She for her part was fiercely devoted to him, grateful as she was to be treated well after the many horrors she had endured in her short life.

She became his constant companion as he spent the next few years meandering through various lands, and when he turned homeward he was determined to take her with him. But his fears that Lucie would object to this were soon confirmed. She had tolerated countless amours, but this was different, for despite the light-hearted references to Machbuba in his letters she instinctively grasped how deep the attachment really was. Moreover, she was unwilling to face the scandal and injury to her pride of sharing her home with an African mistress. She and Pückler had a tense meeting in Budapest in autumn 1839 that resolved little, and then he travelled to Vienna, where he placed Machbuba in a finishing school to be taught European manners. Although a number of Viennese great ladies took a charitable interest in her, she found it difficult to adapt to European society and the cold climate. Her health began to decline, and when it became apparent that she had contracted tuberculosis Pückler took her to Marienbad to take the cure. But there was nothing the doctors could do for her, and, with Lucie having relented, he finally returned to Muskau with the emaciated girl in September 1840. A few weeks later she died.

Another source of discord between the errant prince and his long-suffering ex-wife was Muskau itself. Though his earnings as a writer were essential income they barely made a dent in his debts, and, while still abroad, he resolved to sell the estate. It would be a wrench to relinquish the park, but by now his desire to be free of money troubles had acquired a desperate urgency. However, Lucie had become so attached to Muskau that she reacted furiously, accusing him of trampling her underfoot and even killing her. She went as far as imploring Prussian government ministers to intercede and considered trying to block the sale by legal means. Pückler was horrified by these embarrassing manoeuvres, and wondered sadly if she loved Muskau more than him, but her ferocity checked him and they stayed put. Indeed, once he had recovered from his grief over the decline and death of Machbuba his creation reasserted its claims and he resumed his planting. But the time came when he faced the certainty of personal bankruptcy if he did not sell up, and so in 1845 he accepted an offer of 1,170,000 thalers. Lucie renewed her lamentations, but this time he would not listen. Now sixty, he paid off his creditors and enjoyed an ecstasy of relief that outweighed the sadness of passing his work into other hands.

The loss of Muskau did not spell an end to Pückler's career as a gardener, as he moved to his paternal inheritance Branitz, near the town of Cottbus, and began reshaping its flat, sandy, treeless terrain. Only a fraction of Muskau's size, Branitz forced him to live up to his axiom that hinting at expanses where none exist is the true mark of a landscaper. He rose to the challenge, and by the end of his life had turned Branitz into a gem of gleaming lakes, woods and meadows, at its centre the delicate rococo house set in an English garden. People of all stations came to see 'my oasis in the desert', as he proudly called it. He also worked for others, such as the Grand Duke of Weimar at Ettersburg and Prince William of Prussia (later William I) at Babelsberg, where what he achieved can still be admired. Finally he sought, vainly, to interest Frederick William IV in his idea of a garden city, 'a more ideal urban design than heretofore, including landscapes, without any straight roads, and interspersing trees and buildings'.[5] For all that his patrons were crowned heads, he believed park design was not a rich man's indulgence, rather a useful activity, providing employment and fashioning beauty that ennobled all who saw it.

He also continued his roving, albeit within the bounds of Europe, acting as a supernumerary courtier to various minor monarchs and mixing with the *haute volée* at watering places. He liked to pass a few days in stimulating company, make a good impression himself and then move on before the acquaintance grew stale. On his travels he often encountered groups of English tourists, identifiable by their linguistic incompetence, engrossment in their guidebooks and proprietorial behaviour—like the ladies on a Rhine cruise who avoided relinquishing their deck chairs by hobbling from one spot to another with them pressed against their bottoms. The best thing about the English abroad, in his view, was the marvellously improving effect they had on food and cleanliness wherever they stayed. He was often taken for one himself, perhaps because at inns he came down for dinner with his own bottles of Harvey Sauce and English mustard. In France innkeepers mistaking his nationality would double their attentions but also his bill, and at a provincial theatre in the same country a poor actress in need of a protector addressed him enticingly in English until he informed her of her error and gallantly pointed out a real Englishman sitting nearby.

His attitude to the island nation changed little over the years. Its technical achievements and mastery of the art of living never ceased to impress him. He often employed an English groom, and at Muskau and later Branitz he adopted the relaxed, unobtrusive style of English hospitality, very unlike the stilted etiquette of German country house visiting. Nonetheless his old grudge was easily stoked: by a sneering article on Frederick the Great in *Blackwood's Magazine*; by predatory trading expeditions from Britain to China; and by the narrowly averted scheme of British railway speculators to lay track through his park. The nation's animating spirit was, he said, 'the most unadulterated, most vigorous, and most highly developed *self-interest*'. After Britain triumphed over Prussia in a commercial dispute in the early 1840s, he wrote wearily to a friend, 'These people are too clever for us, and sheep will never liberate themselves, for their destiny is to be shorn until the world ends. If in my next life I cannot be an Englishman I should just as soon stay in my grave.'[6]

He visited England one more time, arriving on 5 October 1851. This time the crossing, from Calais to Dover, took only 2½ hours, followed by a speedy journey in an express train to London, where he once again stayed at the Clarendon Hotel, now in new hands. He was delighted to be in the pulsating capital again. He visited the Great Exhibition in the Crystal Palace and Sir Charles Barry's new Palace of Westminster, and wrote Lucie daily reports of his doings. It was not the Season but he saw a few English acquaintances, while his evenings he spent at the theatre, opera or a restaurant, often in the company of Count Blücher, a grandson of the great field marshal attached to the Prussian Embassy. After seeing his fill of sights and eating his fill of dinners, he went back over the Channel on 3 November.[7]

In 1854 Pückler was in Paris, where he went into society and was received at the court of Napoleon III. Ever a Francophile, he hoped that the increasingly likely attainment of German unity would be followed by what he called 'the mutual saturation, unification and eternal friendship of the French and German peoples'. Their qualities were, he felt, complementary—vivacity, grace and clarity of thought on the one hand and emotional depth and rich imaginative life on the other (rather immodestly he considered himself, with his half-French mother, to be a good advertisement for this fusion). At the political level too Franco-German understanding would yield great things, maybe even the germ of a future union of European states. To the statistician César Moreau he wrote, 'If the peoples of Europe ever form one single family, it will be to France that the credit is mainly due.'[8]

In winter he often spent a few weeks in Berlin, where he saw old friends and gave gourmet lunches in his flat in the Hotel de Russie. Here and elsewhere he was still regularly stung by Cupid's arrow, but he paid the price for not renouncing love once he ceased to inspire it by falling victim to adventuresses and blackmailers. Lucie was understanding during these episodes, having forgiven him for Machbuba and the sale of Muskau, but she required much sympathy herself, since although she grew fond of Branitz and helped in its beautification her last years were full of sadness. She lived to see both her daughter Adelheid and her ward Helmina predecease her, and was herself in constant poor health. Pückler did his best to cheer her up: one night he created a flowerbed beneath her window in the shape of an 'S' for Schnucke, so that she would see it on waking. They spent their evenings talking and playing whist, and during his ever shorter wanderings he sent affectionate letters. In 1852, feeling close to death, she wrote, 'Farewell, Lou, my son, my life! Lead me gently to the grave.

There I shall rest, and my soul, filled with memories of you, will await a new holy union of the spirit.' She suffered several strokes but lingered on until May 1854. For the cross by her grave he chose a simple inscription: 'I think of you in love.'[9]

She had played a huge part in Pückler's life, and he was often lonely in his remaining seventeen years. One by one he lost his friends, and, after a long tenure of youth and vigour, he felt old at last. Lucie had always insisted that he dye his hair, but after her death he admitted to his white locks. He still sought out amusing company and liked receiving guests at Branitz, where he cut an eccentric figure in his Turkish costume among Oriental knick-knacks and a collection of exotic birds. In July 1858 Varnhagen, now a widower, paid a weeklong visit with his niece Ludmilla Assing, and in his diary he describes convivial days spent drinking champagne, talking of art, politics and memories, playing chess and billiards and looking through the English travel albums. He was also given a tour of the park and, as before in Muskau, was astonished by its splendour. Later that year Varnhagen died, and to his grieving niece Pückler wrote, 'Your uncle could hardly have known (much less believed) how much I loved him, and how high among men I felt he stood.' To another he described the dead man as 'a master, teacher and loyal, ever-consistent friend'.[10]

In this case death brought forth new life, as Varnhagen bequeathed his friendship for Pückler to Ludmilla Assing, who enlivened his last years with her intellectually rich, mildly flirtatious letters, some of them concerning the biography of him she proposed to write. A workmanlike but necessarily incomplete treatment had appeared in 1843, but the hope of a full account nourished his never-sleeping vanity, and he set about ordering his voluminous papers. As he pondered his life he felt sure that his real achievement was as a gardener, for he had worked hard and overcome many obstacles to achieve something of practical value. He continued to believe that landscaping was an art form, and the last entry in his diary, written a month before he died, expresses this conviction: 'Art is the noblest and highest of life's goods, for it is creative work for the benefit of mankind. Throughout my long life, I have practised art, according to my abilities, in the realm of nature.'[11]

Although he never gave up writing or dictating letters the child-less old man suffered greatly from the solitude of his declining years, a feeling exacerbated by the intrigues of potential heirs and the dishonesty of servants. He was ready for the end before it came. After Christmas 1870 a bad cold destroyed his appetite, sapping his frame of its final strength. He died in his eighty-sixth year just before midnight on 4 February 1871. On a bitterly cold, snow-flurried morning five days later his coffin, accompanied by family members and various dignitaries, was carried to the tumulus in the park that he had built for the purpose.

ಉ

Ludmilla Assing was as good as her word. In the years after Pückler's death she produced a biography, which is unsurpassed by the four that have followed it, and edited a selection of his letters in nine volumes. Since then several of his individual correspondences have been published, most of the travelogues have been reissued, and critical interest in him has grown markedly in the last two or three decades. The mainstay of his fame as a travel writer remains the book on England, of which there have been annotated editions from three major publishers since 1986, one still in print at the time of writing. Also in print is *Hints on Landscape Gardening*, and it is as a designer of parks that Pückler is principally known in Germany today, his work celebrated in countless books, exhibitions and radio and television programmes.

Unfortunately the landscaper's art is vulnerable to the ravages of time and human folly, and Muskau, his greatest creation, has suffered much. In 1846 the estate was bought by Prince Frederick of the Netherlands, who sensitively continued Pückler's work on the park, and in 1883 his daughter sold it to the Arnim family, which barring a few questionable new buildings kept the property largely intact during their sixty-two year ownership. Disaster struck at the close of the Second World War, when the chateau was burnt down and the park disfigured by heavy fighting. The River Neisse transecting it became the new Polish-German border, and in the ensuing decades the three-fifths of the park in Poland returned to a state of nature, while the chateau on the other side, now state property of the German Democratic Republic, remained an empty, roofless shell, though some work was done on the park and other buildings. In 1989 the restoration of Muskau to its former glory began in earnest with the cooperation of the Polish authorities, and in 2004 UNESCO added the whole 560-hectare site to its World Heritage list. In 2008 Pückler's beloved home, still incompletely renovated, was finally opened to the public. It now contains exhibits on its former owner, a tourist office and a landscaping school.

Branitz has had a less troubled history. After Pückler's death it passed into the hands of his cousin Count Heinrich von Pückler, who together with his head gardener Georg Bleyer further embellished the park, and then his son Count August von Pückler, who was mostly held back from further work by financial difficulties. Following the family's dispossession in 1945 the estate became the responsibility of the German Democratic Republic, which took good care of it. Today it is an immaculately presented visitor attraction, and it is here, more than Muskau, that Pückler's spirit now seems to reside. The house is divided between rooms furnished in period style, including a library and family portrait gallery, and a permanent exhibition on the prince's life and work. Both near the house and dotted around the grounds are several other buildings, including hothouses and a pineapple house. Many of these buildings have been put to new uses: the farmhouse and the stables hold regular exhibitions on Pückler and related themes; the 'cavalier's house', formerly accommodation for his guests, is a restaurant; and the park forge is now the home of the Pückler Archive.

By a twist of posthumous fortune that would have amused him, even Germans with no interest in literature, parks or historical personalities have probably heard of Pückler, for, like the Australian soprano Nellie Melba, he has given his name to an ice-cream dessert.[12] Outside Germany, however, the dessert and its eponym are little known. In England Pückler was forgotten by the time of his death, and few of his contemporaries recall him in their memoirs. Despite Eliza M. Butler's biographical study *The Tempestuous Prince* of 1929 and the three abridged editions of his English travel book in translation since then, it is fair to say that he is now familiar mainly to the writers on Regency life who trawl through the latter in search of colourful quotes. Even the fascinating exhibition at Muskau and Branitz in 2005 on his stay in England had no resonance in that country.

And yet he is, or should be, more than just a purveyor of quotable gobbets to social historians. His time in England, unusually well documented in published and unpublished sources, is the story of a deepening acquaintanceship such as the English themselves make in discovering their past; for just as he was a foreigner in Regency London by nationality, so are they by the passage of time. As a guide he has faults as well as merits, of course, but he is always lively and perceptive. It would be hard to capture his essence better, or give a more balanced verdict, than the critic who noticed his book in the *American Quarterly Review*:

> The information [. . .] which he displays, is not of the most profound kind; nor do his faculties strike as much for their solidity and depth, as for brilliancy and variety. In disposition we should judge him to be vivacious, affectionate, and generous, rather volatile, perhaps, and capricious, and somewhat given to self-indulgence and egotism—in character high-toned and honourable—in temperament enthusiastic, but irresolute, with an infusion of sentimentalism and romance, of a kind well adapted to act as an *ignis fatuus* to his reason, and a source of hypochondriacal disquietude of soul. One thing, at all events, we can confidently assert; it would be difficult to find a more pleasant companion within the two covers of a book.[13]

EPILOGUE

After Pückler's failure to propose to her Mary Gibbings continued her search for a husband, and in 1835 the gossipy Mrs Calvert reported that 'Lord Oxmantown consents at last to marry Miss Gibbings—fifty thousand down—and fifty more at her father's death.' This was not a match, as it turned out, but in 1838, aged thirty-nine, she became the third wife of the sixty-four-year-old former cavalry commander Viscount Combermere. Other than that it was clearly an exchange of a title for money (£40,000 according to the diarist Frances Williams Wynn), little is known of their childless marriage, and Lady Combermere largely effaces herself from the biography she wrote of her husband after his death in 1865. She filled her time with charitable work, composing songs, sketching and watercolour painting, and also published a volume of nonsense verse and a study of human psychology. She seems to have had a golden old age in her home in Belgrave Square, where she entertained younger generations of social and literary lions. She died aged ninety in 1889.[1]

Harriet Kinloch and Georgiana Elphinstone also had long lives. The former married the Reverend Lord Thomas Hay, the sixth son of the Marquess of Tweeddale, in 1833, and they spent most of their wedded life at Rendlesham in Suffolk, where Lord Hay was dean and then rector and their five children were born. Lady Hay died in 1891, a few months after her husband. As for Miss Elphinstone, she justified her reputation as a flirt in the years after Pückler knew her by toying with the perennial fortune hunter Charles de Mornay, the diarist Henry Edward Fox and Augustus Villiers, a younger son of the Earl of Jersey, before accepting Villiers at the second time of asking in 1831. After his early demise she married Lord William Osborne, a brother of the Duke of Leeds. She had children by neither man and lived until 1892.

Little Harriet Bonham, who had offered Pückler a posy of forget-me-nots as he bade her goodbye at Titness Park, never married, and when her elder brother Edward was appointed consul-general at

Naples she went with him as his hostess. She did not reach old age, dying, according to *The Times*, 'much beloved and deeply lamented' in 1863. As for her lovely sister Rosabel Garvagh, she had twelve more years of marriage with her middle-aged husband followed by half a century of widowhood until 1891. Her later years were clouded by estrangement from at least one of her sons and early mental decline, and we last hear of her as a victim of theft and physical cruelty at the hands of her servants.[2]

Sad reverses were also the lot of the wealthiest heiress, Elizabeth Hamlet, whose father lost his whole fortune as a result of disastrous speculations in pearl fisheries and the building of the Princess's Theatre in Oxford Street. In 1841 he was declared bankrupt, his shop closed and his stock sold. He is supposed to have spent a period in the Charterhouse, though when he died in 1853 it was in his own home. His still unmarried daughter stayed at his side throughout these trials, and at the time of his death was fifty-seven years old.[3]

Pückler had no further contact with any of these women after 1828, nor with his first betrothed Lady Lansdowne, who spent her last years living quietly at Wycombe Lodge in Kensington and died there in 1833; nor with his old antagonist Clanwilliam, who after brilliant beginnings fell out with too many powerful men to prosper in public life and saw his career fizzle out in his mid-thirties. He did, however, meet the Duke of Cumberland, now King Ernest Augustus of Hanover, while on his way to London in 1851. Any anger on the score of his stymied wife-hunting had long since cooled. On his way home he passed through Hanover again just after the old king's death and attended his funeral. He also renewed contact with Princess Lieven, and a friendly exchange of letters shows that with her too old differences were forgotten.[4]

Letitia Bonaparte-Wyse, whom he saw briefly in Paris in 1834, passed her time in various places and in increasingly raffish company. She was often short of money and even had a spell in a debtor's prison, but her luck improved when her cousin Louis Napoleon became emperor and she, like other members of the clan, was granted a pension. She died in 1872. As for Henriette Sontag, Countess Rossi, Pückler's diary records that he heard her at a private concert in 1846, but not the impression she made on him. Three years later her husband lost his job and she returned to the stage after an absence of twenty years to support him and their children. She went on gruelling tours of Germany, Britain and the United States, and died aged forty-eight of cholera while singing in Mexico.

APPENDIX

1
FOREIGN MARRIAGES

The light of scholarship has yet to be trained on 'foreign marriages', as they were known, and statistical analysis, even for 1814-40, is beyond the scope of this book. Gathering data is hampered by the lack of civil registration of marriages in England and Wales before 1837, throwing the researcher back on the diffuse evidence of parish registers; and by the fact that the first census, taken in 1841, does not indicate country of birth. Information on marriages contracted elsewhere is even more scattered, much of it, presumably, in town hall archives across the Continent. There is some evidence in the 'Miscellaneous Foreign Marriage Returns' at the Family Records Centre: RG 43/8 (1826-70), but it is too haphazard to be useful. A better source is the Bishop of London's Registry, which collates records of weddings celebrated by chaplains at British embassies after 1816 and is held under the rubric 'International Memoranda' at the Guildhall Library: MSS 10926/1 (1816-24), 10926/2 (1824-32) and 10926/3 (1832-40). This registry has details of hundreds of foreign marriages, permitting some rudimentary comparative analysis. What emerges is that while British men and women marry foreigners in more or less equal numbers, marriages between titled foreign men and British women outnumber marriages between British peers or sons of peers and foreign women many times over. Newspaper marriage notices, which would also be a part of any serious investigation of this topic, seem to confirm this trend.

2
EXTRACTS FROM *BRIEFE EINES VERSTORBENEN*

The following definitions of 'gentleman' and 'temper' show how finely tuned Pückler's perception of contemporary English usage, social and linguistic, can be.

'A "gentleman" is neither a nobleman, nor a noble man; strictly speaking (though in everyday language the term is used for anyone of respectable appearance) it applies only to a man who, by fortune and close familiarity with the customs of good society, is *independent*. Whoever provides a service to the general public, or works for it in any way, with the exception of higher government officials and poets and artists of the first class, is not a gentleman, or at any rate not a full gentleman. There is a man here known to at least every lover of horseflesh at home and abroad, who is wealthy, enjoys great esteem, and is on terms of intimacy with many a lord and duke, but sells horses by auction in a large establishment once a week and is thereby in a sense beholden to the public [*viz*. Richard Tattersall]. Recently I was astonished to hear this man say, "I cannot understand why the Duke of B— has charged me with presenting his challenge to the Earl of M—. He ought to have selected a gentleman for the task, for such things are no business of mine."

A really *poor* man, who is not in a position to make debts, can on no account be called a gentleman, for he is the least independent of all. A rich knave, on the other hand, as long as he has a well-bred air and does enough to avoid losing his good name, can pass for a perfect gentleman.'

Briefe, II, 182-83

'On the way home my young companion spoke unceasingly of Mrs [Mansell], to whose company he had long been drawn as eagerly as a moth to light, and with the same results. Among other things he said, "Never, for all her vivacity, have I remarked even a moment's bad mood or impatience in her—no woman ever had a better temper." This word, like "gentle", is untranslatable. Only a nation that could coin the word "comfort" could have come up with "temper", for temper is to the mind what comfort is to the body. It is the pleasantest state of the soul, and the highest happiness for those who possess it or enjoy it in another. In its complete form it is perhaps only found in women, as their disposition is more passive than active, but it must not be confused with apathy, which either causes tedium or actually aggravates irritation and anger, whereas temper calms and conciliates. It is a truly pious, loving and cheerful principle, mild and soothing like a cloudless day in May. With gentleness in his character, comfort in his home, and temper in his wife, a man's earthly happiness is complete.'

Briefe, II, 225-26

The following anecdote, almost certainly apocryphal, may be set alongside those in the same genre told by Captain Gronow.

'One thing that adds greatly to the dullness of social life in England is the supercilious way Englishmen, who are expansive enough when abroad, in their own country never speak to a stranger, and if spoken to by one almost take it as an insult. Sometimes they poke fun at themselves for this, but without ever changing their habits when the opportunity arises. There is a story that a lady, having seen someone fall into the water, pleaded with the dandy at her side, who was known to be a good swimmer, to go to the unfortunate's rescue. With the imperturbability that is one of the chief requirements of the current fashion he put his lorgnette to his eyes, looked earnestly at the drowning man, whose head was just appearing above the surface for the last time, and then turned calmly to his companion and said, "It's impossible, Madam. I was never introduced to this gentleman."'

Briefe, I, 387

Unhappy at the domination of bureaucrats over landowners in Prussia, Pückler waxes lyrical on the circumstances of the propertied classes in England.

'Is it not pleasing to think that hundreds of thousands of people in England live like this in the comfortable, substantial luxury of their own peaceful homes? In the bosom of their hearth they are as free as kings, calm in the certainty that their property is inviolate. Happy mortals, you are never molested by oppressive letters from uncivil authorities, which want to extend their sway into your living rooms and bedrooms, and think they have rendered the state a great service if they put you to thousands of thalers of expense in unnecessary postage; which are never content to stand above you but must also stand against you, uniting as best they can the roles of prosecutor and judge. You, happy ones, never suffer extractions from your purse or indignities against your person; you know nothing of the pointless importunities of bureaucrats revelling in their own power, or the avarice of an insatiable blood-sucking state. On your own properties you are absolute masters, obliged only to obey laws you yourselves have had a hand in drafting. When one ponders all this, one must concede that England, though not perfect, is a blessed land.'

Briefe, II, 142-43

3
OTHER TESTIMONIES

During his tour of Ireland Pückler visited the Kerry home of Daniel O'Connell, the founder of the Catholic Association. Naturally the anti-Catholic Age *was disgusted.*

'The *Globe*, of Friday, contains the following tit-bit of intelligence:—"Prince Puckler Muskaw, said to be a General in the Prussian army, and a relation of the Buonaparte family, has been on a visit with Mr. O'Connell, at Derrinane Abbey. He was introduced to the Limerick Independent Club, with whom he promised to dine."

In the first place, Prince Pickle and Mustard is *not* a General in the Prussian army; secondly, Prince Pickle and Mustard is no relation to the Buonaparte family, more than having flirted with Madame Buonaparte Wyse, at the Horticultural Fete, and elsewhere; and thirdly, Prince Pickle and Mustard would dine with anyone who would pay for his dinner.'

Age, 28 September 1828

In his new edition of Assing's Pückler biography Dr Nikolaus Gatter lists a single English response to it, in the Saturday Review, *of which the following in an extract.*

'Muskau, in Lusatia, according to *Murray's Guide*, was lately the residence of "a German Prince who wrote a coxcombical book about England." Madlle. Ludmilla Assing holds, on the contrary, that the authorship of the aforesaid book crowned the Prince "with immortal laurels." The truth seems to lie between the two. The Prince, take him all in all, could not be much more fitly described than by the appellation of coxcomb; the book, on the other hand, has enough literary merit to be read with pleasure even now that the affected title "letters of a Dead Man" has become actually applicable. We fancy, however, that a more durable title to renown will be derived from the secret history of this celebrated work as revealed by the indiscretion, or rather the scandalous recklessness, of Madlle. Assing. We question at least whether the records even of German divorce can produce anything *aut simile aut secundum*. Prince Pückler, one of the most extravagant men of his age, was married to a daughter of Chancellor Hardenberg, one of the most extravagant of its women. When the impossibility of making both ends meet became apparent, the princely pair, we are told, agreed to raise ways and means by a divorce. Pückler, it was arranged, was—such is the almost incredible story—to proceed to England and espouse the richest, and, we may take the liberty of adding, the silliest Englishwoman he could find, discharging his debts with a portion of her fortune, and devoting or being supposed to devote (the point being trusted to his honour) the remainder to the weal of his discarded but still adored Princess. The transaction seems to have presented itself to their minds in the light of one of singular magnanimity: –

Lucy felt that she was sacrificing herself for Pückler's sake, and Pückler that he was sacrificing himself for Lucy's, undergoing the inconvenience of a disagreeable and fatiguing course of fortune-hunting for the advantage of her purse as well as his own. And as in his childhood he had been accustomed to pray that it might be vouchsafed to him to win at cards, even so now did he offer up orisons that he might obtain a rich heiress, for his own good, and that of his beloved Lucy!

The strangest part of the whole affair is that this incontrovertibly real live Prince did not get an English wife or any second wife at all, although he dyed his hair and bought a new hat, and within eight months after his arrival in England had paid one thousand four hundred morning calls, arrayed in the full glory of "a green cravat, a yellow cassimere waistcoat with metal buttons, an olive-coloured frock-coat, and iron grey pantaloons." English gentlemen regarded him as a fortune-hunter; English ladies, with less reason, as a Blue Beard; and neither could comprehend how he could have got legally separated from Madame la Princesse without an action for *crim. con.* So far from this, he was sending her a most affection-ate correspondence, with ample details of his honest endeavours to find her a successor, and minute descriptions of his most killing toilets. "I enclose," he says, "a pattern of the waistcoat." From these particulars it will probably be inferred that the book in which they are chronicled is, designedly or otherwise, a withering exposure of the heartlessness, frivolity, and general worthlessness of Continental fashionable society; and such is the case, this being but one out of a number of equally edifying histories related in its pages. It is just to add that the Prince is also an instance of how a naturally excel-lent disposition may be spoiled by unfavourable circumstances of birth and education.'

Saturday Review, 34 (21 December 1872), p. 801

Dr Eugene Oswald (1826-1912), a German-born teacher and writer who settled in England in 1852, recalls the vogue for Pückler's writings in the Germany of his youth.

'Prince Pückler-Muskau, a north Prussian nobleman, was rich, rather well-informed, and with considerable facility of writing—not a great writer. He went all over Europe, then along the south-ern coasts of the Mediterranean into Egypt, which after Buonaparte's expedition had sunk again into darkness, and he wrote in a chatty style, frivolously enough to attract many and not to deter others. He was, besides, owner of considerable lands, and passion-ately given to picturesque gardening. For many years, writing in a mixed style of allusions to society matters, of politics, in a highly aristocratic sense, and of scandal, he pleased, in a long series of volumes, a numerous public composed of those who could not or would not travel themselves. It was *the* thing to admire him. And he preserved a semi-mystery by calling his many volumes the work *eines Verstorbenen* [of a dead man].'

Reminiscences of a Busy Life
(London: Moring, 1911), pp. 80-81

Notes

Prologue

1. *Morning Post*, 18 October 1826 quoted in Butler, 58; Trant, 210; *Court Journal*, 23 (3 October 1829), 360; *Fraser's Magazine*, 5/29 (June 1832), 533–34.
2. Anon., 'Proposals', 46 (on Irish adventurers); Montgomery, 63–64 (on French émigrés); *Quarterly Review*, 46/92 (1831), 520; *Fraser's Magazine*, 5/29 (June 1832), 533.
3. Grant, I, I, 259–60; Duncombe, I, 27.
4. Gronow, I, 33–34; Ziegler, 218 (Duchess of Dino); Custine, I, 438; D'Avot quoted in Jones, 161.
5. *New-York Mirror*, 4 April 1835 (Willis); Pichot, I, 185; *London Magazine*, new series 13 (January 1826), 40.
6. On the Strachans: Buckle, 97; Falk, 134–39, 182–83; Greville, V, 18–21; Raikes, II, 20.
7. *Fraser's Magazine*, 5/29 (June 1832), 537; *Quarterly Review*, 59/117 (July 1837), 134.
8. On Mornay: Granville, I, 411–12; Blessington, I, 114, 128; Fox, 360, 364; *Court Journal*, 23 (3 October 1829), 360; Buckle, 43–44; Greville, I, 312.
9. See appendix (1).
10. *Morning Herald*, 14 April 1828; Vincent, 242 (Pepoli, Pecchio).
11. For Anglo-French marriages in this period see Elkington, 98–99. On the Flahauts: Arbuthnot, I, 224; Bernardy, *passim*; Emden, 152–53; Fox, 68, 165; E. Holland, 17–18; Williams Wynn, 202. On the San Antonios: Arbuthnot, II, 348; Byrne, II, 57–58; Glenbervie, 144; Gronow, II, 1; Moore, IV, 1620.
12. On the Blüchers' marriages: *Morning Chronicle*, 28 September 1826; *Courier*, 10 October 1828.

Chapter 1

1. *Briefwechsel*, IV, 330–31. Other than his published letters, my main sources for Pückler's early life are Assing's biography and Arnim and Boelcke's history of the Muskau estate.
2. *Briefwechsel*, VI, 493.
3. At the time 6½ thálers were the approximate equivalent of £1.
4. *Briefwechsel*, VI, 323–24.
5. *Briefwechsel*, IV, 340–43.
6. *Briefwechsel*, IV, 401–02, 413, 414, 418.
7. *Jugend-Wanderungen*, 191; *Briefwechsel*, I, 405–76.

8. *Briefwechsel*, VII, 285–86; IV, 295.
9. Dorow, IV, 102 (letter of August 1834 from Nostiz to Varnhagen).

Chapter 2

1. Tsar Alexander quoted in Priestley, 117; Frampton, 202.
2. Gronow, I, 54.
3. VS 177/39/13/217–25 (theatre visits); EB 1/31 (Duke of York's dinner).
4. Goethe quoted in Assing, I, 146.
5. Figures kindly provided by Christian Friedrich of the Pückler Archive.
6. Wolff's unpublished diary quoted in Arnim, 26; Wolkan's 1886 article is the source for Pückler's letters to Schefer. Then in Wolkan's private collection, these letters are now lost.
7. Ilchester, 131; Gower, II, 74. Estimates of Lady Lansdowne's age by her contemporaries are very contradictory, and the true date of her birth is unknown.
8. Glenbervie, 214–15; Gower, II, 409. The Lansdowne 'castle' stood for only seventeen years.
9. Stirling, 153–54. The names of Lady Lansdowne's five daughters are given in her will of 1821 (National Archives, Prob 11/1817).
10. H. Holland, 238; VS 106/126/28/491–515 (Lauderdale–Lansdowne–Pückler correspondence).

Chapter 3

1. VS 177/39/13/226–39, 243–45 (letters from Blum to Pückler); VS 177/39/13/263–66, 273–95, 299–311, 318–21 (letters from Hunt to Pückler).
2. *Briefwechsel*, V, 151; IV, 242.
3. *Briefwechsel*, IX, 19.
4. Brey and Brey, 'Gartenpracht', 77 (on Repton in Muskau).
5. Petzold quoted in Assing, I, 212.
6. *Briefwechsel*, VIII, 245.
7. *Briefwechsel*, IV, 227, 210.
8. *Briefwechsel*, V, 258.
9. R. Varnhagen, 418.
10. *Briefwechsel*, VI, 306; K. A. Varnhagen, *Blätter*, III, 194–95; IV, 18–19; Clanwilliam/Meade Papers D3044/F/13 (microfilm 588.8.2399). K. A. Varnhagen, *Blätter*, IV, 207–08.
11. *Briefe*, II, 552.
12. K. A. Varnhagen, *Blätter*, IV, 88, 152–53, 157, 212–13, 219; Heine, III, 114.

13. On Pückler's finances at this time see Arnim and Boelcke, 187. The information on incomes in England, with special reference to Austen's novels, is in Copeland, 133–37.
14. *Briefwechsel*, V, 415.
15. Entry for 25 December 1840 from Lucie's unpublished diary in Schäfer, 72; *Briefwechsel*, VI, 223, 241.
16. On the Biel and Maltzan marriages see Doetinchem, 15–17, 19–20.
17. VS 177/39/13/318.
18. *Briefwechsel*, VI, 330.

Chapter 4

1. *Briefe*, I, 60–61.
2. *Briefe*, I, 71.
3. *Briefe*, I, 77.
4. *Briefwechsel*, V, 196; EB 1/31.
5. *Briefwechsel*, V, 149.
6. EB 1/36; *Bell's Life*, 24 June 1827; *Satirist*, 2/43 (29 January 1832), 37; Wilson, II, 601–05; Neumann, *passim*.
7. EB 1/30 (Pückler records Rothschild's English).
8. *Briefe*, I, 93–94.
9. *Briefe*, I, 101–04. The original account, which names Chippenham Park and the people he met there, is in VS 163/76/18/302–08.
10. *Briefe*, I, 99, 100.
11. Tharp Papers R.55.7.21.1, pp. 24–28 (8–13 July 1817); *Briefe*, I, 99–100.
12. *Briefe*, I, 106.

Chapter 5

1. Pückler's copy of Mavor's book, with his ex-libris label, is held by the Stiftung 'Fürst-Pückler-Park', Muskau; *Briefe*, II, 380 (unspecified newspaper quoted in English by Pückler); *Literary Gazette*, 15 (1831), 760; VS 163/76/18/267.
2. The visiting books Pückler kept in England are lost.
3. *Briefe*, I, 188.
4. On tips as an early form of visitor charge see Perkin, 78.
5. *Briefe*, I, 210.
6. *Briefe*, I, 267.
7. *Briefe*, I, 557.
8. *Briefe*, I, 215.
9. EB 1/65 (Pückler on Brown). This summary of Pückler's land-scaping principles in their relationship to the 'picturesque debate'

draws heavily on Goodchild, 'Fürst Pückler'.

10.*Briefe*, II, 19.

11.*Briefe*, I, 34–35.

12.*Briefe*, I, 72–73.

13.Hyde's *Anecdotes* extracted in *Morning Chronicle*, 3 November 1827; Ziegler, 293; Apperley, 98–99; Spencer, I, 43–44.

14.*Briefe*, II, 198–99.

15.VS 164/77/19/118–19 – transcribed by the Pückler Archive; *Briefwechsel*,VI, 496.

Chapter 6

1. Thackeray, *Vanity Fair*, 211–13; Musgrave, 50–52 (on Dr Russell).
2. EB 1/121.
3. VS 164/77/19/167.
4. *Briefwechsel*,VI, 363.
5. *Briefe*, I, 362–65.
6. *Briefe*, I, 346, 377, 347; Kelly, 131–34 (on German praise for the beauty of Englishwomen).
7. See *Brighton Gazette*, 15 February 1827; *Brighton Herald*, 24 February 1827; *Morning Chronicle*, 19 & 26 February, 14 March 1827; *Morning Post*, 5 & 12 February, 10 March 1827.
8. EB 3/8r.
9. VS 164/77/19/215, 225.
10.Fremantle Papers, D–FR/82/12 (31 January, 5, 7 & 9 February 1825).
11.Sala, I, 29; Bulwer-Lytton, 118.
12.Combermere, *Friar*, 141; *Our Peculiarities*, 258.
13.VS 177/40/13/122.
14.VS 164/77/19/216, 225, 227.
15.VS 164/77/19/245–46; *Briefwechsel*,VI, 364.
16.VS 164/77/19/261.

Chapter 7

1. Scargill, II, 1.The novels of the Silver Fork School (c.1825–1840) seek to depict the speech, customs, dress and material reality of the elegant world with the greatest possible precision.
2. Stendhal, 225.
3. Berkeley, III, 12; Lady Morgan's diary quoted in Stevenson, 260; Letter of April 1827 from Pückler to Lucie printed in Brey and Brey, 'Exclusives', 58 (on his costume);VS 164/77/19/111–12 – transcribed by the Pückler Archive (on his cabriolet).
4. VS 164/77/19/326; *Briefe*, I, 369–70.

5. VS 164/77/19/510.
6. *Morning Post*, 12 May 1827.
7. *Times, New Times, Courier*, 5 March 1827; *Brighton Gazette*, 8 March 1827; *Sunday Times*, 11 March 1827; *Fraser's Magazine*, 12/72 (December 1835), 718; Pecchio, 151.
8. *Briefe*, I, 134; Clanwilliam/Meade Papers D3044/F/13 (microfilm 588.8.2397). On Clanwilliam in Berlin see Gleig, 229–30; Airlie, I, 137; K.A.Varnhagen, *Blätter*, III, 232, 237–38; IV, 41–42.
9. Butler, 15; *Briefe*, I, 131. Unfortunately Clanwilliam's Berlin diary contains almost nothing of a personal nature. Apart from the steeplechase (VS 162/74/17/269), Pückler's letters have nothing relevant either. The mockery of Clanwilliam's pursuit of Henriette Sontag and his other misadventures is in Ludwig Rellstab's *Henriette, oder die schöne Sängerin* of 1826.
10. EB 2/39.
11. Gronow, I, 31; *Briefe*, I, 432.
12. *John Bull*, 13 May 1827; *Morning Post*, 13 June 1827.
13. *Briefe*, I, 729–30.
14. *Briefe*, I, 749.
15. *Briefe*, I, 746.
16. *Briefe*, I, 183. A wide range of visitors' testimonies to the absence of a 'culture' of conversation and sociability in England is given in Langford, 184–98.
17. Gronow, I, 227; *Briefe*, I, 743.

Chapter 8

1. VS 164/77/19/282–83, 456–57, 484; *Morning Herald* excerpted in *Courier*, 22 March 1832.
2. VS 164/77/19/442, 333, 379, 391.
3. VS 164/77/19/414–15.
4. VS 164/77/19/422; Creevey, 300; Leconfield and Gore, 186 (Lady Holland); Louisa Smythe's diary, 15 & 29 November 1827.
5. VS 164/78/20/69, 164/77/19/408.
6. *Briefwechsel*, VI, 365; VS 164/77/19/484.
7. I am grateful to John Wardroper for identifying the artist of this caricature.
8. VS 164/78/20/67–68, 159–60.
9. Letter of 12 January 1837 from Charlotte Williams Wynn to Varnhagen, VS 282; *Court Journal*, 150 (10 March 1832), 156; Louisa Smythe's diary, 20 January 1828; Trant, 234; VS 164/78/20/361.
10. For example Crusius, 105, 107; Fox, 164–65; Gronow, II, 325–26; Pichot, I, 188; Stendhal, 220 (primary sources) and Langford,

107–08, 219–27; Letts, 153–55; Muncker, 32, 42 (secondary sources).

11. *Foreign Quarterly Review*, 16/31 (1835), 148; *Court Journal*, 143 (21 January 1832), 38; *Satirist*, 2/45 (12 February 1832), 55; Berkeley, III, 13; VS 164/78/20/80.

12. VS 164/78/20/108–09; Anon., *St James's*, 149; Anon., *Fortunate Youth*; VS 164/78/20/109.

13. Figures and quote in Brey and Brey, 'Bewegte Welt', 30.

14. VS 164/78/20/70, 158–59.

15. EB 2/32.

16. The scholar Grenville Pigott remarked in 1828 that 'it certainly will not be Danneskield's fault, if he does not add some solidity to his title of Excellency. I understand that he made four proposals here, but that his fascinations were resisted': Williams Wynn Letters, VIII, 26.

17. VS 164/79/21/214.

18. VS 164/77/19/304–07. The painting in question is Titian's *Venus of Urbino* of 1538, in which the subject employs her left, not her right hand in the manner described.

19. VS 164/78/20/77–78; 177/40/13/14–15.

Chapter 9

1. *Courier, Morning Herald*, 22 May 1827; *British Traveller, New Times*, 23 May 1827.

2. Heine quoted in Prawer, 43 (his translation); Heine, II, 434.

3. Heine, II, 435. This summary of German impressions of London owes much to Fischer, *Reiseziel*, 600–37.

4. Spencer, II, 345–49; Carlyle, *Sartor*, 4, 178.

5. *Briefe*, I, 82, 385, 517.

6. *Briefe*, I, 71, 440–43, 76, 179.

7. *Briefe*, I, 507.

8. EB 1/61, 29.

9. This view of Lawrence's style was shared, it seems, by his patron George IV: Croker, 133.

10. EB 1/50; VS 164/78/20/455.

11. See Kelly, 65–66.

12. EB 1/55; *Briefe*, II, 211.

13. *Briefe*, I, 519.

14. *Briefe*, I, 480. The famous letters of the fourth Earl of Chesterfield (1694–1773) to his natural son Philip contain cynical advice on how to succeed in politics and society. A German mile equates to about four English miles.

15. EB 2/11–14.

16.*Briefe*, II, 458–59.

Chapter 10

1. *Briefe*, I, 543.
2. *Briefe*, I, 550–53.
3. EB 2/47–48.
4. *Briefe*, I, 468–69.
5. VS 164/78/20/200.
6. Hakewill, 309.
7. *Briefwechsel*,VI, 370; VS 164/78/20/201.
8. *Briefwechsel*,VI, 370.
9. VS 164/78/20/203.
10. VS 164/78/20/204–05.
11. VS 164/78/20/206–07.
12. *Briefwechsel*,VI, 370–71.
13. *Briefwechsel*,VI, 372.
14. VS 177/39/13/335–37.
15. *Briefwechsel*,VII, 63.
16. *Briefwechsel*,VII, 46 (incorrectly attributed to 'Miss Hamlet'); EB 2/57. Titness Park was demolished and the estate divided up in the 1930s. At the end of the twentieth century a new house with the same name was built on a nearby site.

Chapter 11

1. Letter from Nathan Mayer Rothschild to Messrs Cobb of Margate, 18 August 1827 (surviving copy of a letter sent to several bankers): Cobb Papers, EK–U1453/B3/15/1641.
2. *Briefe*, I, 599.
3. He would have been amused by the information given in the *Sheffield Courant* soon afterwards that 'Prince Puckler Muskau, whom we stated in our last week's paper to have passed through this town and visited the show-rooms of Messrs. Joseph Rodgers and Sons, was a companion of arms of his Grace the Duke of Wellington, having commanded the left wing of the army at the battle of Waterloo': reprinted in *Morning Chronicle*, 15 October 1827.
4. VS 164/78/20/357 – transcribed by the Pückler Archive.
5. Thackeray, *Diamond*, 8, 23–27.
6. Gronow, I, 135. The best single source on Thomas Hamlet is Culme.
7. Berkeley, III, 48.
8. *Age*, 12 August 1827.

9. VS 164/78/20/363; *Briefwechsel*,VII, 45 (Pückler's, or, more likely, his agent's, English).
10. VS 164/78/20/387–88.
11. VS 164/78/20/391, 398–99; *Briefwechsel*,VI, 374.
12. VS 164/78/20/410–11.
13. *Briefwechsel*,VII, 45 (Pückler's English).
14. *Briefwechsel*,VII, 47.
15. VS 164/78/20/443.
16. VS 177/39/13/341–52 – printed by Butler, 68–78.
17. VS 164/78/20/474, 443.
18. *Briefwechsel*,VI, 376.
19. Butler, 71.
20. *Briefwechsel*,VI, 377.
21. *Briefwechsel*,VI, 377.

Chapter 12

1. VS 164/78/20/475.
2. Here he stayed until April 1828, when he moved along the street to no. 16, his last London address.
3. *Briefwechsel*,VII, 254.
4. VS 164/78/20/495–96.
5. VS 164/78/20/543–44. *La chaude pisse* refers to the painful urination caused by sexually transmitted infections. Pückler had an episode of the same condition, probably herpes, in 1823 (VS 164/74/17/212).
6. VS 164/79/21/124–25; *Briefwechsel*,VII, 67–70.
7. The Travellers Club incident: *Athenaeum*, 225 (18 February 1832), 105–06; *Court Journal*, 152 (24 March 1832), 177; *Town*, 5 (29 January 1832), 37; VS 177/39/13/474, 476–78, 501–02 (letters from committee members to Pückler); *Briefwechsel*, III, 109. The incident is noted in the committee minutes for 11 April 1832 (information supplied by Sheila Markham).
8. VS 164/77/19/208.
9. Wardroper's recent biography lays all doubts about these matters to rest (see bibliography).
10. *Briefwechsel*,V, 431–32.
11. These insinuations are described in Butler, 20.
12. VS 164/78/20/511–12.
13. *Briefwechsel*,VII, 252.
14. *Briefwechsel*,VI, 386.

Chapter 13

1. *Briefwechsel*,VI, 332.
2. Eberty, 42.
3. Gautier translated in Anon., *Life of Henriette Sontag*, 51.
4. Holtei quoted in Pirchan, 55; K. A.Varnhagen, *Blätter*, IV, 207–08; *John Bull*, 17 June 1827. See also *Age*, 17 June 1827 and *New Times*, 14 June 1827.
5. *Morning Chronicle*, 12 April 1828; *Morning Herald*, 16 April 1828; *Athenaeum*, 25 (1828), 394–95.
6. On the 'Souvenir de Londres' see Pirchan, 101.
7. Letter of April 1828 printed in Stümke, 124.
8. *Briefwechsel*,VI, 395.
9. *Briefwechsel*,VI, 397.
10. *Briefwechsel*,VI, 398.
11. *Briefwechsel*,VI, 398–99.
12. VS 164/79/21/245; *Briefwechsel*,VI, 400.
13. *Briefwechsel*,VI, 403.
14. *Briefwechsel*,VI, 417–19.
15. *Briefwechsel*,VI, 432–33.
16. Maria Malibran quoted in Christiansen, 98; Granville, II, 40–41.

Chapter 14

1. *Briefwechsel*,VI, 421.
2. VS 164/78/20/69; *Briefwechsel*,VI, 401.
3. VS 164/79/21/315–16.
4. Bonaparte-Wyse, *Brood*, 74.
5. *New Times*, 13 February 1828; *Morning Herald*, 14 February 1828; *Sphynx*, 27 February 1828; Richardson, 99.
6. VS 164/79/21/311–13.
7. *Sphynx*, 25 June 1828; reprinted in *The Times* and the *New Times* on 27 June 1828 and the *Age* on 29 June 1828; there is a shorter account in *John Bull* of 29 June 1828.
8. Bonaparte-Wyse, *Brood*, 77; *Issue*, 20–27. On the liaison with Buckingham see also *Satirist*, 2/46 (19 February 1832), 61 and 2/55 (22 April 1832), 133.
9. VS 164/79/21/326–27.
10. Assing, II, 2.
11. *Briefwechsel*,VI, 416.
12. *Briefwechsel*,VI, 446.

Chapter 15

1. K. A. Varnhagen, *Blätter*, V, 101–02.
2. On Varnhagen's role in making Pückler turn author see Assing, I, 240.
3. Goethe, XVIII/2, 194–99; *Briefwechsel*, VII, 202.
4. Heine, II, 499; K. A. Varnhagen, *Geschichtschreibung*, 311–33; Goethe, XVIII/2, 962.
5. Tilman Fischer counts 157 travelogues and travel guides on England published in Germany in the forty years after Pückler's book: *Reiseziel*, 46.
6. *Briefwechsel*, III, 34.
7. Hamburger and Hamburger, 81–82. This study prints parts of the correspondence between Sarah Austin and Pückler, together with related material.
8. Hamburger and Hamburger, 100.
9. Hamburger and Hamburger, 103–05.
10. *Atlas*, 7/302 (26 February 1832), 189; *Courier*, 27 February 1832; *Morning Chronicle*, 24 March 1832.
11. Carlyle and Carlyle, *Letters*, VIII, 43; Pickett and McCulloh, 78.
12. *Westminster Review*, 16 (January 1832), 228.
13. *Court Journal*, 156 (21 April 1832), 242.
14. *Fraser's Magazine*, 5/29 (June 1832), 534; *Quarterly Review*, 46/92 (1831), 531; *Metropolitan*, 3/9 (January 1832), 7; *Edinburgh Review*, 54/108 (December 1831), 395.
15. *Foreign Quarterly Review*, 9/18 (1832), 292; *Monthly Repository*, 5 (1831), 837; *Atlas*, 6/287 (13 November 1831), 763; *Metropolitan*, 3/9 (January 1832), 7.
16. VS 180/46/15/423–24 (E. Wilson); *Briefwechsel*, VIII, 211 (Lady Shrewsbury); Lyttelton, 272; Jacobs, 27 (H. Taylor); Madden, III, 269 (Lady Blessington's friend); Fischer, *Reiseziel*, 298 (the sightseer was Woldemar Seyffarth).
17. Morgan, 360, 456.
18. Hook, *Gilbert Gurney*, I, 304ff.; *Jack Brag*, II, 274.
19. Dickens, 203.
20. White, II, 66–74.
21. Butler, 21 (Leveson Gower) – I have found no trace of a performance of this play; *Court Journal*, 152 (24 March 1832), 177; 158 (5 May 1832), 273; 160 (19 May 1832), 314; *New Monthly Magazine*, 41 (July 1834), 306–12; 42 (September 1834), 64–68.
22. Kaser, 123–24; *North American Review*, 36/78 (January 1833), 1–2; *Briefwechsel*, III, 156.
23. Hamburger and Hamburger, 108, 124. My account of Pückler's relations with Sarah Austin is drawn almost entirely from this source.

24. *Briefwechsel*, IX, 304; Hamburger and Hamburger, 118.
25. Hamburger and Hamburger, 121, 147.

Chapter 16

1. *Briefwechsel*, VI, 432.
2. *Andeutungen*, 37.
3. Goodchild, 118–20 (on Loudon); *Hints*, iii.
4. *Briefwechsel*, I, 327.
5. *Briefwechsel*, IV, 108; IX, 182.
6. *Tutti Frutti*, III, 42; *Briefwechsel*, VI, 109.
7. VS 168/92/23/262–344 (Pückler's letters to Lucie of 1851 from London).
8. *Briefwechsel*, VI, 33; VIII, 356.
9. Assing, II, 266, 268.
10. K. A. Varnhagen, *Tagebücher*, XIV, 310–20; *Briefwechsel*, IV, 4; VIII, 27.
11. *Briefwechsel*, IX, 367.
12. To create *Fürst-Pückler-Eis*, vanilla, strawberry and chocolate ice-cream are made from fresh ingredients and frozen in superimposed layers in a pan. Once hard, the ice-cream 'loaf' is sliced into three-coloured fingers, which are each dipped in chocolate. Six fingers are arranged from a central point on each plate and garnished with whipped cream, macaroon or wafer biscuits and a cherry.
13. *American Quarterly Review*, 12/24 (December 1832), 324–25.

Epilogue

1. Richardson, 227; Williams Wynn Letters, X, 201. Lady Combermere's books are listed in the bibliography, and the British Library holds three printed piano scores: refs A.868.n. (3.), G.807.vv. (31.) & h.3282.uu. (12.).
2. *Times*, 1 June 1863 (Harriet Bonham); 27 August 1877 (Rosabel Garvagh).
3. Culme does not give Miss Hamlet's first name. Pückler called her 'Harriet', but as there are two other Harriets in our story I have followed the 1851 Census in calling her Elizabeth.
4. VS 108/127/28/178-82 (Pückler–Lieven letters).

Notes on Sources

From 1826 to 1828 Pückler sent long letters from England to his ex-wife Lucie in Muskau. These are written in diary form, with entries for each day. He also filled four albums, which he called 'Erinnerungsbilder' ('Pictorial Reminiscences'), with images and notes. *Briefe eines Verstorbenen* (*Posthumous Letters*), his published account of his English tour, includes reworked passages from the albums, but its main source is the original letters, which he cut drastically, partially rewrote, and cleansed of all sensitive personal details. A small amount of the omitted material is printed in the *Briefwechsel und Tagebücher* (*Correspondence and Diaries*) edited by Ludmilla Assing, but most is only to be found in the manuscript letters. These form part of the Varnhagen-Sammlung (Varnhagen Collection) held at the Jagiellonian Library, Cracow, with a set of copies at the Pückler Archive, Branitz. Also available at Branitz are the albums, two of them loaned by Hermann Graf von Pückler. In consulting the albums I have benefited from scans of the images and a transcript of Pückler's comments prepared by the Archive's staff. In the chapter notes I refer to the above sources using the following abbreviations:

VS: Varnhagen-Sammlung
EB: 'Erinnerungsbilder'
Briefe: *Briefe eines Verstorbenen* (ed. Vaupel)
Briefwechsel: *Briefwechsel und Tagebücher* (ed. Assing)
Reference to VS documents is made, in order, by:
i) the box containing the document at the Jagiellonian Library;
ii) the microfilm to which it was first copied;
iii) the CD-Rom to which that microfilm was transferred;
iv) the scan number.
References to Pückler's writings are usually given only for direct quotations. Unless otherwise indicated, all translations are my own.

Bibliography

Unless stated otherwise place of publication is London.

MANUSCRIPT SOURCES

PÜCKLER ARCHIVE, BRANITZ, COTTBUS
i) 'Erinnerungsbilder' ('Pictorial Reminiscences')
ii) Pückler's correspondence with Rudolph Ackermann, Lady
Elizabeth Bligh, John Blum, Charlotte Elizabeth Bonham, Henry
Bouverie, George Bulkeley, Anne Chambre, the Marquess of
Conyngham, the Earl and Countess of Darnley, Mary Woolley
Gibbings, Robert Gibbings, Elizabeth Hamlet, Thomas Hamlet, W.
M. Hunt, Lady Isabella Kinloch, the Marchioness of Lansdowne, the
Earl of Lauderdale, Princess Lieven, Lady Morgan, John Murray,
Bessy Niles, Friedrich Oding, Sir Gore Ouseley, Princess Lucie von
Pückler-Muskau, Leopold Schefer, Edmund Spencer, Effingham
Wilson etc.

JAGIELLONIAN LIBRARY, CRACOW
Varnhagen Collection: Letter from Charlotte Williams Wynn to
Varnhagen, 12 January 1837

CAMBRIDGE COUNTY RECORD OFFICE
Tharp Papers: Diary of Captain John Tharp during a Journey to Paris
and Baden, 1817

CENTRE FOR BUCKINGHAMSHIRE STUDIES, AYLESBURY
Fremantle Papers: Diary of Thomas Francis Fremantle for 1825

EAST KENT ARCHIVES CENTRE, DOVER
Cobb Papers: Letter from Nathan Mayer Rothschild to Messrs Cobb,
18 August 1827

GUILDHALL LIBRARY, LONDON
International Memoranda

LLANGEDWYN HALL, POWYS
Typescript letters to and from Sir Henry Watkin Williams Wynn and
other members of his family (10 vols)

NATIONAL ARCHIVES, KEW
Wills of Henry Bonham, Robert Gibbings and the Marchioness of
Lansdowne

NATIONAL LIBRARY OF SCOTLAND, EDINBURGH
Saltoun Papers: Will of Sir Alexander Kinloch

PUBLIC RECORD OFFICE OF NORTHERN IRELAND,
BELFAST
Clanwilliam/Meade Papers

SOMBORNE PARK, HAMPSHIRE
Diary of Louisa Smythe

PRINTED SOURCES

1. NEWSPAPERS
The Age; The Atlas; Bell's Life in London; The British Traveller; The Courier;
The Court Journal; The Examiner; John Bull; The Mirror of Literature,
Amusement and Instruction; The Morning Chronicle; The Morning Herald;
The Morning Post; The New Times; St. James's Chronicle; The Spectator;
The Sphynx; The Standard; The Sunday Times; The Times

2. WORKS BY PÜCKLER
Briefe eines Verstorbenen: Ein fragmentarisches Tagebuch aus England, Wales,
Irland und Frankreich, geschrieben in den Jahren 1828 und 1829, 2 vols
(Munich: Franckh, 1830); trans. Sarah Austin, *Tour in England, Ireland,*
and France, in the Years 1828 and 1829. With Remarks on the Manners
and Customs of the Inhabitants, and Anecdotes of Distinguished Public
Characters. In a Series of Letters. By a German Prince, 2 vols (Wilson,
1832 [1831])
Briefe eines Verstorbenen: Ein fragmentarisches Tagebuch aus Deutschland,
Holland und England, geschrieben in den Jahren 1826, 1827 und 1828,
2 vols (Stuttgart: Hallberger, 1832 [1831]); trans. Sarah Austin, *Tour*
in Germany, Holland and England, in the Years 1826, 1827, and 1828.
With Remarks etc., 2 vols (Wilson, 1832)
Briefe eines Verstorbenen, ed. Therese Erler, 2 vols (Berlin: Rütten &
Loening, 1987)
Briefe eines Verstorbenen, ed. Günter J. Vaupel, 2 vols (Frankfurt am Main:
Insel, 1991)
Briefe eines Verstorbenen, ed. Heinz Ohff, 2nd edn (Berlin: Propyläen, 2006;
1st edn Berlin: Kupfergraben, 1986)
Tour in England, Ireland and France, in the Years 1826, 1827, 1828 & 1829;

With Remarks on the Manners and Customs of the Inhabitants, and Anecdotes of Distinguished Public Characters. In a Series of Letters. By a German Prince (Zurich: Massie, 1940) [abridged edition of the Austin translation with a preface by an anonymous editor]

A Regency Visitor: The English Tour of Prince Pückler-Muskau Described in his Letters 1826–1828, ed. E. M. Butler (Collins, 1957) [abridged edition of the Austin translation]

Puckler's [sic] *Progress: The Adventures of Prince Pückler-Muskau in England, Wales and Ireland as Told in Letters to His Former Wife*, trans. Flora Brennan (Collins, 1987)

Tutti Frutti: Aus den Papieren des Verstorbenen, 5 vols (Stuttgart: Hallberger, 1834)

Andeutungen über Landschaftsgärtnerei, verbunden mit der Beschreibung ihrer praktischen Anwendung in Muskau [1834], ed. Günter J. Vaupel (Frankfurt am Main: Insel, 1988); trans. Bernhard Sickert, *Hints on Landscape Gardening* (Boston: Houghton Mifflin, 1917)

Jugend-Wanderungen. Aus meinen Tagebüchern; für mich und Andere (Stuttgart: Hallberger, 1835)

Semilassos vorletzter Weltgang: Traum und Wachen [1835–36], ed. Heinrich Conrad, 3 vols (Munich: Müller, 1913-14 [vols 1-2]; Berlin: Harz, 1923 [vol. 3])

Aus Mehemet Alis Reich: Ägypten und der Sudan um 1840 [1844], ed. Günther Jantzen (Zurich: Manesse, 1985)

Briefwechsel und Tagebücher, ed. Ludmilla Assing, 9 vols [1873-76] (repr. Berne: Lang, 1971)

3. ENGLISH REVIEWS OF *BRIEFE EINES VERSTORBENEN*

Age, 8 January 1832

Athenaeum, 211 (12 November 1831), pp. 732–33; 225 (18 February 1832), pp. 105–07

Atlas, 6/287 (13 November 1831), p. 763; 7/302 (26 February 1832), p. 189; 7/306 (25 March 1832), p. 204

Courier, 8 November 1831; 27 February 1832

Court Journal, 135 (26 November 1831), p. 797; 143 (21 January 1832), p. 38; 150 (10 March 1832), pp. 156-58; 151 (17 March 1832), p. 173

Edinburgh Review, 54/108 (December 1831), pp. 384-407

Examiner, 1831, pp. 739-40 (20 November); 1832, pp. 147-49 (4 March)

Foreign Quarterly Review, 9/18 (1832), pp. 290-312 [Charles Buller]

Fraser's Magazine, 5/29 (June 1832), pp. 533-44

Gentleman's Magazine, 101/2 (1831), pp. 609-10; 102/1 (1832), pp. 432-34 [Thomas Crofton Croker]

John Bull, 19 February 1832

Literary Gazette, 15 (1831), pp. 705-07, 726-28, 744-46, 759-61; 16

(1832), pp. 114–17, 165

Metropolitan, 3/9 (January 1832), pp. 6–10

Mirror of Literature, Amusement, and Instruction, 18/523 (17 December 1831), pp. 421–23

Monthly Repository and Review of Theology and General Literature, 5 (1831), pp. 837–40 [Harriet Taylor Mill]

Monthly Review, 3/4 (December 1831), pp. 579–98; 4/4 (April 1832), pp. 503–24

New Monthly Magazine, 32 (December 1831), pp. 500–06 [Edward Bulwer-Lytton]

Quarterly Review, 46/92 (1831), pp. 518–44 [Theodore Hook]

Satirist, 1/32 (13 November 1831), p. 250; 2/48 (4 March 1832), p. 74

Spectator, 4 (1831), pp. 1097–1101; 5 (1832), pp. 185–86, 207–08, 282–83

Times, 15 November 1831; 10 January 1832

Town, 5 (29 January 1832), p. 37

Westminster Review, 16 (January 1832), pp. 225–43 [Henry Southern]

American Quarterly Review, 12/24 (December 1832), pp. 315–54

North American Review, 36/78 (January 1833), pp. 1–48

4. NOVELS AND SATIRICAL VERSES

Anon., *The Fortunate Youth; or, Chippenham Croesus*, 2nd edn (Johnston, 1818)

Anon., *St James's: A Satirical Poem, in Six Epistles to Mr Crockford* (n.publ., 1827)

Becke, Richard, *The Prima Donna, a Tale of To-Day* (Bull, 1828)

Dickens, Charles, *The Posthumous Papers of the Pickwick Club* [1837] (Oxford: Oxford UP, 1987)

Hook, Theodore, *Gilbert Gurney*, 3 vols (Whittaker, 1836)

——, *Jack Brag*, 3 vols (Bentley, 1837)

Morgan, Sydney, Lady, *The Princess; or, The Beguine* (Paris: Baudry, 1835)

Rellstab, Ludwig, *Henriette, oder die schöne Sängerin* (Leipzig: Herbig, 1826)

Scargill, William Pitt, *Rank and Talent*, 3 vols (Colburn, 1829)

Sternberg, Alexander von, *Tutu: Phantastische Episoden und poetische Exkursionen* [1846] (Meersburg: Hendel, 1936)

Thackeray, William Makepeace, *Vanity Fair* [1848] (Guild, 1980)

——, *The Great Hoggarty Diamond* [1849] (Wells Gardner, Darton, 1902)

White, Charles, *The Adventures of a King's Page*, 3 vols (Colburn, 1829)

5. DIARIES, CORRESPONDENCES, MEMOIRS AND TRAVELOGUES

Anon., *Life of Henriette Sontag, Countess de Rossi, with Interesting Sketches by Scudo, Hector Berlioz, Louis Boerne, Adolphe Adam, Marie Aycard, Julie de Margueritte, Prince Puckler-Muskau, and Theophile Gautier* (New

York: Stringer and Townsend, 1852)

Adrian, Johann Valentin, *Bilder aus England* (Frankfurt am Main: Sauerländer, 1827-28)

Airlie, Mabell, Countess of, *Lady Palmerston and Her Times*, 2 vols (Hodder and Stoughton, 1922)

Apperley, Charles James, *Nimrod's German Tour* (Wismar: Godewind, 2006)

Arbuthnot, Harriet, *Journal 1820-1832*, ed. Francis Bamford and the Duke of Wellington, 2 vols (Macmillan, 1950)

Berkeley, Grantley F., *My Life and Recollections*, 4 vols (Hurst and Blackett, 1865-66)

Bernardy, Françoise de, *Son of Talleyrand: The Life of Comte Charles de Flahaut 1785-1870*, trans. Lucy Norton (New York: Putnam, 1956)

Blessington, Marguerite, Countess of, *The Idler in France*, 2 vols (Colburn, 1841)

Bonaparte-Wyse, Olga, *The Spurious Brood: Princess Letitia Bonaparte and Her Children* (Gollancz, 1969)

——, *The Issue of Bonaparte-Wyse: Waterford's Imperial Relations* (Waterford: Waterford Museum of Treasures, 2004)

Buckle, Richard, ed., *The Prettiest Girl in England: The Love Story of Mrs Fitzherbert's Niece* (Murray, 1958)

Bulwer-Lytton, Edward George, *Letters of the Late Edward Bulwer, Lord Lytton, to his Wife*, ed. Louisa Devey (Swan Sonnenschein, 1884)

Byrne, J. C., *Gossip of the Century: Personal and Traditional Memories – Social Literary Artistic etc.* (New York: Macmillan, 1892)

Carlyle, Thomas and Jane Welsh, *Collected Letters*, ed. Charles Richard Sanders and Kenneth J. Fielding (Durham, NC: Duke UP, 1970-)

Creevey, Thomas, *Creevey's Life and Times*, ed. John Gore (Murray, 1934)

Croker, John Wilson, *The Croker Papers*, ed. Bernard Pool (Batsford, 1967)

Crusius, Friedrich Lebrecht, *Reise eines jungen Deutschen in Frankreich und England im Jahre 1815*, ed. Georg Brand (Leipzig: Wigand, 1909)

Custine, Astolphe de, *Mémoires et Voyages*, 2 vols (Paris: Vezard, 1830)

Doetinchem, Bia von, *Biel-Nachlese: Beiträge zu Persönlichkeiten der Familie* (privately publ., 2005)

Dorow, Wilhelm, *Denkschriften und Briefe zur Charakteristik der Welt und Literatur*, 5 vols (Berlin: Duncker, 1838-41)

Duncombe, Thomas Slingsby, *Life and Correspondence*, ed. Thomas H. Duncombe, 2 vols (Hurst and Blackett, 1868)

Eberty, Felix, *Jugenderinnerungen eines alten Berliners* (Berlin: Hertz, 1878)

Falk, Bernard, *'Old Q's' Daughter: The History of a Strange Family* (Hutchinson, 1937)

Fox, Henry Edward, *Journal*, ed. the Earl of Ilchester (Thornton Butterworth, 1923)

Frampton, Mary, *Journal 1779-1846*, ed. Harriot Georgiana Mundy (Low, Marston, Searle & Rivington, 1886)

Gleig, George Robert, *Personal Reminiscences of the First Duke of Wellington, with Sketches of Some of His Guests and Contemporaries* (Edinburgh: Blackwood, 1904)

Glenbervie, Sylvester Douglas, Baron, *Journals*, ed. Walter Sichel (Constable, 1910)

Gower, Lord Granville Leveson, *Private Correspondence 1781 to 1821*, ed. Castalia, Countess Granville, 2 vols (Murray, 1916)

Granville, Harriet, Countess, *Letters 1810-1845*, ed. F. Leveson-Gower, 2 vols (Longmans, Green, 1894)

Greville, Charles, *Memoirs 1814-1860*, ed. Lytton Strachey and Roger Fulford, 8 vols (Macmillan, 1938)

Gronow, Rees Howell, *The Reminiscences and Recollections of Captain Gronow* (Nunney: Surtees, 1984-85)

Hamburger, Lotte and Joseph, *Contemplating Adultery: The Secret Life of a Victorian Woman* (New York: Fawcett Columbine, 1991)

Holland, Elizabeth, Lady, *Letters to her Son, 1821-1845*, ed. the Earl of Ilchester (Murray, 1946)

Holland, Henry, *Recollections of Past Life* (Longmans, Green, 1872)

Ilchester, Earl of, *The Home of the Hollands 1605-1820* (Murray, 1937)

Jacobs, Jo Ellen, *The Voice of Harriet Taylor Mill* (Bloomington: Indiana UP, 2002)

Leconfield, Maud, Lady, and John Gore, eds, *Three Howard Sisters: Selections from the Writings of Lady Caroline Lascelles, Lady Dover and Countess Gower, 1825-1833* (Murray, 1955)

Lyttelton, Sarah Spencer, Lady, *Correspondence 1787-1870*, ed. Mrs Hugh Wyndham (Murray, 1912)

Madden, Richard Robert, *The Literary Life and Correspondence of the Countess of Blessington*, 3 vols (Newby, 1855)

Moore, Thomas, *Journal*, ed. Wilfred S. Dowden et al, 6 vols (Newark: U of Delaware P, 1983-91)

Neumann, Philip von, *Diary 1819-1850*, ed. E. Beresford Chancellor, 2 vols (Allan, 1928)

Pecchio, Giuseppe, Count, *Semi-Serious Observations of an Italian Exile, During His Residence in England* (Wilson, 1833)

Pichot, Joseph J. M. C. A., *Historical and Literary Tour of a Foreigner in England and Scotland*, 2 vols (Saunders & Otley, 1825)

Pickett, T. H., and Mark McCulloh, 'Sarah Austin's Letters to K. A. Varnhagen von Ense', *Euphorion*, 82/1 (1988), pp. 63-88

Pirchan, Emil, *Henriette Sontag: Die Sängerin des Biedermeier* (Vienna: Frick, 1946)

Raikes, Thomas, *Portion of the Journal Kept by Thomas Raikes, Esq.*, 2 vols (Longman, Brown, Green, Longmans & Roberts, 1858)

Richardson, Ethel M., *Next Door Neighbours (at 9 and 10 Grafton Street, W.)* (Hutchinson, 1926)

Sala, George Augustus, *Life and Adventures*, 2 vols (Cassell, 1895)

Seymour, Lady, ed., *The 'Pope' of Holland House: Selections from the Correspondence of John Whishaw and his Friends, 1813-1840* (Unwin, 1906)

Spencer, Edmund, *Sketches of Germany and the Germans*, 2 vols (Whittaker, 1836)

Stendhal, *Souvenirs d'égotisme*, ed. Pierre Martino (Paris: Presses de l'Imprimerie Nationale, 1954)

Stevenson, Lionel, *The Wild Irish Girl: The Life of Sydney Owenson, Lady Morgan (1776-1859)* (Chapman & Hall, 1936)

Stirling, A. M. W., ed., *The Letter-Bag of Lady Elizabeth Spencer-Stanhope*, 2 vols (Bodley Head, 1913)

Stümke, Heinrich, *Henriette Sontag* (Berlin: Gesellschaft für Theatergeschichte, 1913)

Trant, Clarissa, *Journal 1800-1832*, ed. C. G. Luard (Bodley Head, 1925)

Varnhagen von Ense, Karl August, *Blätter aus der preußischen Geschichte*, ed. Ludmilla Assing, 5 vols (Leipzig: Brockhaus, 1868-69)

——, *Tagebücher*, ed. Ludmilla Assing, 15 vols [1861-70; 1905] (repr. Berne: Lang, 1972)

Varnhagen von Ense, Rahel, *Briefwechsel mit Pauline Wiesel*, ed. Barbara Hahn and Birgit Bosold (Munich: Beck, 1997)

Vincent, E. R., *Ugo Foscolo: An Italian in Regency England* (Cambridge: Cambridge UP, 1953)

Wardroper, John, *Wicked Ernest: The Truth about the Man who was almost Britain's King* (Shelfmark, 2002)

Williams Wynn, Charlotte Grenville, Lady, *Correspondence*, ed. Rachel Leighton (Murray, 1920)

Wilson, Harriette, *Memoirs*, ed. Thomas Little, 2 vols (Eveleigh Nash, 1909)

Ziegler, Philip, *The Duchess of Dino*, 2nd edn (Collins, 1986)

6. BOOKS AND ARTICLES ON PÜCKLER

Anon., 'Muskau, in Silesia, the Residence of Prince Pichler [*sic*] of Muskau', *Ackermann's Repository*, 11/66 (1 June 1828), pp. 313-14

Arnim, Hermann Graf von, *Ein Fürst unter den Gärtnern: Pückler als Landschaftskünstler und der Muskauer Park* (Frankfurt am Main: Ullstein, 1981)

—— and Willi A. Boelcke, *Muskau: Standesherrschaft zwischen Spree und Neiße* (Frankfurt am Main: Propyläen, 1992)

Assing, Ludmilla, *Fürst Hermann von Pückler-Muskau* [1873-74], ed. Nikolaus Gatter, 2 vols (Hildesheim: Olms, 2004)

Bowe, Patrick, 'Pückler-Muskau's Estate and its Influence on

American Landscape Architecture', *Garden History*, 23/2 (1995), pp. 192-200

Brey, Nicole and Michael, 'Die bewegte Welt des Reisenden – Mit vier PS durch England', in *Englandsouvenirs: Fürst Pücklers Reise 1826-1829*, no ed. (Zittau: Graphische Werkstätten, 2005), pp. 17-30

——, '"Exclusives, Beaux und Dandies" – Lebensbilder des Regency', in ibid., pp. 43-68

——, 'Gartenpracht und "Landschaftsepopöen" – Die englische Parkjagd', in ibid., pp. 69-104

Buruma, Ian, *Voltaire's Coconuts; or, Anglomania in Europe* (Weidenfeld & Nicolson, 1999), pp. 86-110

Butler, Eliza Marian, *The Tempestuous Prince: Hermann Pückler-Muskau* (Longmans, Green, 1929)

Ehrhard, Auguste, *Le Prince de Pückler-Muskau*, 2 vols (Paris: Plon, 1927-28)

Fischer, Tilman, 'Literatur und Aristokratie: Zur Debatte um Fürst Hermann von Pückler-Muskau', *Jahrbuch der Charles-Sealsfield-Gesellschaft*, 14 (2002), pp. 181-224

Friedrich, Christian, 'Ein alliierter Oberstleutnant im Reich der Queen – Die erste Englandreise des Fürsten Hermann von Pückler-Muskau', *Cottbuser Blätter*, Sonderheft 2004, pp. 17-19

Goodchild, Peter, 'Fürst Pückler und die Gartenkunst im England des Regency (1800-37)', trans. Ralf Jaeger, in *Englandsouvenirs: Fürst Pücklers Reise 1826-1829*, no ed. (Zittau: Graphische Werkstätten, 2005), pp. 105-30

Gruenter, Rainer, 'Der reisende Fürst: Fürst Hermann Pückler-Muskau in England', in R. G., *Vom Elend des Schönen: Studien zur Literatur und Kunst* (Munich: Hanser, 1988), pp. 83-100

Hermand, Jost, Introduction to Pückler, *Briefe eines Verstorbenen* (New York: Johnson Reprint, 1968)

Im Spiegel der Erinnerung: Hermann Fürst von Pückler-Muskau: Gartenkünstler, Schriftsteller, Weltbummler, no ed. (Branitz: Fürst Pückler Museum, 1995)

Jäger, August, *Das Leben des Fürsten von Pückler-Muskau* (Stuttgart: Metzler, 1843)

Jelaffke, Cordula, *Fürst Pückler: Biographie* (Berlin: Neues Leben, 1993)

Just, Klaus Günther, 'Fürst Hermann von Pückler-Muskau', in K. G. J., *Übergänge: Probleme und Gestalten der Literatur* (Berne: Francke, 1966), pp. 153-88

Krebs, Gérard, '*Der Lebendigste aller Verstorbenen* – Zum wieder-erwachten Interesse an Fürst von Pückler-Muskau', *Jahrbuch für finnisch-deutsche Literaturbeziehungen*, 27 (1995), pp. 193-202

Marx, Reiner, 'Ein liberaler deutscher Adliger sieht Englands Metropole: Die Wahrnehmung Londons in Pückler-Muskaus

"Briefen eines Verstorbenen"', in *Rom-Paris-London: Erfahrung und Selbsterfahrung deutscher Schriftsteller und Künstler in den fremden Metropolen*, ed. Conrad Wiedemann (Stuttgart: Metzler, 1988), pp. 595-610

Neuhaus, Stefan, 'Das fehlerhafte Vorbild: Zur Darstellung Großbritanniens in Hermann Fürst von Pückler-Muskaus Bestseller "Briefe eines Verstorbenen"', *Neophilologus*, 83 (1999), pp. 267-81

Ohff, Heinz, *Der grüne Fürst: Das abenteuerliche Leben des Hermann Pückler-Muskau* (Munich: Piper, 1991)

Rippmann, Inge, 'Tradition und Fortschritt: Das frühindustrielle England aus der Perspektive eines aristokratischen Individualisten', *Recherches Germaniques*, 25 (1995), pp. 159-79

Schäfer, Anne, '"Die Fürstin Pückler wie sie leibt und lebt aber nicht meine Schnucke" – ein Bildnis der Fürstin Pückler', *Cottbuser Blätter*, Sonderheft 2004, pp. 71-74

Schnirch, Paula, 'Fürst Hermann von Pückler-Muskau und K. A. Varnhagen von Ense' [typescript] (U of Vienna Dissertation, 1914)

Steinecke, Hartmut, '"Reisende waren wir beide": Pückler-Muskau und Heine, London, Frühjahr 1827. Aspekte der Reiseliteratur vor der Julirevolution', in *Vormärz und Kritik*, ed. Lothar Ehrlich et al (Bielefeld: Aisthesis, 1999), pp. 163-80

Tausch, Harald, 'Vom Bild der Natur zum imaginären Bilderbogen der Vergangenheit: Hermann von Pückler-Muskaus *Andeutungen über Landschaftsgärtnerei* und die Literarisierung des englischen Landschaftsgartens', *Archiv für das Studium der neueren Sprachen und Literaturen*, 233 (1996), pp. 1-19

Wolkan, Rudolf, 'Fürst Pückler-Muskau und Leopold Schefer', *Neues Lausitzisches Magazin*, 62 (1886), pp. 130-48

7. OTHER TITLES

Anon., *Proposals for Redressing Some Grievances Which Greatly Affect the Whole Nation: With A Seasonable Warning to Our Beautiful Young Ladies Against Fortune Hunters; And A Remedy Proposed in Favour of the Ladies* (Johnson, 1740)

Carlyle, Thomas, *Sartor Resartus: The Life and Opinions of Herr Teufelsdröckh*, ed. Rodger L. Tarr and Mark Engel (Berkeley: U of California P, 2000)

Christiansen, Rupert, *Prima Donna: A History* (Bodley Head, 1984)

Combermere, Mary Woolley, Viscountess, *Our Peculiarities* (Smith, Elder, 1863)

——, *A Friar's Scourge: Nonsense Verses* (no publ., 1876)

—— and W. W. Knollys, *Memoirs and Correspondence of Field-Marshal Viscount Combermere*, 2 vols (Hurst and Blackett, 1866)

Copeland, Edward, 'Money', in *The Cambridge Companion to Jane Austen*, ed. E. C. and Juliet McMaster (Cambridge: Cambridge UP, 1997), pp. 131-48

Culme, John, *The Directory of Gold & Silversmiths, Jewellers & Allied Traders 1838-1914*, 2 vols (Woodbridge: Antique Collectors' Club, 1987), I, pp. 205-06

Elkington, Margery E., *Les relations de société entre l'Angleterre et la France sous la restauration (1814-1830)* (Paris: Champion, 1929)

Emden, Paul H., *Regency Pageant* (Hodder & Stoughton, 1936)

Fischer, Tilman, *Reiseziel England: Ein Beitrag zur Poetik der Reisebeschreibung und zur Topik der Moderne (1830-1870)* (Berlin: Erich Schmidt, 2004)

Goethe, Johann Wolfgang von, *Sämtliche Werke nach Epochen seines Schaffens*, ed. Karl Richter et al (Munich: Hanser, 1985-)

Grant, James, *The Great Metropolis*, 1st series, 2 vols (New York: Saunders and Otley, 1837); 2nd series, 2 vols (Philadelphia: Carey & Hart, 1838)

Hakewill, James, *The History of Windsor and its Neighbourhood* (Lloyd, 1813)

Heine, Heinrich, *Werke*, ed. Hans Meyer et al, 4 vols (Frankfurt am Main: Insel, 1968)

Jerrold, Clare, *The Beaux and the Dandies* (New York: John Lane, 1910)

Jones, Ethel, *Les voyageurs français en Angleterre de 1815 à 1830* (Paris: Boccard, 1930)

Kaser, David, ed., *The Cost Book of Carey & Lea 1825-1838* (Philadelphia: U of Pennsylvania P, 1963)

Kelly, John Alexander, *England and the Englishman in German Literature of the Eighteenth Century* (New York: Columbia UP, 1921)

Langford, Paul, *Englishness Identified: Manners and Character 1650-1850* (Oxford: Oxford UP, 2000)

Letts, Malcolm, *As the Foreigner Saw Us* (Methuen, 1935)

Mann, Kay, *London: The German Connection* (Bridgwater: KT Publishing, 1993)

Montgomery, Robert, *The Age Reviewed*, 2nd edn (Wright, 1828)

Muncker, Franz, *Anschauungen vom englischen Staat und Volk in der deutschen Literatur der letzten vier Jahrhunderte*, vol. 2 (Munich: Verlag der Bayerischen Akademie der Wissenschaften, 1925)

Musgrave, Clifford, *Life in Brighton: From the Earliest Times to the Present* (Faber, 1970)

Perkin, Joan, *Women and Marriage in Nineteenth-Century England* (Routledge, 1989)

Prawer, S. S., *Frankenstein's Island: England and the English in the Writings of Heinrich Heine* (Cambridge: Cambridge UP, 1986)

Priestley, J. B., *The Prince of Pleasure and His Regency 1811-1820* (Heinemann, 1969)

Varnhagen von Ense, Karl August, *Zur Geschichtschreibung und Litteratur* (Hamburg: Perthes, 1833)

It is not customary to include reference works in bibliographies of this sort, but I must at least acknowledge my indebtedness to the *Oxford Dictionary of National Biography*, various peerage books, the *Annual Register* for 1827 and 1828, and *The London Encyclopaedia* (ed. Weinreb and Hibbert).

Index

'P' indicates Hermann von Pückler-Muskau. The subheadings under his name relate to his life and character. For his opinions on particular subjects see the relevant heading.

Also from Signal Books—

LONDON OBSERVED
A Polish Philosopher at Large, 1820-24
Krystyn Lach-Szyrma
Edited and annotated by Mona Kedslie McLeod
Foreword by Neal Ascherson

The philosopher and writer Krystyn Lach-Szyrma came to Britain in 1820 as tutor to two Polish princes, as their Grand Tour took them to Enlightenment Scotland, where they spent two years studying at Edinburgh University. After a short tour of continental Europe they returned in 1822 to England to enjoy the delights of London and observe its monuments and people.

Over a period of 18 months they visited prisons, hospitals and factories as well as art galleries and museums and were entertained by individuals of the calibre of Elizabeth Fry and Robert Owen. The philosopher and his princely charges familiarised themselves with the Houses of Parliament the Stock Exchange and Westminster Abbey, but were also intrigued by London's inns and theatres. Looking at the capital's financial, religious and academic institutions, they analysed its class system and law-and-order problems, pondering such issues as the origins of the term 'Cockney' and the nature of English breakfasts.

With insatiable curiosity and good humour, Lach-Szyrma recorded his impressions of London and Londoners in perceptive and readable style. Of peasant origins, Lach-Szyrma was no snob. His observations are shrewd, witty and irradiated by the enthusiasm of a Romantic.

On his return to Poland Lach-Szyrma published his *Reminiscences of a Journey through Scotland and England*, of which this book forms the second part. The earliest description of British society to be written in Polish, it aroused great interest at a time when both English and Scottish institutions were widely admired and London had become the most vibrant city in Europe.

Mona Kedslie McLeod is a retired lecturer from the Extra Mural Department of Edinburgh University.

November 2009
ISBN: 978-1-904955-64-1
Price: £12.99 paperback